GLOBAL WARMING

and the Sweetness of Life

GLOBAL WARMING

and the Sweetness of Life

A TAR SANDS TALE

MATT HERN AND AM JOHAL

WITH JOE SACCO

The MIT Press - Cambridge, Massachusetts - London, England

Grant funding provided by Furthermore: a program of the J. M. Kaplan Fund.

Furthermore:
a program of the J.M. Kaplan Fund

This book was set in Chaparral Pro by The MIT Press. Printed and bound in the United States of America.

Library of Congress Cataloging-in-Publication Data

Names: Hern, Matt, author. | Johal, Am, author. | Sacco, Joe, illustrator.
Title: Global warming and the sweetness of life : a Tar Sands tale / Matt Hern and Am Johal ; with Joe Sacco.
Description: Cambridge, MA : MIT Press, [2018] | Includes bibliographical references and index.
Identifiers: LCCN 2017031167 | ISBN 9780262037648 (pbk. : alk. paper)
Subjects: LCSH: Oil sands—Environmental aspects—Alberta—Fort McMurray Region. | Petroleum engineering—Social aspects—Alberta—Fort McMurray Region. | Alberta—Social life and customs.
Classification: LCC TD195.P4 H47 2018 | DDC 338.2/72830971232—dc23
LC record available at https://lccn.loc.gov/2017031167

10 9 8 7 6 5 4 3 2

CONTENTS

—

Territorial Acknowledgments - vii | Gratitude - ix

1 – EAST VANCOUVER
səlil'wətaɁɬ (Tsleil-Waututh), S̲kw̲x̲wú7mesh (Squamish),
and xʷməθkʷɔ̓y̓əm (Musqueam) Territories   1

2 - EDMONTON
Cree, Saulteau, Blackfoot, Métis, and Nakota
Sioux Territories - 31

3 - BITUMEN OR BUST - 71

4 - FORT MCMURRAY
Dene, Woodland Cree, and Chipewyan Territories - 81

5 - LITTLE BUFFALO
Lubicon Territory - 115

6 - FORT MCMURRAY AND JANVIER
Dene, Woodland Cree, and Chipewyan Territories;
East Vancouver: səlil'wətaɁɬ (Tsleil-Waututh), S̲kw̲x̲wú7mesh
(Squamish), and xʷməθkʷəy̓əm (Musqueam) Territories - 143

Notes - 177 | Index - 207

TERRITORIAL ACKNOWLEDGMENTS

—

This book was built around multiple road trips that took us many thousands of kilometers as we crisscrossed through lands held by multiple and overlapping nations.

We have made our best attempt throughout the text to note those whose lands we were passing through and the territory where we reside. That project, though, is complicated, in part because many Indigenous nations' relationships to the land do not easily translate into simple Westphalian languages of ownership and sovereignty. It is true, for example, that Vancouver is the territory of the səlilwətaɬ (Tsleil-Waututh), Skwx̱wú7mesh (Squamish), and xʷməθkʷəy̓əm (Musqueam) peoples. But acknowledging that does not mean that one entity holds exclusive title to the land here; it is much subtler and more complicated than that.

Essentially no treaties have been signed in British Columbia until very recently, and the vast bulk of the province remains unceded. Most Indigenous nations in Alberta, on the other hand, signed treaties with the Canadian government at some point over the past 150 years—which does not mean they *ceded* their territories, but rather that they agreed to share them under certain conditions. These are

Treaty 6, Treaty 7, and Treaty 8, with small areas covered by Treaty 4 and Treaty 10; the Lubicon Nation, however, was overlooked and has signed no treaty to this day. The language of *unceded* and treaty numbers neither substantiates the dichotomy between *unceded* and *ceded* that is sometimes invoked, nor does it suggest the legitimacy of treaties, but this is how the territories are currently acknowledged and delineated by the state.

These lands have never been simply *owned* by one Indigenous nation or another; Edmonton (often referred to by its Cree name Amiskwacîwâskahikan), for example, has perhaps always been best described as a place where multiple and diverse nations pass through, use the land in various ways, and share responsibility for it. Throughout we have tried our best to acknowledge the Indigenous territories and people whose land we were crossing, consulting numerous experts in this attempt, with special thanks to Khelsilem for his guidance. Any mistakes, inaccuracies, or misacknowledgments are our own.

The complexity and nuance of the task of acknowledging territory underlines one of our core contentions: that global warming, and more importantly *ecology*, is at heart a matter of land and sovereignty. The anticapitalist and decolonizing politics with which Indigenous claims to land might be honestly answered are the exact same politics required to confront global warming and find a sweetness of life.

GRATITUDE

—

A big thank you to all the friends, colleagues, and allies who gave us thoughtful advice and incisive feedback as we worked through our ideas. They include: Geoff Mann, Mark Jacobs, Yoo-Mi Lee, Andrea Curtis, Jeff Derksen, Imre Szeman, participants of the 2016 Banff Research in Culture residency, Rabi Kadri, Matthew Huber, Samir Gandesha, Sheena Wilson, Jeff Diamanti, Selena Couture, Althea Thauberger, Ernst Logar, Bethany Barratt, Louis Helbig, Arthur Ray, Jane Heather, Matt Wildcat, Carmen Aguirre, and Khelsilem. Jordan Kinder was hugely helpful with his rigorous research support.

Special thanks to Ashley Dornan, Vanessa Elie, Gita Levine, the Isaac family (Dawit, Seble, Abigail, Naomi, and Leah), Reinalie Jorolan, Ana Maria Mendez, everyone in Little Buffalo, Auntie Lillian, Maggie Cairns, Diane Herman, Ja-Nene Herman, and Alberto Acosta, for their time and generosity. Several other people deserve particular thanks for their generosity, insights, and significant blocks of time they shared with us. We owe Glen Coulthard, Melina Laboucan-Massimo, Melissa Herman, and Dennis Herman all our most sincere thanks (and beers). And more than anyone, our thanks and praise is due to Leanne Simpson who offered brilliant analysis to us on multiple occasions, and so kindly helped us think past our most entrenched blind spots and see in new ways. It was only in conversation with these friends that the task of the book gradually became clear to us. We learned so much from all of them, and thus, any failings or deficiencies in the text are wholly their responsibility.

We are tremendously thankful to the MIT Press for their eagerness to publish this work, to Judith Feldmann for her eagle-eyed editing, and most especially to Beth Clevenger. Beth has been consistently critical, supportive, kind, and challenging. This book would not exist without her.

1

EAST VANCOUVER

—

səlil'wətaɁɬ (Tsleil-Waututh), Sḵwx̱wú7mesh (Squamish), and
x^wməθkʷəy̓əm (Musqueam) Territories

Leanne looked across the table, paused long and hard, gazed out the window, then turned back to us: "I think that's asking the wrong question." We had asked her about development in a time of global warming. She told us about a conversation she'd had with an elder from her community about sustainable development: he'd said the concept didn't make any sense to him.

We were sitting with Michi Saagiig Nishnaabeg scholar, theorist, and author Leanne Betasamosake Simpson in the restaurant of the Sylvia Hotel in downtown Vancouver, eating breakfast and looking out onto English Bay.[1] It was a sparkling spring morning, the kind of day that's purpose-built for touristic promotional materials and real-estate advertising. The sun bounced off the bay in a thousand directions, waves of joggers and strollers washed past, the coffee tasted freshly brewed, the mountains still had a dusting of snow, and baby deer frolicked on the hotel lawn (well, almost). It was also April 9, 2015, and literally as we spoke (though we didn't know it at the time) the Greek-owned, Cypriot-registered bulk-carrier grain ship *MV Marathassa* was resting at anchor several hundred yards offshore from where we sat, spewing tanker fuel into the bay.

The *Marathassa* was a brand-new boat on its maiden voyage. It remains unclear exactly what went wrong, but on that lovely morning and all through the previous night, fuel had been draining from its tanks, dumping more than 2,700 liters into the bay.[2] And it wasn't just regular old oil; it was notoriously toxic Bunker C fuel. Officials immediately warned everyone not to touch it, not to let your pets sniff it, just stay the hell away from it.[3] As we peacefully ate breakfast, cleanup crews had begun to scramble all over the water, Coast Guard ships were hustling to clear civilian watercraft, environmental containment crews were somewhere out there dropping booms, wildlife specialists were on the beaches trying to protect any unlucky animals—and faster than anyone, communications, spin, and legal teams were readying their defenses.

We saw none of that from our restaurant window. The City of Vancouver was issuing a string of ominous tweets and various levels of media were in full roar, but under that bright blue sky, at least from our table, everything appeared tranquil. Plenty of pleasure-craft boats were still out on the water, people and their dogs blanketed the beaches—nothing seemed amiss in the least. No alarm bells were sounding, we sensed no panic in the air, and most everyone seemed to be carelessly enjoying the sun.

The days and months that followed saw flurries of recriminations and admonishments between various levels of government, the Coast Guard, port authorities, and the shipping company, each blaming one another, backing away from responsibility, and posturing theatrically. In the end, after everything settled down, it became evident that the *Marathassa* incident was a relatively pedestrian, garden-variety industrial accident that most everybody responded to as best they could. It was the sort of accident that just happens from time to time—that *has* to happen, given probability vectors. There is only so much volume of industrial activity—all relying on material integrity and human culpability—that can be undertaken without accidents, no matter how many risk-management strategies or accident-prevention protocols are in place.

FIGURE 1.1

Toxic fuel spill in Vancouver's English Bay, April 9, 2015.
Photograph by Chad Dey for NEWS 1130. Used with permission
of Rogers Media Inc. All rights reserved.

Vancouver is a classic gateway city: the entry and exit platform for
Asia and the American West Coast to and from Canada. Perched on
the edge of the Pacific Rim, it is emerging as a full-fledged global city,
flush with visitors and migration, tourism and investment, flows
and circulations, progress and growth. Forty percent of the people
living in the metro area were born outside the country.[4] The airport
and port are expanding frenetically, new freeways are busting
through and around the city to transport goods, and every level of
government can scarcely find words sufficient to express their en-
thusiastic welcome of international capital.

Despite a culturally liberal and environmentally progressive reputation, Vancouver articulates neoliberal urbanism as comprehensively as any city anywhere. For more than a decade, Canada has been among the world's most tax-competitive countries for business according to KPMG's ranking system, coming in second behind only Mexico in 2016. Vancouver lands consistently in the very upper echelon of their international scoring system for cities, mostly on the "strength" of extremely low corporate tax rates, placing fifth (out of 100) in 2016.[5] Vancouver's mayor, Gregor Robertson, is a perfect exemplar of the city's ability to speak out of both sides of its mouth. A pleasant, bicycle-riding organic-juice tycoon, he was lifted into his position in 2008 by a powerful consortium of real estate and development interests working hand in hand with green/soft-left/labor coalitions: the perfect amalgam of capital accumulation sutured to sensitive eco-performative politics.

All of this makes it hardly surprising that the seaport here is a going concern, to put it delicately. Vancouver is the third-largest port in North America, with twenty-seven major marine cargo terminals, three Class 1 railroads, and 1.5 million containers passing through four terminals every year. The Port of Metro Vancouver's deep-sea terminals have what is (delightfully) called "Super Post-Panamax capacity with virtually no draft restrictions," and its five core business sectors—automobiles, breakbulk, bulk, container, and cruise—trade with more than 170 countries.[6]

Given this level of activity, some marine accidents are indeed inevitable. Despite the high visibility of the *Marathassa* incident (which was not an oil tanker), the Port of Vancouver is not moving a lot of oil. Of all its traffic, oil and chemical tankers make up a pretty small piece, something like 1.5 percent of the total, with only about 100 rolling through these waters annually. If all the new pipeline infrastructure that has been proposed over the past few years is completed, that number will quadruple, but those are still small numbers compared with the big dogs in the shipping world. For reference, the world's two biggest tanker ports, Singapore and Rotterdam, handle 22,280 and 8,206 tankers a year, respectively.[7]

Even if oil transport is a minor piece of the local economic puzzle, Vancouver, like pretty much all of Canada and really the rest of the globe, is convulsed by debates over fossil fuel. It's hard to overemphasize how simultaneously volatile and intractable much of the contention is here, and how—as it does everywhere—oil, and thus global warming, seeps into every political question.

A quick note here: throughout the book we use the term *global warming* rather than *climate change*. *Climate change* is now the more common term to describe a whole range of historical and emerging climate disruptions, but the contemporary changes are *caused* by global warming. The average temperature of the Earth is increasing, with fifteen of the sixteen warmest years on record occurring since 2000, and 2016 ranking as the hottest on record.[8] It is global warming, caused by rising greenhouse gas emissions (the amount of greenhouse gases released into the atmosphere hit record highs in 2016),[9] that is precipitating the broader phenomenon of climate change. Thus, in our view, the term *global warming* is more accurate and useful in describing what is happening. We are also using it as a political term, not a scientific argument. *Climate change* is a more inclusive evocation that can get its arms around the global-weirding of the contemporary climate, and we sympathize with its use; but climate change is really just global warming with all the rough edges sanded off: a move to more depoliticized and unfocused narratives. *Climate change* opens the door to denialisms, obfuscations, and waffling.[10]

When you start talking about the relationships between global warming and oil in North America, at some point you inevitably end up talking about the tar sands of Alberta: perhaps the world's biggest single industrial site, and to many, our era's defining extractive project.[11] Northern Alberta is home to immense oil reserves, by most estimates the third largest in the world.[12] Industry and governments badly want to get that oil to market somehow, and pipelines are by far the cheapest and most efficient technique. There already are pipelines, sublines, feeder lines, and gathering lines moving synthetic crude, bitumen, and natural gas in every direction out of Alberta—far more existing infrastructure than most people know. In some parts of North America, pipelines are a glaring intrusion, the oil economy made visible in their own backyards, but for most us, oil production is hidden away in the hinterlands. We certainly didn't realize just how many pipelines are already in operation until we saw them up close and personal, a spider-web lattice thrown across the continent. As of early 2017, for example, just the Alberta Energy Board was regulating 431,000 kilometers of lines, all running exclusively within the province.[13]

The pipelines that cause the most consternation and public resistance, though, are those that cross provincial and national borders, and newly elected governments in both Canada and the United States have swiftly resurrected and approved new lines that had been previously stalled. Donald Trump quickly reversed the Obama administration's 2015 denial of permits for the Keystone XL running from Alberta to Nebraska and revived the stalled Dakota Access Pipeline (DAPL) project running through the Standing Rock Indian Reservation in North and South Dakota. Canadian Prime Minister Justin Trudeau, while developing a highly controversial national carbon tax, has also enthusiastically approved multiple pipeline projects.

In late 2016, the Kinder Morgan Trans Mountain Expansion line running essentially from Edmonton to Vancouver was approved, as was the Enbridge Line 3 project, a massive expansion of existing lines running from Alberta to Wisconsin. Trudeau displayed a deft political touch in announcing the approvals, framing them in clear class terms: "I have said many times that there isn't a country in the world that would find billions of barrels of oil and leave it in the ground while there is a market for it. ... [These pipelines] will give much needed hope to thousands of hard-working people in Alberta's conventional energy sector, who have suffered a great deal in the past two years. ... And as I said in making the announcement, these approvals are a major win for Canadian workers, for Canadian families and for the Canadian economy."[14]

When that *Marathassa* oil spill happened in April 2015—even if it wasn't from an oil tanker or even directly affiliated with the oil and

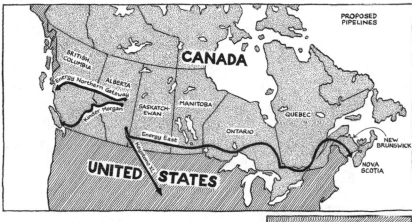

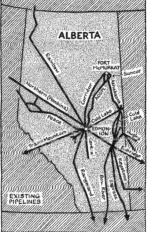

FIGURE 1.2
–
Some of the key and recently proposed tar sands pipeline infrastructure.
Map by Joe Sacco.

gas industry—it was a spark-to-tinder reaction for many people in Vancouver, as the repercussions of extractivism hit home for once. The spill itself was apparently mopped up quickly and effectively, and a month later only two beaches remained closed to the public. There seemed to be no calamitous effects for sea life or birds, and less than two months later we were happily swimming away at the next beach over, joking about toxicity, tasting the water and finding it saltily familiar, without too much of that Bunker C aftertaste. All the dire enviro-catastrophe narratives that had spilled out in the aftermath of the *Marathassa* situation seemed unwarranted, and Vancouver's pristine green veneer was left unspoiled. For many, especially those embedded in industry, it was exactly the example they were looking for: sure, accidents happen, but look—we have the skills and technology to clean them up. Whether it's Deepwater Horizon or Fukushima or something a lot smaller, good old human ingenuity and technology can avert or at least tidy up pretty much any disaster.

That oil spill was hardly the first environmental calamity that required cleaning up in Vancouver. Just a month before the *Marathassa* spill, a fairly major port fire had broken out in (still) unexplained circumstances. Huge plumes of vicious-looking smoke had cascaded across the whole eastern side of Vancouver, billowing out from the downtown container port. A six-meter shipping container of trichloroisocyanuric acid, an industrial disinfectant, had arrived from China and was waiting to be loaded onto a train bound for Eastern Canada when it caught fire. The city's downtown core was immediately put on lockdown: officials quickly warned residents to stay inside, lock the windows, not breathe the air (!), and if anyone had respiratory issues to get out of Dodge ASAP. The warning was lifted after a few hours, the fire was controlled, the smoke subsided that same day, and by late afternoon everything had returned to normal. The incident presented itself as potentially catastrophic, then just as quickly was dealt with, and the whole thing was almost immediately forgotten.[15]

These two incidents underline quite starkly that even in Vancouver—the self-styled Greenest City in the World,[16] bathed in a clean,

FIGURE 1.3
—
Smoke billowing from the 2015 Vancouver Port fire.
Photo by Ryan Stelting.

naturally wholesome reputation—*normal* is still toxically tenuous. In any given year, something like five hundred containers of that same industrial disinfectant pass through that same Vancouver port, and at any given time three or four containers of trichloroisocyanuric compounds are sitting around on the docks, among thousands of other containers of various hazardous substances that stream through the city every year.[17] None of them seem to catch fire very often, and no one seems to know what caused that particular container to blaze in March 2015; but, as with the oil spill, most everyone seems more or less satisfied with the hazmat emergency responses. These two situations were just another couple of incidents that elicited possible emergency and upheaval and were then handled smoothly.

The chemical fire and the bunker fuel spill were relatively small and harmless in and of themselves (especially compared to so many industrial disasters in the Global South), but symbolically and ideologically they revealed a great deal. Much of the subsequent local analyses tended to fall into two clearly defined and full-throated antagonistic camps. For some, these incidents were singular markers of the ecological perils in front of us and harbingers of the increasingly desperate need to limit industrial development. For others, they were just minor occurrences that were cleaned up quickly and effectively, providing demonstrable evidence that with sound management we can handle the extractive economy safely. But these two positions present a false dichotomy—in reality, most of us believe both things simultaneously, and a whole lot in between.

Vancouver is hardly the only jurisdiction in the grip of these debates. Every city, every town, every watershed, every bioregion is bound by the same recursively deepening choices that are presented as the inevitabilities of development versus the intractabilities of ecological decline. Our relationships with the other-than-human world are seeping into every social and economic conversation. Increasingly (and with accelerating speed) political cartographies are being shaped by environmental imperatives, and overwhelmingly those conversations are now necessarily entangled with global warming. Debates that were once exclusively local concerns now have planetary repercussions. In other words, the tar sands are not just an Albertan affair: they are *everyone's* business.

The scientific debate about global warming was essentially settled by the late 1970s, and decades of subsequent research have confirmed and nuanced the original claim that anthropogenically produced carbon levels in the atmosphere would precipitate calamitous warming of the climate, as well as other grim repercussions. Running alongside this research, and often entwined with it, wave after wave of sophisticated evidence has been documenting biodiversity collapses, watershed precarity, species extinctions, and air, water, and soil pollutants. There is no reasonable, reality-based argument that can be marshalled to counter the fact that we are in a world-historical epoch of environmental peril.

The battles we now face are most typically framed as fossil-fuel industries versus more sustainable developmental strategies; oil versus solar/wind/electric; industrial versus postindustrial. These dichotomies are part of it, for sure, but we suspect that such questions function to obscure deeper and more troubling questions about tradition and change, nostalgia and imagination, duration and place. Our suspicion, like that of so many others, is that we have to excavate further, to look to the narratives of development and progress entangled within the two dominant thematics of our time—capitalism and colonialism—if we are to have much hope of getting our arms around an ecological future.

FOR THINGS TO STAY THE SAME, EVERYTHING HAS TO CHANGE

Most conventional definitions of ecology revolve exclusively around biological relationships. The word emerged in Germany in the nineteenth century, coined by zoologist Ernst Haeckel as *oecologie*; its etymology derives from the Greek *oikos*, a dwelling or a house, and *logie*, the study of something. Dictionary definitions describe ecology as "the branch of biology that deals with the relations of organisms to one another and to their physical surroundings."[18] Overwhelmingly, everyday uses of the word take ecology to be a fundamentally scientific endeavor rather than a political one. Conservation narratives, for example, tend to draw a circle around specific aspects of the other-than-human world (a forest, a watershed, a certain species under threat) in an attempt to preserve their integrity. The problem, in most every circumstance, is that the threats to the inside of the circle exist *outside* of it.

This begins to sketch out the ongoing schism within ecological discourses between science and politics, but beyond that, it is remarkable how little confluence or clarity there is in describing what ecology is: "No consensus as to what constitutes 'ecology' has ever emerged."[19] Thinkers from every ideological and disciplinary tradition have deployed the term to instrumental ends: systems and population ecologists, eco-socialists and eco-anarchists, social and political ecologists, environmental justice movements, and green political parties have all tried to mobilize *ecology* for particular purposes. We rely on many of these traditions in shifting and flexible ways, but it is striking how difficult it is, even for thinkers we admire, to cleanly articulate what they mean when they use the word.

And now the velocity of global warming has thrown so much of ecological scholarship into disarray as planetary-scaled climate disruptions accelerate, adding new and emergent vectors as contemporary theorists grapple with how to define the term. Philosopher Michel Serres in the *The Natural Contract* argues that in the face of this new form of global environmental crisis, science overtakes law and politics as the space of decision making, to a place where adjudication of human problems is no longer possible in the same way.[20] As Serres writes, what is new in the questions of today is that "At stake is the Earth in its totality, and humanity, collectively. Global history enters nature; global nature enters history: this is something entirely new in philosophy."[21]

Ecology is often framed exclusively by rationalist and scientific discourses, and is all too rarely grounded in politics. This tendency simultaneously externalizes and marginalizes politicized claims as irrelevant to ecological integrities. Colonialism, capitalism, and environmental degradation are inextricably bound together, and in our view, struggling with that entanglement is essential to understanding and redefining ecology.[22]

Our central claim here is that by definition, any questions of ecology are immediately questions of land politics and sovereignty: who gets to make what decisions for what land? Here in Vancouver, for example, we live in the territories of the səlil'wətaʔɬ (Tsleil-Waututh), Sḵwx̱wú7mesh (Squamish), and xʷməθkʷəy̓əm (Musqueam) people.

The experience of colonialism is so recent in Canada, and especially here on the West Coast (where it is still very much in progress), that trying to think about what an ecological future could look like has to place the relationships between settlers and Indigenous people at its center. That imperative is true everywhere, regardless of how recent the displacement and dispossession.*

The root of the genocidal rationalities colonized people face is always the attempt to eliminate connections to the land: to dislodge, exterminate, and/or assimilate people and their subjectivities—sometimes gently, most often brutally—into enforcing narratives of progress and modernization, private property and markets, states and borders. And thus, thinking about ecology or natural resource extraction or economic development has to encounter Indigenous displacement, and dispossession, both theoretically and materially. In Canada, as in several other parts of the globe, we've seen highly publicized efforts by the government over the past decade at apology and reconciliation with Indigenous people, but the one key ingredient—land—almost always stays off the agenda. As Leanne puts it: "Land has never been part of the Canadian reconciliation discourse, and Indigenous peoples will not survive as Indigenous peoples without homelands."[23]

Leanne writes about her experiences with elders and the spheres of knowledge they hold, ways of thinking about and comprehending the world that are often difficult to translate into Western frames of progress.[24] So when we ask her about development it often feels like we are reaching past each other. Part of Leanne's scholarly work calls for a reclamation of land as pedagogy and a centering of Indigenous stories, processes, and protocols that derive from the land as part of the creation and mobilization of knowledge.

---

*Colonialism is not enacted everywhere in the same way with the same goals or strategies: there are many colonialisms. Numerous scholars have done extensive work taxonomizing, categorizing, and analyzing the effects of specific colonial articulations, but in this book we are speaking of colonial rationalities as a comprehensive worldview. Here in North America the mode is best described as *settler colonialism*, where colonial settlers come to stay and do not leave.

She writes, "Intelligence flows through relationships between living entities."[25] Crucially, she insists that it is not the task of Indigenous knowledge to be recognized by Western institutions. She writes that knowledge keepers, cultural producers, and activists need to look away from the academy and reestablish a relationship to the land as a part of being in the world, and to restore a resurgent Indigenous nationhood. She writes: "We need to be able to articulate in a clear manner our visions for the future, for living as Indigenous Peoples in contemporary times. To do so, we need to engage Indigenous processes, since according to our traditions, the processes of engagement highly influence the outcome of the engagement itself. We need to do this on our own terms, without the sanction, permission or engagement of the state, western theory or opinions of Canada."[26]

Other Indigenous scholars who speak about the politics of refusal have much to offer ecological conversations from a radically decolonizing perspective, particularly in foregrounding Indigenous approaches to jurisdiction, sovereignty, and justice. Audra Simpson talks about a productive place of *refusal*—particularly refusal of forms of recognition offered by the colonial state.[27] This stance has a strong relationship to Dene scholar Glen Coulthard's critiques of liberal forms of state recognition and reconciliation. Coulthard's definition of *grounded normativity* is useful here: "The modalities of Indigenous land-connected practices and longstanding experiential knowledge that inform and structure our ethical engagements with the world and our relationships with human and nonhuman others over time."[28]

In discussing the work of Audra Simpson and Coulthard, Leanne Simpson asks, "What does that mobilization look like? What happens when we build movements that refuse colonial recognition as a starting point and turn inwards building a politics of refusal that isn't just productive, but that is generative?"[29] These three scholars, among many others, would argue that the relationship to land is essential to building an understanding of domination, both between humans and between humans and other-than-humans. In that sense, a decolonized horizon is a crucial starting point to any contemporary discussions of ecology.

The vast majority of land here in British Columbia, apart from that covered by a few modern-day treaties, was brazenly stolen.[30] In the rest of North America where lands have been subject to treaty, overwhelmingly those agreements have been manipulated, ignored, and violated so repeatedly that they would never stand any test of international law or morality.[31] The Canadian and US experiences echo those in countries across the planet: colonized people overpowered or betrayed, their lands stolen, their lives imperiled. The ironies run deep: we live in nations ruled by law, governed by systems of legal obligations that fixate on property rights. Yet each system rests on a dogged denial of originary land theft. Leanne puts it wryly: "You know what, when an individual even within Canadian law steals a really expensive car and gets caught—they still have to give it back! They don't get to keep it even if it's worth a lot of money and they really like it."[32] And it's not just land as a national narrative that the colonial state covets. It is a material lust: the oil and gas, the minerals, the hydroelectric power, the timber, the animals. The battles to reclaim colonized homelands can seem so daunting that it is sometimes easy to miss the Indigenous resurgences all around us.

Putting decolonization at the center of thinking about land, and thus ecology, opens up possibilities for *all of us*—not in a nostalgic sense, but in a resurgent sense. We need these creative resistances and affirmative visions of the future now more than ever, in a time when narratives of inevitability are trotted out with relentless predictability. Nearly every day we hear ever-direr warnings from some UN body or scientific panel that we have *this* many years left and *these* targets to hit before the tipping points when the whole world unravels. The languages at hand to think through and beyond global warming seem consistently inadequate, and sometimes it feels impossible to think *outside* the exhaustions of dominant narratives. This is part of why Indigenous insistences on land are so vital: not just because of the *justice* of rectifying land thefts, but because so many of us feel a simmering desperation to find new ways to think about and relate to land and the other-than-human world.

Leanne describes the alternative to alienation, poverty, and dispossession not as development, but as "rebuilding the original intentions of my ancestors, which was for me and the ancestors who haven't been born yet to live as Mississauga Anishnabec unfettered and unharassed on our homeland." That sounds beautiful for her and her people, but by implication really great for the rest of us too. Not because many of us have clearly delineated cultural milieus or homelands or original intentions that we might seek to return to, but because the political conditions in which Leanne's claims to her territory could be answered are the exact same circumstances within which we might be able to grasp the meaning of ecology.

The only way colonial states are ever going to take Indigenous claims seriously is if they are willing to think about land very differently. As long as land is positioned as a *resource*, the discussion can only be about *how much* it is exploited, *how much* should be taken from it, whether it is done profligately or more modestly, and on what timelines. Within this frame, all there can be is *exploitation*—of human and other-than-human alike: their futures are thoroughly entangled.

The hopefulness of anticolonialism informs an ecology beyond domination, an ecology that necessarily confronts displacements and seeks reparations. Decolonization cannot hope for simple reconciliation—to offer colonized people some new rights or acknowledgments and call it even. It has to trouble every notion of sovereignty—of who gets to make what decisions about what land, and why. Ecology demands justice, but most environmental thinking wants to peripheralize and externalize those claims. This is among the core questions we're struggling with here: how to put land politics in the heart of ecological thinking in a politically transformative way.

Housing and planning scholar Lisa K. Bates helps with this question considerably when she speaks of the relationships between "land stolen from people, and people stolen from land." If most of us do not have originary homelands, as is the case for so many Black people, who have been violently displaced via slavery and ongoing oppression, how can ecology demand a connection to land? What land, whose land? How can Black struggles for justice and reparations connect to Indigenous land struggles, and to ecology? We suspect that thinking beyond ideologies of development and exploitation are an inescapable part of that project.

Development starts with the stance that all land needs to be improved—that it can do better and be bettered, that it can relinquish its wealth, that it can be made useful for particular human desires. Progress and development are perhaps the central animating narratives of capitalism, and both rest on particular renditions of *scarcity* and *anxiety*: that we do not have sufficient resources, that we are vulnerable, that we always need more. Leanne talks a lot about the anxiety that haunts capitalism and colonialism, about how nothing is *ever* enough for settlers, how settlers always want more.*

This dissatisfaction—this hunger—has been noted as a characteristic of colonial pillage all over the world. Here on Canada's West

---

*We want to highlight our use of the word *settler* here and throughout the book. A loaded term that has come under increasing and rightful scrutiny, it refers to non-Indigenous arrivals and residents on Indigenous territory who are afforded their legitimacy by the settler state. It is a blanket term that obscures the vast array of differentiation among non-Indigenous inhabitants and the routes by which they came to be here, and reduces the entire population to a simple Indigenous/settler binary. The landscape is far more complicated than that, with vast differences in access to resources and privileges. To call refugees and recent arrivals, for example, who have escaped disastrous circumstances elsewhere, *settlers* tends to whitewash their displacements and expulsions. Similarly, rendering Black people in North America as *settlers* papers over a history of slavery and violent relocations and suggests a tenuous legitimacy. These are intensely complicated and fraught distinctions, which we are not going to delve into here. But we do want to acknowledge the complexities of the term and note that the three of us are clear that (for now, anyway) *settlers* is the best word we have to describe ourselves.

Coast, historian Keith Thor Carlson, working with the Stó:lō Nation Heritage Trust and cultural advisor Albert (Sonny) McHalsie, uses the term *Xwelitem* to refer to non-Indigenous arrivals to Stó:lō territory, and explains it in this way: "This indigenous term, which literally translates as 'hungry ones' or 'starving ones,' has a long history and is still in widespread, popular use among Stó:lō people." He explains that it rose to common use in gold rush times when miners were literally starving along the Fraser River's banks, but the word "has relevance among contemporary Stó:lō people because the immigrants to their country continue to display hunger for Stó:lō resources to which they have no moral or legal rights."[33]

The two of us (Am and Matt) both certainly qualify as settlers here in Canada, if from very different backgrounds. Matt is a fourth-generation settler: his Euro-mongrel family (Irish, English, Scottish, French) has been here in the southwest of the province since the early 1900s, arriving via the shipping industry. Am's family originates in what is today Pakistan, near Faisalabad and Sialkot. With colonial partition in the late 1940s, Sikh families were uprooted to the Indian side of the Punjabi border to rural farming villages—his father was born before partition and his mother after. They eventually immigrated—his father first in the 1960s to work in the forest industry, and his mother in the early 1970s—and settled in Williams Lake, in British Columbia's interior.[34]

We are both nerdy, activist types. We both have PhDs with research focuses on ecological discourses. We both spend a lot of time speaking and writing in public, we've written books about ecology, displacements, and sovereignties, and we both have an abiding interest in critical theory. Though we both occasionally draw paychecks from universities, neither of us is an academic; we both identify primarily as community organizers who spend the vast bulk of our time doing work outside the academy.

We also both grew up in small resource towns in British Columbia, and so, entwined with our critiques of extractivist capitalism, we have a pretty deep well of sympathy for people who find themselves employed in fishing, mining, oil, and forestry. Both of us have buddies, family members, and colleagues who make their living working in and with extractive industries. It's not all that hard to imagine alternative life trajectories that might have found ourselves making our money working in the tar sands, or someplace like it.

So if we are in pursuit of a new way to define ecology, the question arises: why, exactly? Thinking very differently about ecology and trying to redefine it is not just a theoretical task: it is also a strategic and tactical one. In short, we are seeking a politicization of ecology.

We both have reflexive sympathies for "green" tendencies, but so many of those conversations rub us the wrong way. The eco-performances of capital, the blissfully ignorant privilege so many environmentalists flaunt, the futile (and deeply counterproductive) tactics of shame and behavioral discipline—all of it begins to explain why ecological claims so often fall on deaf ears. Ecology has to speak to *class* directly: to explicitly confront inequality with believable claims that a different world is possible. The startling impasses today around global warming specifically, and ecology more generally, suggest that current progressive strategies and discourses are nearing exhaustion.

The domination of the other-than-human world by humans is predicated on the domination of humans by humans, and thus any ecological claims must be rooted in *social* change. A critique of capitalism is not enough; it has to be a decolonizing politics. Capitalism may well be able to solve global warming and carry on happily. Environmental thinking habitually points to capitalism and its rhetorical stand-ins—growth, greed, consumption, and the like—as the core driver of biospheric degradation and global warming, but it is very clear that capitalism can outlive global warming, and equally, that global warming can outlive capitalism. We might well see a time when state and capital have essentially solved, or at least mitigated the threat of, global warming in the same way that they have apparently averted the threat of chlorofluorocarbons (CFCs),[35] while leaving all the core pillars of capitalism—profit, exploitation, surplus labor value, and all the rest—intact.[36] Capitalism has proven spectacularly malleable and agile; it has always been willing to work with and through the state, and it will be able to exist long after any climate crisis is ameliorated, if the crisis is framed only as that—only as one of climate.

This is one of the key contributions we hope to make: that a critique of capitalism is necessary, but insufficient, for an ecological analysis. Ecology requires an interrogation of the colonial and predatory rationalities that dominate contemporary relationships with land, and the anxious, restless yearnings that underpin them. We suggest that the politics with which decolonizing claims might be realized are the *exact same politics* needed to confront global warming. Decolonizing claims are inextricably entangled with ecology, and the possibility of that politics then opens us up to a reconstituted understanding of what the sweetness of living might mean today: a renovated way of being in the world.

This is the ecological future we are trying to imagine. But we're really struggling with it—we're as bound up with the contradictions as anyone. As we researched and wrote this book, we found ourselves returning time and again to the relationship between political subjectivities and planetary-scale crises, not so much as a strategic problematic, but as a corporeal one. Global crises demand we act, *right now*—but our everyday efforts are so inconsequential. Our performances of recycling and climate-justice marching are matched by our relentless fossil-fuel consumption. We're self-aware carbon pigs, climate villains, and walking biohazards, bifurcated into self-disciplining, self-renouncing selves, one part constantly monitoring and castigating the other.

One of our strategies here as we try to break out of our own impasses is to speak closely with people whose jobs and fortunes depend directly on extractivism. At the same time, we try to listen carefully to people who are being directly and materially damaged by the oil and gas industry, especially Indigenous people whose land is under threat. In that, we are searching for some affirmative routes, some forward motion to propel us out of our general inertia. We're especially interested in the idea of change in the context of tradition.

The historical record is certainly very strong on the ability of technoscientific modernist intelligence to solve specific types of problems, especially in overcoming barriers to production. But the contemporary record is just as bleak when it comes to the other-than-human world, and there is ample evidence that much of what is frequently described as capitalist triumph is actually catastrophic loss. It has become increasingly clear that more of the same thinking and acting will not suffice to avert biocollapses: "If we want things to stay as they are, things will have to change."[37]

TIME KEEPS ON SLIPPING, SLIPPING, SLIPPING*

But what might that mean, for everything to change? Reimagining tradition—reconsidering our most entrenched, most established and inherited modes of thinking and acting—is unwelcome work for most of us. It would be so much easier if there were just a *solution* to all this global warming trouble. The will to panacea is endlessly attractive across ideological spectrums, and the search for something, *anything*, that can save us from ourselves has so much pull: walls of rechargeable batteries, geo-engineered carbon-eating drones, giant reflective mirrors in the sky to deflect the sun's rays, or albedo enhancement or stratospheric aerosols? Something?

If a technological solution is not on the near-enough horizon, then surely there is a similarly scaled political solution. Surely the UN or some world-government bodies with sufficient authority can compel global populations to reduce their emissions, stop polluting, and save biohabitats. A planetary authority—or what Geoff Mann and Joel Wainwright have called a "Climate Leviathan," a global

---

*With regards to Steve Miller.

superagency for pollution

climate regime that usurps national or local powers on a sweeping level—is more frequently advocated than one might think. Consider the seminal book *Ecoscience* by Paul and Anne Ehrlich with John Holdren (Harvard physicist and once National Science Advisor to former President Obama), written in 1977:

> Perhaps those agencies, combined with UNEP and the United Nations population agencies, might eventually be developed into a Planetary Regime—sort of an international superagency for population, resources, and environment. Such a comprehensive Planetary Regime could control the development, administration, conservation, and distribution of all natural resources. ... Thus the Regime could have the power to control pollution not only in the atmosphere and oceans, but also in such freshwater bodies as rivers and lakes that cross international boundaries or that discharge into the oceans. The Regime might also be a logical central agency for regulating all international trade, perhaps including assistance from DCs to LDCs, and including all food on the international market. The Planetary Regime might be given responsibility for determining the optimum population for the world and for each region and for arbitrating various countries' shares within their regional limits.[38]

While this particular prescription is terrifying, mass-scale authoritarianism travels in various guises, and such calls are repeated often by sincere (as well as many less benign) environmentalists who despair at the unwillingness of national governments, let alone transnational capital, to seriously address global warming.[39]

The desire for clarity, for finality, for relief from anxiety has led many others to abandon democracy as a political operating principle. James Lovelock, the originator of the Gaia hypothesis, has been plainly skeptical about democracy and openly pines for authoritarian control: "We need a more authoritative world. We've become a sort of cheeky, egalitarian world where everyone can have their say.

It's all very well, but there are certain circumstances—a war is a typical example—where you can't do that. You've got to have a few people with authority who you trust who are running it."[40] Neo-Malthusians like Garrett Hardin have long-advocated for forced sterilization, eugenics, and overtly racist immigration control.[41] Far-end deep ecologists like Pentti Linkola in Finland are explicitly fascist,[42] but many other more moderate climate scientists and commentators easily shade or gesture that way when prompted. In a 2010 issue of *Environmental Politics*, for example, political scientist Mark Beeson wrote that forms of authoritarianism "may become not only justifiable, but essential for the survival of humanity in anything approaching a civilised form."[43] Dale Jamieson, professor of environmental studies, philosophy, and law at New York University and author of 2014's *Reason in a Dark Time*, calls global warming "the largest collective action problem that humanity has ever faced"; he claims that evolution has equipped humans and our political institutions poorly for the problem and that, "sadly, it is not entirely clear that democracy is up to the challenge of climate change."[44]

Such calls to authoritarianism in the name of the climate are hardly an isolated or surprising phenomenon, which is part of why it's important to be suspicious of the languages of crisis. In some ways we *are* facing a climate crisis that *does* demand immediate collective responses. But *crisis* invokes an emergency where debate is suspended, reflection limited, and objections marginalized. The implications of invoking a *climate crisis* are all too vivid: it is into this breach where hegemonic states and capital step so easily and so reassuringly. There is in fact a novel peril in front of us, a newly constituted, only recently fully understood confluence of events and circumstances, but it is only one in a long series. Declaring a crisis creates a state of exception that allows authorities to impose measures or rationalities that would not be possible during a conventional or "normal" period. Global warming, unfortunately, could very much create—perhaps is already creating—a set of emergency-fueled discourses that are foreclosing possibilities all around us.

While global warming generates a seductively enveloping urgency, we need to resist calls to planetary discipline. The work of ecology has to be done *by* people, not *to* people, and any paths to ecological futures will rest on rooted experimentations that can build new ways of acting out of new traditions. Resistance has to be the product of insistent, relentless inventions of new traditions in the present.* Somewhere between the people and the state lies the possibility of a new modern tradition—or, as French philosopher Alain Badiou would say, *the possibility of the possibility of something new.*[45]

Any egalitarian economic and political movement is not a linear construction. It is much messier and more complicated, with myriad regressions and atemporal tendencies. As Badiou once put it: "Today, we know that it's not so simple. We have really to understand that sometimes under the name of progress, we have, in fact, something that is often against human life, against human beings. ... The dialectical relationship between progress and tradition is completely different today."[46] He argues that "tradition is something that does not organize change but rather organizes a sort of struggle against the change."[47] The task "is to organize in the subject the return to the good repetition, or the good life inside the repetition."[48] In other words, interrogating the specific relationships between tradition and change asks: what should continue on, what ought to be abandoned?

Throughout this book, we use the theoretical work of scholars such as Simpson, Simpson, and Coulthard to think through ecological questions, and on our journey we make some links between their scholarship and theorists from the radical continental tradition, not

---

*When we use the word *tradition* here, we are talking about the repetition of certain ideas and practices that are materially produced and constructed in the present. We understand that our use of the word echoes certain nostalgias and ossified forms, but we are talking about tradition in a much more active sense. Our argument is not that answers lie in the past, but rather that we should reproblematize the term *tradition* as something far beyond a simple, reactionary conservative idea. Lots more on this to come.

as means of validation or recognition, but as an attempt at productive, critical, and generative solidarity. For example, Alain Badiou's critiques of private property and the state are not the same as those of Coulthard or either Simpson, but they all allow for a critique of the existing apparatus of state and capital, albeit in very different ways. When calling for a politics of solidarity, it's important to understand these differences, similarities, entanglements, and frictions. It is also our contention that Indigenous worldviews and theorists have a lot to teach traditional forms of Western philosophy, particularly in highlighting their gaps and their historical connections to colonialism.

So that's our project here: to search for new definitions of ecology that can articulate relationships *to* and *with* land. When we are talking about land, it is not just forest or the bush or rural areas—we are talking about *all* land. Land is an urban phenomenon just as much as anywhere else: the sidewalk, the city block, the backyard, just as much as mountains, jungles, tundra and rivers. All land has been subject to logics of domination, and thus all relationships with land are immediately forced to confront colonialism.

Decolonization cannot be reduced to discourse, though: it has to be material. As Eve Tuck and Wayne Yang put it: "Decolonization is not a swappable term. ... Decolonization doesn't have a synonym. ... Decolonization is not a metonym for social justice."[49] They continue:

> Decolonization as metaphor allows people to equivocate these contradictory decolonial desires because it turns decoloniza tion into an empty signifier to be filled by any track towards liberation. In reality, the tracks walk all over land/people in settler contexts. Though the details are not fixed or agreed upon, in our view, decolonization in the settler colonial context must involve the repatriation of land simultaneous to the recognition of how land and relations to land have always already been differently understood and enacted; that is, *all* of the land, and not just symbolically. ... Settler colonialism and its decolonization implicates and unsettles everyone.[50]

No truly ecological society—a society that is rooted in nonexploitive, nondominatory relationships with land and other-than-humans— can be financed by land theft. Thus any search for ecology has to start with decolonization and a grappling with capital, instigating assiduous renovations of how all decisions about land allocation, control, and access are made.

REORDERING

Capitalism is nothing if not a sophisticated ordering operation of a given population: a secular religion with a theological belief in markets and their myriad disciplinary methods. Capital's ability to constantly create and re-create itself wipes away the trauma and memory of disaster. Tradition under capitalism is constantly being reinvented to suit new languages of accumulation and dispossession, and accumulation *by* dispossession.

In our view, conversations around oil, global warming, and crisis are potentially very dangerous when they are defined by capital and the state because, ultimately, they reveal a particular faith: a faith in a capitalist paradigm of beautiful destruction. From the perspective of capital, global warming is seen as an opportunity that should be faithfully exploited.

Walter Benjamin often described capitalism as religion. In a 1921 essay, he wrote that "Capitalism is entirely without precedent, in that it is a religion which offers not the reform of existence but its complete destruction. It is the expansion of despair, until despair becomes a religious state of the world in the hope that this will lead to salvation."[51] It's difficult not to think of such an apocalyptic vision of capitalism as simultaneously one of religion and destruction, and how this idea reveals the antagonistic relationship between capital and the other-than-human world.

We're intrigued by the idea of change as a kind of tradition. Wrapped in the history of modernity, beyond the desire for newness, is the reflex of progress that holds so much of history in contempt. Any history that doesn't fit with capitalist narratives is cast as an obstruction, a blockage to the flow of the new, to be discarded and forgotten.

Presenting capitalism and development as the only possible form of progressive social ordering is a move toward closure in thinking about change. Today, what is being presented, at least in the narrow frame of the Global North, is that there is no modernity other than a capitalist one. Theorizing an ecological future requires a rupture between capitalism and modernity. The challenge is to construct new ideas of change while reimagining what we talk about when we talk about tradition, especially when we (and we mean that in the general "we," but more pressingly in the particular—i.e., the two of us) carry so many contradictory, confusing, and often revanchist traditions with us.

Among the most central narratives of capital is *exploitation*, a close cousin of domination. We get a clearer glimpse of an ecological future when the classical Marxist rendition of exploitation is extended beyond human relations. As Glen Coulthard articulated: "We have to extend our concern with exploitation of labor to other-than-human communities. Exploitation is an instrumental relation to the other. It's a condition that views all other things as existing for our consumption and gain. The main problem with exploitation is a lack of consideration of others as agents themselves, and a corresponding lack of informed consent to the power relations that affect them."[52]

Understanding the exploitation of labor—the extraction of surplus value from human bodies—is foundational to understanding capitalism. It is necessary but insufficient for understanding the task of ecology. Coulthard continues: "Marxists tend to focus too much on accumulation, too much on the body and labor: it's too anthropocentric an understanding, in my view. In presenting class struggle as universal struggle, it is very parochial because we have to face the larger ecological life sphere that we all live within." Extending our understanding of exploitation opens up a wider set of political possibilities and can help us think through global warming to larger ecological questions:

What if we start to think about exploitation that doesn't just happen to labor? What is exploitation? Decisions made over another without their substantive input or consent. It's the extraction from another without a consideration of them, or our ethical relationship to them as such. They're just instrumental—just a means to an end. We have a language of exploitation that needs to be stripped of its narrower definition in the anthropocentric Marxist sense. The alternative would be nonexploitative, nondominating relationships governed by ethical relationships to the other. Others being comrades, conationals, neighbors and crucially, in a wider sense, other-than-human relations. Exploitation gives us a language that crosses political and anthropocentric ideas.[53]

Reaching past narrow definitions of exploitation to consider the other-than-human world allows us to speak of domination more broadly. It opens us up to what nonexploitative, nondominating relationships might require politically, but it also demands alternatives. How can we deploy existing languages and understandings of exploitation to build new definitions of ecology?

One route to answering that question that we are especially fond of is Italian philosopher Giorgio Agamben's speculative invocation of Alexandre Kojeve's use of the term *la dolce vita* or *douceur de vivre*— *the sweetness of living*, *the good life*, or *the sweet life*. These ideas describe what he argues is a common attitude in Spain, Italy, and southern Europe that is qualitatively different from the Protestant work ethic of northern European countries.[54] Agamben claims this attitude describes a wholly different relationship to the future, a recovery of time, a resistance to capitalism, and the preservation of a significant way of living: the capacity to define life as something outside of work. He notes that the ongoing, recurring, and deepening economic crises in Europe are being used as instruments of rule, but might be better thought of as one rendition of the sweetness of life resisting discipline.[55]

Our point here is not to argue for or against Agamben's thesis per se, but that his articulation of a *different way of being in the world* is a particularly relevant rupture.[56] Just its invocation is a powerful claim. It is these ruptures in capitalist certainties that are so critical: articulating alternative possible relationships to each other, to other species, to the land, and to the future. Every alternative to the logics of domination, every practiced alternative worldview constructs the outlines of potential new modern traditions that are called for today and the possibilities for constructing new kinds of freedom. In a time when even the unconscious is being colonized by capital, radical articulations of change become indispensable acts of resistance.[57]

For the past century, capitalism has ingested Marxism and let out a satisfying burp. For some, there is no crisis today; for them, the world can happily go on as it is. Capital, in its own narrative construction, has historically solved its ecological problems by counting the other-than-human world as externalities, mere objects for our use. For many, freedom is nothing more than *the freeing of capital from constraints*—but any progressive renovation of the idea of freedom has to be affirmative: a freedom *to*, not a freedom *from*. Ecology has to speak to all kinds of people in all kinds of circumstances, as a change that can be materially exercised in the concrete world by masses of people.

The challenge of global warming often feels overwhelming and disorienting, and confuses traditional political cartographies. We're faced with a dismaying constellation of political responses ranging from straight denial to geo-engineering to authoritarian state solutions to consumerist pressure to state led transitionalism to supranationalism to relocalization—and so much else. The existing categories of responses are neither exclusive nor exhaustive, and most people occupy multiple positions at once: we all often believe many discordant things simultaneously. There are often real gaps between where our beliefs lie and our actions land. Positions and solutions are liquid; they tend to overlap and bleed into one another, and move across boundaries.

The vast majority of global warming scholarship, however, marginalizes or ignores the politics of land, its historical trajectory and its practical consequences. We are convinced that linking the domination of people to the domination of land and the other-than-human world is a key to grasping an ecological future. We would go even further to suggest that any robust ecological discourses *have* to start with decolonization and thoroughly renovated land politics.

The right question here might be: "How do our relationships with land inform and order the way humans conduct relationships with each other and other-than-human beings?"[58] New modern traditions today need to define freedom *through* equality, *through* differentiation and complexity, *through* a relationship with land and other-than-human beings. In so doing, we can recover a reconstituted understanding of what *the sweetness of living* might mean today.

This is our starting point for grappling with ecology, but as we embarked on this project we weren't entirely sure what that might mean to our everyday lives. We wanted to search further: beyond our keyboards, beyond our familiar milieus and tidy consensual nods. We wanted to think about global warming and the possibility of an ecological future in conversation with people who have very different politics from our own. We wanted to find definitions of ecology that place land at its center. So we decided to head to the tar sands.

2
EDMONTON

—

Cree, Saulteau, Blackfoot, Métis, and Nakota Sioux Territories

That's how we found ourselves traveling through Alberta, heading to Fort McMurray and the Athabasca tar sands. Canada harbors what is often described as the world's third-biggest oil reserves, with at least 172 billion currently confirmed barrels untapped, 98 percent of which is in the Alberta tar sands.[1] Fort McMurray, or the Mac—Fort McMoney, for many—is the piston in the engine of Canada's oil and gas industry. The city is Canada's richest, with an average household income of $191,507,[2] and its population has been growing, then booming, for the last four decades, as thousands of people from across the globe have converged on this isolated little spot in the northeast of the province.

It hasn't always been this way. It wasn't until the 1970s that the oil and gas industry took serious notice of what Indigenous people had known for millennia: the ground all through the region is saturated with sticky, tar-like bitumen, creating the oil sands. It took years of experimentation and generations of new extractive technologies to figure out how to efficiently get the bitumen out of the sand, but now the sheer volume of oil that is available in the area is staggering. Industry often throws around numbers in the *trillions* of barrels that might be conceivably available in the near future as innovative advances make more and more of the reserves accessible. Even in the present, Fort McMurray has emerged as perhaps the preeminent capitalist articulation of development in our time—the Alberta tar sands are often called "the world's biggest industrial development project,"[3] even the "largest industrial project in human history."[4] No matter how you measure it or what superlatives you invoke, Fort Mac has emerged as one of the hottest ecological battlegrounds of our time.

FIGURE 2.1
Just off Highway 63. Photo by Selena Couture.

We were definitely eager to see the place, but we needed some re-inforcements. We needed company and someone to help us think things through. So we called our old (and we do mean *old*) pal Joe in Portland, Oregon, and invited him to join us. A journalist by training but a cartoonist at heart, he essentially invented the genre of long-form cartoon journalism. Joe's books *Palestine, Footnotes in Gaza, The Fixer, Safe Area Goražde*, and *The Great War* are classics, and one of the key themes throughout his work is land and the struggles over it. Whether it's the Middle East or Bosnia or India, Joe has a distinc-tively subtle and disarming way of listening to people, of uncovering narratives of dispossession and taking sophisticated and generous looks at dismayingly complex situations. He's a good-humored, con-vivial, and warm friend who's easy to travel and drink with, but we also wanted to learn from his sharp political instincts.

What we are after is a clearly articulated political stance that can attend to the complexities of global warming. All three of us instinc-tively point accusingly at capitalism's rapacious consumption, but that strikes us as inadequate. It's a start, but it's not enough. We're all accountable, and it's not just a malleably defined "capitalism" that is blocking paths to ecological possibilities. We knew we had to listen carefully to some new and sharper ideas.

Suffice to say, then, that despite some obvious differences, the three of us share a lot: basic political frames, journalistic sensibilities, con-flicted and conflicting class and ecological commitments, and general attitudes toward humor. And of course, all three of us are middle-aged, privileged dudes. So while our individual and collective positionalities immediately presented—and presents—a certain range of limitations (all of which we are pretty sure you have noted already!), it became im-mediately evident how useful it was to be on the ground.

It also became clear that much, even most, of the writing about global warming that we had relied on previously was dissatisfyingly inadequate. As soon as we started driving north we knew we were disturbing some of our most entrenched assumptions about global warming and ecology.[5]

BATTLE ROYALE

Environmental activists and writers often like to frame the tar sands as an epic battle, an all-out war where the future of the country, humanity, even the planet is being waged,[6] but that seems like a frustratingly elusive way to think about Fort Mac. It's easy to see though why so many people invoke military metaphors to talk about the conflicts over extractivism in North America—the battles at Standing Rock, for example, feel like harbingers of the decades to come when every pipeline, every mine, every watershed will be bitterly fought over. You don't have to look far from the tar sands to see the everyday damage being done to people. If you spend any in time in, say, Fort Chipewyan, the metaphors seem a lot more realistic.

Fort Chip is 220 kilometers north (downstream) from Fort Mac. It is a town of about a thousand, predominantly Cree, Chipewyan (Dene), and Métis people that is wracked by awful disease and cancer rates. In 2014, Health Canada finally recognized what residents had known for decades. In the words of one researcher: "Something unique is happening in Fort Chipewyan, especially around cancer."[7] The three-year million-dollar study interviewed 94 people and reported 23 cases of cancer, linked directly to high levels of contaminants from bitumen extraction found in the fish and animals residents rely on for food. The report also noted a wide range of other diseases, confirming the findings of multiple previous studies, and linked all directly to tar sands production.[8] Heading into Northern Alberta is not the same as heading into a war zone, but volatile tensions simmer all around, and in the midst of an economic downturn, the pressures felt that much more abrasive.

We converged on Edmonton from three separate directions, landing on the eve of a historic provincial election. Alberta is Canada's Texas. It's a swaggering, unapologetically and historically right-wing, full of itself, defensively aggressive and aggressively defensive, populist prairie-farming, no-apologies-resource-extracting, guns-and-religion kind of place, now emboldened by buckets of oil and gas money. Just like Texas, plenty of other clichés, stereotypes, and jousts are part of the package. But also, just like Texas, all of that is very far from the whole story—in fact, that's really not it at all.

All that oil and gas money has ushered in successive waves of immigration, so that even shit-kicking, stubble-jumping cities like Edmonton that were once derided as full of rubes and cattle and not much else now look a lot more cosmopolitan, with cafés, galleries, global-city pretensions, and university expansions. Calgary, which has a cultural reputation something akin to Houston's, was in the midst of a running love affair with its mayor Naheed Nenshi—a mildly progressive, Muslim, arts-supporting, former business-school instructor who won reelection in 2013 with 73 percent of the vote.[9] And of course, all of that sweet, sweet oil money has funded an avalanche of highly publicized green cultural and social initiatives.

But on that early May day in 2015, when the three of us arrived in Alberta for our first visit to the tar sands, things were decidedly less than rosy. Oil prices had been plunging hard for the previous eleven months,[10] and halfway through 2015 Bloomberg reported that energy was the worst-performing industry in the S&P 500 index over the past year.[11] When we stepped off our respective planes, the price of a barrel of oil had fallen to under $59 USD (which at the time was considered catastrophically low—hah!), throwing Albertans' thoughts for their budget and future financial prospects into disarray, with almost no contingency planning for oil's continued free fall and volatility, and almost no cushion in the face of apparently intractable price instabilities and glut. In the election spin-frenzy, the projected budget deficit was $5 billion for the 2015 fiscal year, a prospect that soon emerged as far too optimistic.[12] (By mid-2016, Alberta's annual deficit was projected at $11 billion; "the once debt-free province will be $32-billion in debt by the end of the current fiscal year."[13] By 2017, that debt was forecasted to balloon to $45 billion in 2017–18 and $71 billion by 2019–20.[14]) And so the bloodletting began: by the evening of May 5, 2015, the unthinkable had happened, the quasi-leftist New Democratic Party (NDP) had won a huge provincial majority, and the dynastic Progressive Conservative Party was reduced to a distant third.

It's hard to emphasize how disorienting that election result was, not just for Alberta but for all of Canada. It was as if Michelle Obama had won the Texas governor's race running on a Green Party platform. Or Elizabeth Warren had won Wyoming. Or Jesse Ventura had become the governor of Minnesota (wait, what?). Or Donald Trump had won the White House. (Too soon? That joke will always be too soon.) The Alberta NDP is possibly the most conservative variant of the NDP imaginable; they are nothing like socialist (as is often alleged) or even really all that leftist. They are resolutely in support of the oil industry and aggressively proselytize for pipeline construction, but they are socially progressive on a number of fronts, and the fact that they could be elected in Alberta with such a decisive majority was mind-bending. Not mind-bending in a Trump way, but reflective of the volatility that oil economies engender everywhere.

It was clear that the specter of global warming and Alberta's reputation as Canada's most abject and unapologetic environmental villain exerted real and significant pressure on the election—some of it political, some economic, some of it cultural.[15] In the months and years to come, the shine of Alberta's newly liberal-leaning political landscapes dimmed as brute realities and compromises became clearer; but that time and that election represented a sea change in how Albertans viewed themselves, and even more, how the rest of Canada and the world viewed Alberta.

Our multiple trips to Northern Alberta coincided with what would prove to be a vivid snapshot of a petro-economy in disarray. The price of oil (of course) continues to experience consistent volatility—the bottom has and will drop out more than once, there will be swift market lifts and false recoveries, Alberta will continue to hemorrhage jobs and money and then encounter sudden oases; but in 2015, the landscape had been shaken to its core. And Alberta's economic foundations will continue to wobble as long as the province depends so thoroughly on oil in a time of climate and energy turmoil. The coming years will surely see heavy doses of both good and bad news—conflicting economic numbers, anxious consumer confidence, and wild swings of stock prices in the oil and gas sector—as well as other characteristics of a traditional boom-and-bust economy. What makes this different from other crises (say, the oil shocks of the 1970s or the early 1980s) or other periods of economic flux are the multiplying instabilities of global warming. The volatility of economies so deeply reliant on oil closely mirror the accelerating volatility of climate disruptions.*

But when the three of us first dropped anchor in Edmonton that spring day before the election, most of the political turmoil was in the future. We had come to Alberta to see the tar sands, to think about the implications of oil and not to report on provincial (in both senses) politics. The oil sector holds such a confluence of power and money, and enjoys such a total lack of transparency, that it's often really hard to understand what's going on. We wanted to see the hyperbole for ourselves. We wanted to see the most fulsome expression

*Volatility is a constant theme in all resource towns and industries. Through 2015 and 2016 on our initial trips, the low price of oil was causing crises throughout Alberta, and OPEC-induced oil gluts were the popular villain. By 2017, when we returned to Fort Mac, the threat posed by fracking was more front and center in people's minds. In the first fiscal quarter of 2017 major players ExxonMobil, Royal Dutch Shell, and Marathon Oil substantially pulled out of their tar sands commitments, citing dwindling profits, unstable futures, and better energy prospects elsewhere (http://www.bnn.ca/companies-leaving -canada-s-oil-sands-acting-in-own-interest-trudeau-1.693314). Much of that investment was being impacted by regulatory environments, new interest in renewables, and continuing oil surpluses, but the reason most people on the ground cited was the amazingly profitable new fracking fields (especially in the US). As Charles E. Olson put it, "Fracking is where it's at. It's simpler and less risky. Oil companies just aren't willing to take the risks they were willing to take in days gone by." Olson noted that fracking is vastly less capital inten- sive, far more agile, and comparatively "a sure thing," meaning that energy giants are aggressively shifting their investments (https://www.rhsmith.umd .edu/news/why-shell-has-all-given-canadas-oil-sands).

of development ideology we could think of—to see the show up close and personal.

You don't have to actually go to the tar sands to encounter them. Every part of the Canadian economy is entangled with petrologics, and you can get a particularly heavy dose of it in Edmonton, a city built by and for oil. It's not hard to fly directly into Fort Mac, but the easiest route is through Edmonton, about a five-hour drive south, and it's a gentler way to ease yourself into the pool. Drop into the YEG airport at Edmonton, and it looks and feels like every other airport you've been to, but with a distinct petro-vibe. Long lists of flights to Fort McMurray, Firebag, Fort Hills, Fort Chip, East Tank Farm, and other tar sands sites flash and scroll down the Departure displays. Oil-celebrating art grins from display cases, murals, and ads. You can immediately spot the roving packs of guys just out of the oil patch throughout the terminal. They're everywhere, uniformed with their wrap-around sunglasses propped up on the bills of their ball caps, oil derrick tattoos, huge duffle bags, and guffaws, crowding the airport bars and ordering morning rounds of shots.

Edmonton is just another mid-sized, million-person, oil-industrial city, and it evinces the same feel as the airport. The city perches on the edge of the North Saskatchewan River in the middle of the Alberta Plains, but you might be in Russia or Brazil or Kazakhstan or any spot that is overtly yoked to oil. Extractive detritus lines the highways in, oil prices are front-page newspaper material every day, radio hosts and editorials jubilantly sneer at environmentalist pratfalls, and apparently, every urinal in town displays an advertisement for careers in the patch. Civic and university buildings are inevitably named after oil company donors. Their NHL team is called the Oilers. The prominent and well-loved junior hockey team is called the Oil Kings. Huge billboards shine with promises of so-called ethical oil produced here in Canada, regulated and safe. Sunny ways indeed.[16] But the tar sands are everywhere in Canada—they are as much in Calgary, Ottawa, or Vancouver as they are in Fort Mac: those are the

capital and regulatory sites of the same extraction processes, and in
Edmonton you cannot miss their prominence.

It's also easy to feel affection for the city. Edmonton is your good-
natured country cousin who has made a bunch of money and comes
into town for the weekend, pockets bulging, ready for action but not
sure where to find it. The place is now full of people from all over the
planet, and with them comes a cosmopolitan energy, one that older
residents have learned to comfortably work with and around. Driving down its wide streets, you can feel the city's agricultural roots,
but all that money hasn't just disappeared. Edmonton is bursting
with transformative new developments: the university is humming with cash, public institutions are flush, and slick, new arenas,

FIGURE 2.2
Petroleum Plaza, downtown Edmonton. Photo by Selena Couture.

condos, and public transit rise under an army of cranes—and all of it speaks to decades of tar sands money funneling south. But you can also feel the city bracing itself, bearing up under the incredible pressure of the tar sands, suffering the last years' oil-market collapse, wondering what's next, wondering if the tar sands' time is up. The sheer volatility of the oil sector means that no one feels secure, no one can quite believe their luck, and everyone knows they had better make hay while the sun shines, before fracking, or OPEC, or shale gas, or new regulations arrive and the market careens again.

The core extractive problem with the tar sands is that the oil is not sitting around in underground reservoirs like most of, say, Saudi Arabia's reserves; it saturates the sand (that's the tar: oil-soaked sand and mud) and is difficult to harvest. This is what makes it an unconventional source of oil and multiplies its environmental effects: the primary methodologies for getting the bituminous oil out of the sand involve huge volumes of water, which after the processing is filthily toxic and is supposed to be contained in tailings ponds but frequently spews into watersheds, rivers, and streams. This whole process requires colossal volumes of energy; according to the Pembina Institute, the input required to make tar sands production profitable creates somewhere between 8 to 37 percent higher greenhouse gas emissions than conventional sources.[17]

The impact of tar sands development is particularly intense in Alberta. It's not just the carbon emissions; it is a cavalcade of in situ and regional environmental calamities. The effects on the land and animals are staggering. Watersheds and rivers flowing north are transmitting awful cancers and diseases, especially in Fort Chipewyan but now also farther downstream.[18] Most of the small glaciers in the nearby Rockies will disappear by mid-century. Water levels in Lake Athabasca could drop 6.5 feet to 9.8 feet. It takes three times the amount of water to produce tar sands oil than conventional oil—anywhere from 0.4 to 3.1 barrels of water for every barrel of oil.[19] In 2013, 15 percent of the Athabasca water flow was used for oil sands production—that number will rise dramatically if the oil sands production increases as hoped from 2 million barrels a day to 5 million by 2030. One-third of the lakes in Alberta could dry up in the next thirty years.[20]

This is why people call oil from the tar sands "dirty oil" or "extreme oil" and why it is so reviled by so many. James Hansen, formerly of NASA, and one of the world's most prominent global warming scientists, claims that putting the Alberta tar sands into full production would mean it's "game over" for the climate. Hansen is divisive and full-throated, but compelling: "We are getting close to the dangerous level of carbon in the atmosphere and if we add on to that unconventional fossil fuels, which have a tremendous amount of carbon, then the climate problem becomes unsolvable."[21] Every serious (i.e., non-oil-corporation-funded) climate scientist and every credible source, from the IPCC to *Nature*,[22] says essentially the same thing: unless the vast majority of the tar sands is left in the ground, disastrous global warming is a near certainty. The calculus is really not all that complex, and in the case of the tar sands it is especially bleak and unequivocal.

Every country in the world needs to make real sacrifices if the global temperature rise is to be controlled at or below 1.5 degrees Celsius over preindustrial levels (the essentially agreed-upon threshold to contain the worst of the damage), but Canada's responsibility is stark and disproportionate because so much of the country's oil is so dirty. A 2015 *Nature* article detailed *exactly* how much of Canada's reserves needs to stay in the ground and that no more than 15 percent (7.5 billion barrels) of the viable reserves and 1 percent of the total bitumen available in the oil sands can be extracted. That is: 85 percent has to be left alone.[23]

Fort McMurray thus sits right in the middle of global warming discourses, and every journalist, every green crusader with a budget, every activist with a pulse wants to get up there. Desmond Tutu, Leonardo DiCaprio, and James Cameron have all been up to talk smack. Neil Young did a tour.[24] Canada's National Film Board produced a technically impressive and critically acclaimed video game/film/documentary hybrid called *Fort McMoney*. The *Guardian* has been reporting on global warming from the tar sands for years. In 2011, *Vice* produced a three-part documentary called *Toxic: Alberta* and has been back often since. The *New York Times*, *The Daily Show*, *Huffington Post*, the *Nation*, *Al Jazeera*, newspapers and magazines from around the world—everybody has taken a good swing.

All too often liberal and leftist types find their way up to the tar sands in search of enviro-porn, looking for photo-ops of ugly messes and background shots for their video-moralizing. If you're interested in an eco-apocalypse tour, Fort Mac is high on your bucket list, and in the rush to document the tar sands, analytical nuance is not often part of the story. Especially galling is that all too often the people working the tar sands are condescended to, patronized, and/or straight up vilified as dimwitted monster-truck-driving mouth-breathers who are wantonly destroying the planet so they can afford one more lap-dance in Vegas.

That narrative gets inscribed repeatedly, both implicitly and explicitly. Condescending to people in places like the Mac, or individualizing responsibility for eco-collapses, is one of contemporary capitalism's prime defensive strategies: reduce ecological imperatives to one more consumer decision, one more atomized set of purchasing choices, thereby isolating governments and capital from culpability. Blaming the choices individual people make in the context of highly limited options and grinding employment pressures is a fool's errand.

Alberta's tar sands, like fracking in the plains, shale gas in the Appalachians, oil rigs in the Gulf of Mexico, or any other concentrations of the fossil fuel industry have been a godsend for so many. People from all over the world have descended on Fort Mac and found unbelievably well-paid employment: tough jobs, hard-working jobs, but jobs that leave you hooting at your paycheck. Jobs that have lifted whole families out of poverty, jobs that have brought kids and wives and grandparents to Canada, jobs that have paid off mortgages, jobs that have sent kids to college.

For whole parts of Canada, the tar sands are pretty much the only thing going. Take Cape Breton, for example, historically one of the country's poorest regions—a rocky island pinned to the far Atlantic coast, stuck in economic decline for generations with the collapse of the fisheries and the departure of coal mining and steel factories. Now the tar sands are the island's primary economic engine, keeping the local economy afloat from thousands of miles away as workers flee en masse for Albertan jobs. As one resident put it, "We're beginning to be a single industry town again. Only this time the industry is in Alberta."[25] Dependent relationships like this, of course, always have a flip side. Now that the tar sands are suffering, the pain is also being felt thousands of miles away, as employees—very often laborers who have traveled great distances—are being rapidly cast aside. The Petrocultures Research Group,[26] in their publication, *After Oil*, identifies this phenomenon: "Energy deepening names the tendency through which capitalist modernization mobilizes natural forms of physical power to optimize, manage and discard human labour."[27]

While the tar sands have a particularly startling visage, we are all implicated in the oil economy; every single one of us is bound up with petro-logics. We are all simultaneously witness, victim, and perpetrator of climate crimes. Here in the Global North the weight of responsibility sits heavy, and yet so few of us do so little to really change much, and apologists for fossil-fuel extraction gleefully point to all the hypocrisy and double-speak of pretentious plane-flying, car-driving, plastic-using, toothpaste-sucking, sour-candy-eating urbanites on our high horses. (Yes, sour candies have oil as a key ingredient, as do scores of other fast foods, chips, candy, packaged food, tooth paste, etc. Not the packaging, the food part. Probably the really good-tasting part, too.)

The argument that if we participate in any oil-burning or ever use a petro-product we are then ineligible to critique the oil industry is absurd troll-speak, but it is absolutely true that we are all entangled with narratives of global warming, oftentimes in highly uncomfortable

ways. How much people claim to care about the climate does seem to correlate with how much they fly: people who are ostensibly most invested in ecological discourses habitually jet off to Paris, Lima, Copenhagen, Durban, or wherever for a very important conference where their attendance is apparently crucial. And we three are very far from clean—our hypocrisies and contradictions are glaring. Who repeatedly flies and drives thousands of miles to find new ways to talk and think about global warming?

Despite all the gloom, there is slim evidence of a bright side. In June 2015 the G7 summit made a collective commitment to decarbonization.[28] That same month, Pope Francis issued a remarkable papal encyclical calling on "the world's rich nations" to begin paying their "grave social debt" to the poor and take concrete steps on global warming, saying that failure to do so presents an undeniable risk to our "common home" that is beginning to resemble a "pile of filth" and charging that "many of those who possess more resources and economic or political power seem mostly to be concerned with masking the problems or concealing their symptoms."[29] Jurisdictions around the globe are making commitments to carbon reduction and sustainable energy. To what degree any of these places hold, or can be held, to these promises is another matter, of course, but still: Norway has promised to go carbon-neutral by 2030.[30] Hawaii has committed itself to 100 percent clean energy by 2045.[31] Quebec has pledged a 40 percent cut in its use of petroleum products by 2030.[32] Mexico says it can cut GHG emissions 22 percent by 2030.[33] Ethiopia says it can reduce carbon pollution by 64 percent by 2030.[34] Many more promises and pledges will follow. Some might be kept. Other new ones will be made. The future of global warming is not fixed or inevitable, no matter how often it seems that way.

FIGURE 2.3
Illustration by Joe Sacco.

WITH CHEESE

The first thing we noticed about Fort Mac, long before we even arrived, was that people have strong opinions about the place. And
they want to tell you about them. In full color. We live in Vancouver
and Portland, two of the most eco-performative cities in North
America, and as soon as we started mentioning our travel plans the
first response was almost always "Good lord, *why*? Why on earth
would you go there? *By choice*?" Other reactions came in varying
shades of opprobrium, dismay, curiosity, and encouragement. But
mainly we met with shock, awe, and not-so-polite distaste.[35]

Fort McMurray occupies a specific position in the Canadian consciousness as well as in the global gaze, and shame is always part of
the package. It is both a spectacular place and spectacularly ordinary.
It is a fulcrum of global warming and probably is doing as much damage to our collective futures as any municipality on earth. But we
take Fort Mac and its claims seriously.

Wandering through the Edmonton airport, we were startled to
notice the huge piles of Naomi Klein's 2014 book *This Changes Everything* in the bookstore.[36] It is a little difficult to figure out why and
how this book has become popular enough to make its way into massive chain-store-scaled pyramids.[37] It is an unabashedly radical political polemic: Klein is explicitly arguing for a wholesale reassessment
of capitalism:

> Our economy is at war with many forms of life on earth, includ-
> ing human life. What the climate needs to avoid collapse is a
> contraction in humanity's use of resources; what our economic
> model demands to avoid collapse is unfettered expansion. Only
> one of these sets of rules can be changed, and it's not the laws
> of nature.[38]

The book's subtitle is *Capitalism vs. the Climate*, and throughout
she insists on challenging the "fundamental logic of deregulated

capitalism," claiming that there is no other way to adequately combat catastrophic global warming. The book stands out easily from the
raft of contemporary climate change titles in part because of its anticapitalist heart, in part because it is positional rather than simply
analytic, but mainly for its optimistic sheen.

Klein spends most of her time documenting the devastations and
predations of global warming, locating the research in stories across
the globe with measured yet dire predictions of where all this is
headed. Unlike most others, though, her politics take an almost jar-
ringly positive twist. She suggests that in the face of catastrophe, we
are presented with an unparalleled opportunity to rethink and remake almost everything, from how we generate power and energy
and food, to how we conceive of employment and land allocations, to
reconfiguring societies as more equitable. She claims that global
warming, "if treated as a true planetary emergency ... could become
a galvanizing force for humanity, leaving us all not just safer from
extreme weather, but with societies that are safer and fairer in all
kinds of other ways as well."[39]

Maybe it's the book's essential hopefulness (especially coming
from someone who is best known for her searing critiques of capitalism via No Logo and The Shock Doctrine), tempering its stark
warnings, that has attracted so many readers. Klein is calling for
something that is very hard to hear, let alone imagine: a "managed
degrowth," a radical reduction of consumption, a renunciation of
extraction and profit. She is clear that antagonism is required: the
changes have to be immediate and deep, and will invoke severe
compromises. She takes particular issue with mainstream environmental organizations and the vast bulk of commentators who are
hoping against hope that climate solutions can be found within the
context of existing capitalism—that just a few tweaks and innova-
tions here, a tax and an incentive there, and we can all carry on
more or less as per usual: "Hard-core ideologues understand the
real significance of global warming better than most of the 'warm-
ists' in the political center, the ones who are still insisting that the

response can be gradual and painless and that we don't need to go to war with anybody."[40]

It is on this point that Klein has attracted the most trenchant critiques and even outright denunciation from credible reviewers.[41] Among the most prominent of these has been Elizabeth Kolbert, best known for her environmental writing in the *New Yorker* and her best-selling books *Field Notes from a Catastrophe* and *The Sixth Extinction: An Unnatural History* (which won the 2015 Pulitzer Prize for General Non-Fiction). Suffice it to say that Klein and Kolbert are heavyweights, and their disputes articulate the intricacies and convictions so common to global warming debates and so recognizable from our own conversations. These two authors have been quoted, published, and invoked repeatedly. While their wide coverage runs the risk of exhaustion, it is worth considering their positions not just because their differences are emblematic of much of the progressive left's gridlock on global warming, but because they highlight critical ecological fault lines and offer an orienting cartography.

Kolbert largely concurs with the foreboding assessments at the heart of *This Changes Everything*,[42] but she sharply diverges from Klein after that. Kolbert claims that while *This Changes Everything* is correct on the desperate need to reduce carbon loads and emissions, it has little to offer beyond telling a useful fable. She writes that Klein

> avoids looking at all closely at what this [reducing emissions] would entail ... [and] vaguely tells us that we'll have to consume less, but not how much less, or what we'll have to give up. At various points, she calls for a carbon tax. ... Near the start of the book, Klein floats the "managed degrowth" concept, which might also be called economic contraction, but once again, how this might play out she leaves unexplored. ... [Then in] place of "degrowth" she offers "regeneration," a concept so cheerfully fuzzy I won't even attempt to explain it.[43]

At the core of both of their arguments, like so many others, is the insistence in framing global warming as a planetary emergency. But does it help or hurt to call it an emergency? Does that mobilize or paralyze?

Our era consistently presents itself with Frankensteinian paradoxes and uncontrolled ecological visages. The scope of these threats—often described as existential—surpasses our reach. Their possibilities are so calamitous as to demand concrete, immediate responses, but scaled so monstrously as to defy realistically effective personal, or even collective action. Our agency is scarcely a question—*everything* any of us do is ineffective, or worse, exacerbates the damage. This dissonance extrapolates to the social: just as global warming calls on us to present our better selves, it also calls on us to discipline those of us who cannot or will not abide by necessary limits. A planetary emergency cannot wait for everyone to get with the program. A state of emergency is just that, a time when the law can be suspended, *should be* suspended, when every newsflash begs for a sovereign authority to take charge and save us from ourselves.

Wandering the streets of Edmonton in the midst of an economic downturn, you don't have to listen hard to hear the word *crisis*. As the price of oil slumped, everyday conversations quickly turned anxious and fatalistic, but the invocations of emergency had nothing to do with the climate: the crises in Edmonton were all about mortgages and jobs. We love Klein's work and are on her side about most everything, but Kolbert has a point here. Who *exactly* are we supposed to be going to war with? Resisting extractivism sounds correct, and capital is the villain, but that battle is going to mean damaging real people. Let's not be cheerfully fuzzy about any of this. It's not CEOs or upper-level engineers who will feel the pain of that war—not for a very long time, anyway. It's people with kids and grandparents, and rents they can't afford, and car payments they will miss, and savings they don't have, and a whole lot worse. It's the people who are the least culpable who will suffer first and worst. If an ecological future requires a battle, let's be sure who we are fighting.

POWER SOURCES

Timothy Mitchell, in his book *Carbon Democracy*, argues that the move to coal during the industrial revolution uprooted hierarchies and forms of political power that existed in the nineteenth century. Utilizing their power to withdraw labor (via strikes and work disruptions) in an era of coal-powered development, social movements and especially organized labor were able to make massive material advances for a century and half based on workers' centrality to and irreplaceability in production. Mitchell's argument is that the move from coal to oil as the predominant energy source, and the resulting decentering of labor, disrupted that direction of social advances by the middle of the twentieth century. While the transitions from coal to oil was and is uneven—and still incomplete—the structural changes are still flowing through. In particular, the financialization of the global economy that followed the oil crisis in the early 1970s had a direct relationship to the rise of neoliberalism. In other words, Mitchell argues that energy supplies shape political and economic structures more than we think. Each energy source, be it coal or oil or whatever, has been part of the dominant mentality of its time, and there's good reason to think that whatever new energy source becomes the hegemon by the mid-twenty-first century will be its own type of monster.

Oil froze the intellectual currents of mainstream economics for most of the twentieth century, as most models assumed infinite resources of oil. That's all being thrown into question now, of course, and the valuations and returns of oil companies are being reevaluated in a profound way as new forms and extractive technologies challenge every predictive vector. New energy sources will certainly emerge, subsidized and advanced by both state and private interests, and the future of energy, even in the short term, is far from clear. In this sense, we are far from a toppling of capitalism; rather, a shapeshifting reorganization and reentrenchment of neoliberalism is unfolding—driven by change, but unfazed by it.

The pace of energy shifts over the last seventy years has been astounding. In 1945, the United States produced two-thirds of the world's oil. Over half of the remaining third came from Latin America and the Caribbean. Alongside the emergence of Bretton Woods, and the creation of the World Bank and the International Monetary Fund (IMF), the International Petroleum Council was created to grease the wheels for Anglo-American influence over Middle Eastern oil. The American relationship between oil, industry, politics, and military is not too hard to paint if you look at the last half of the twentieth century and through the beginnings of the twenty-first. The story that Mitchell tells is of the inevitable link between oil as the prime energy source and the rise of neoliberalism that began in the mid-1950s and accelerated after the early 1970s.[44]

There is no necessary relationship between oil and democracy, or between oil and antidemocracy. Oil production and consumption need order and stability to support the financial instruments required to make the long-term investments that profits rely on. Order and stability can come in many forms.

Oil has produced a narrative of the future, but reductionist narratives that claim that our currently dominant energy supply is the only, or even primary, force shaping our political and economic structures are inadequate. That claim is certainly true in limited ways, but does anyone really doubt that capitalism as presently structured could be left substantially intact with, say, solar power as its hegemonic fuel?[45] It's more interesting to say that there is a widening gyre of relationships between our energy ideologies and our political sensibilities. Mechanical power (the power to organize material) and political power (the power to organize bodies) inform and construct one another, but that is far from the whole story.

The story of our times can be told as the story of oil, and that's not an unconvincing narrative—but spend any time in Edmonton, and that story soon reveals itself as incomplete. Edmonton is an oil city, but one that is hardly ignorant about global warming, and one that would happily accept another dominant power source if it were equally profitable. Oil is essential to Edmonton, just as it is for every city everywhere, but that's not a forever thing. Transitions to new fuel sources will enact reorderings of geopolitical relationships, assist the rise and fall of many fortunes, provide new market opportunities for eager investors, and trigger consequences at many scales. But we're more interested in the logics that made this current set of crises so inevitable. Without understanding those logics, we are just trading one ecological catastrophe for whatever comes next, kicking the can down the road and deepening our debts.

Global warming could well be solved at some grand multinational scale while other forms of biocollapse continue unabated. Our aim is to think of global warming as a lever to something more fundamental than a mere transition to renewables. But if we are not confronting a technical question, or a geopolitical exercise, or a disciplinary governance quandary—then what *are* we facing?

ECOLOGICAL SCENERIES

It has suddenly become commonplace to claim that we have now entered something called the Anthropocene, or the Age of Man, a time period emerging from the Holocene: a new epoch defined by human transformations and disfigurements of the Earth's atmosphere, biosphere, and even geology. The progenitor of the term is typically taken to be Paul Crutzen, a Nobel-prize-winning atmospheric scientist who pronounced the new epoch at a major international conference in 2000, and then followed up over subsequent years with a series of articles, often written with collaborators like Will Steffen and Eugene Stoermer. Since then the name and idea have built up enough velocity among ecologists, scientists, artists, journalists, and casual observers that it is often a taken-for-granted truth that we have entered this new epoch. In August 2016 a working group at the 35th International Geological Congress in South Africa confirmed that the Anthropocene is a new era; as soon as the International Union of Geological Sciences formally agrees, the designation will be formally declared and enter textbooks. The Anthropocene Working Group (AWG), comprising several Leicester University geologists and others, acknowledged the "provisional recommendation" and said: "The Anthropocene concept ... is geologically real. The phenomenon is of sufficient scale to be considered as part of the International Chronostratigraphic Chart, more commonly known as the Geological Time Scale."[46]

It is easy to see why this claim is being made: the basic evidence is unassailable. There is no part of the Earth that does not bear evidence of human impact. We *have* entered an era of unprecedented species extinctions and threats to the biosphere. There *are* hitherto unimagined levels of pollution and perversions of ecosystems. We know, unequivocally, irrevocably, that humans are the cause. Doesn't that equal the Anthropocene, then? That's what Gaia Vince, author of *Adventures in the Anthropocene*, suggests:

> It's a difficult and novel task for the geologists who must try to determine a start date for an era whose palaeontology and geology are still being created —there's no handy stripe in the rock layers to mark the Anthropocene yet.
>
> The mid-20th Century, the beginning of the global Great Acceleration (there are some great graphs for this), makes for a useful marker both scientifically and because it also represents the great social changes that have occurred. This is important because it was an evolution in human society that created this environmental planetary change—and it is the way human society develops that will shape this new age for the decades and centuries to come.[47]

The issue that Vince foregrounds here—the difficulty in pinpointing a start date for the Anthropocene—is both critical to grapple with and deceptively obscuring. Many observers, from the expert to casual, have noted that if a new epoch is going to be anointed, then we need both clear and material evidence of it as an event, and thus definitive acknowledgment of when it began. Or, as the Subcommission on Quaternary Stratigraphy's Working Group on the Anthropocene puts it:

> The "Anthropocene" has emerged as a popular scientific term used by scientists, the scientifically engaged public and the media to designate the period of Earth's history during which humans have a decisive influence on the state, dynamics and future of the Earth system. It is widely agreed that the Earth is currently in this state. ...
>
> A formal "Anthropocene" might be defined either with reference to a particular point within a stratal section, that is, a Global Stratigraphic Section and Point (GSSP), colloquially known as a "golden spike"; or, by a designated time boundary (a Global Standard Stratigraphic Age).[48]

There is nothing like consensus on this issue, nor much conceptual confluence on how a particular point, the so-called golden spike, might be agreed on. Crutzen (among many others) has put forward the dawn of the Industrial Revolution;[49] others have argued for much longer timelines, suggesting that the Anthropocene actually began with the advent of agriculture or the Neolithic era. Still others claim that the Anthropocene is actually of much more recent provenance, starting maybe in 1950, or in 1964,[50] or in 1945 when the first nuclear test occurred, which the International Anthropocene Working Group has offered.[51] Most popular narratives invoke the post–World War II hockey stick graphs[52] and implicate modernity, industrialism, growth, and/or overconsumption.

Some of this parrying is constrained to technical science and relies on huge scales of data and precise measurements to make particular claims for one originary point or another. But the political impact of this project is critical, because where the Anthropocenic timeline is taken to begin drives subsequent political analysis: your chosen historical instigation of the Anthropocene prefigures what you think are the root causes of planetary-scale biodegradations, and thus what you take to be the proper ameliorations or social prescriptions.

The core logic in play here strikes us as essentially correct: claims of a new epoch require a starting point, and it is true that this is an era unlike any other in the planet's history. But in our view, there is a critical, even fatal, problem with the designation of the Anthropocene, far more important than figuring out when and where it started. Two primary objections are entwined here. The first is that any rendition of the Anthropocene requires an absurdly grand narrative, a sweeping conflation of all of humanity into an undifferentiated mass of *we*, one that easily makes claims about what *we* have done, how *we* must change *our* behavior, how *humans* have precipitated these terrible alterations to the biosphere, how *our* stories have to change.

Listen to Mark Lynas, the author of *Six Degrees: Our Future on a Hotter Planet* and *The God Species: Saving the Planet in the Age of Humans*. Lynas was once a conventional antinuclear, anti-GMO environmentalist who flipped the script and is now aggressively pro-both. He is also energetically pro-corporate, pro-geoengineering, and pro-market, and a lead author of the 2015 "Ecomodernist Manifesto": "Calculated globally, human society consumes the equivalent of 400 years' worth of ancient solar energy (expressed in terms of the net primary productivity of plants during previous geological eras) each year through our use of fossil fuels."[53] Later, in *The God Species*, he calls humans "fire-apes" and prophesies, "God's power is now increasingly being exercised by us. We are the creators of life, but we are also its destroyers."[54] Or consider James Lovelock's version of "us": "Unfortunately, we are a species with schizoid tendencies, and like an old lady who has to share her house with a growing and destructive group of teenagers, Gaia grows angry, and if they do not mend their ways she will evict them."[55]

This is absurd. Undifferentiated platitudes about how *we* have to change *our* consumption and lifestyles, *our* ethos and ethics, are totally untenable. These depoliticized prescriptions are beyond grating to, say, Indigenous communities across the planet, societies throughout the Global South, and people everywhere who have been fighting the unapologetic depredations of neoliberal extractionism. Oh, so now *we* all have to change?

Worse, the Anthropocenic narrative that collapses everyone into one humanity easily descends into nihilistically lyrical evocations of humans' (and the Earth's) inevitable demise. Among the most prominent of these is Roy Scranton's *Learning to Die in the Anthropocene*. Scranton is an ex-US soldier who served time in Iraq, and his book is a brief, often beautifully written meditation on living in an era of environmental catastrophe that is animated by a set of conclusions that *we* have torched the Earth and now just have to live with it:

> We're fucked. The only questions are how soon and how badly. … Global warming is not the latest version of a hoary fable of annihilation. It is not hysteria. It is a fact. And we have likely already passed the point where we could have done anything about it. … There is a name for this new world: the Anthropocene. … The rub now is that we have to learn to die not as individuals, but as a civilization.[56]

There is little doubt that Scranton is terrorized by the future he envisions. He posits that "carbon-fueled capitalism" is the culprit, but then extrapolates wildly into Nostradamussing the end of civilization, taking pains to sneer at the efforts of activists and organizers:

> No matter how many people take to the streets in massive marches or in targeted direct actions, they cannot put their hands on the real flows of power, because they do not help produce it. They only consume. …
>
> The problem is that the problem is too big. The problem is that different people want different things. The problem is that nobody has real answers. The problem is us.[57]

It may well be that the Earth has been damaged to the point that human flourishing will be compromised irrevocably: that possibility is not in question. It is also widely understood and accepted that almost every human on the planet bears some responsibility for our contributions to global warming. Wildly differing responsibilities; but every time a computer is turned on, every piece of plastic, every mow of the lawn, every coal-based bit of electricity people use is contributing to the carbon load the atmosphere is being forced to bear. But there is no single global civilization that is doomed to collapse. The problem is not us.

No other species is capable of destroying all the others. No other species has ever held such monstrous power. That is not to say, not even close to saying, that humans reside at the apex of biotic evolutions, nor to intimate that humans are more advanced or more worthy or more valuable than other species. That said, to construe humans as an undifferentiated, amorphous blob, dislocated from entwined interspecies relationships, is pernicious. As Jason Moore puts it:

> The Anthropocene makes for an easy story. Easy, because it does not challenge the naturalized inequalities, alienation, and violence inscribed in modernity's strategic relations of power, production, and nature. It is an easy story to tell because it does not ask us to think about these relations *at all*.[58]

The planetary-scale environmental circumstances facing all humans are the result of real political decisions, of millions upon millions of choices made over the course of hundreds, even thousands, of years, and of choices still to come. Those choices were not preordained, they are not intractable, and they are constantly differentiated and differentiating. The most impactful decisions are those that have been made and are being made by those with disproportionate access to power and privilege. There is no delicate way to put it: we may well be living in a new era, but it is *not* the Anthropocene.[59]

Moore (among many others) suggests our epoch is better named the Capitalocene. "This is an old capitalist trick: to say that the problems of the world are problems created by everyone, when in fact they are problems created by capital. ... We should talk about the Capitalocene. We have an historical era dominated by capital."[60]

It might be more accurate to call it the Corporatocene. Richard Heede's research provides compelling evidence that it's not so much the amorphous designation of "capital" that's responsible—actually it is a very small number of companies and government-run industries that are primarily blame. to Heede demonstrates that between 1854 and 2010, only ninety entities are responsible for 63 percent of all climate-changing emissions, the top twenty responsible for almost 30 percent and the top ten almost 16 percent.[61]

Erick Swyngedouw has suggested the Oliganthropocene (an epoch dominated by the actions of a few men, and even fewer women).[62] In *The Shock of the Anthropocene*, Christophe Bonneuil and Jean-Baptiste Fressoz try a few other possibilities out, playing with the Thermocene, Carbocene, Thanatocene, Phagocene, Phronocene, Agnotocene, and Polemocene (naming fire/burning stuff, carbon, war, consumption, ignoring warnings, ignoring limits, and social contestations as culprits).[63] Not to be outdone, Donna Haraway has made a strong case for the Chthulucene, a title that grounds itself in sympoiesis or multi- and interspecies assemblages that shift the focus from humans to relationships between all species.[64] Many other names are in play (!), and all are fun in that they open up the space that Anthropocenic arguments shut down. Mackenzie Wark agrees and piles on: "Let's invent new metaphors! Personally I like the #misanthropocene, but don't expect it to catch on."[65]

French philosopher Catherine Malabou raises the question of the "current constitution of the brain as the new subject of history, and the type of awareness requested by the Anthropocene."[66] In the fashionable discussions that ensue with the introduction of new and contentious terms, academic and artistic movements begin frothing at the mouth and elbowing for room as they jockey for position and posture for posterity, hoping to ride the next intellectual wave—be they in favor or against, or as they attempt to carve out some other discursive space in relation to the *new term*. It's also illustrative and not particularly surprising that almost all of the voices who are attached to the Anthropocene and its derivative terms are Western and white, and predominantly male.

Métis scholar Zoe Todd identifies the concept of the Anthropocene as yet another white space in her essay "Indigenizing the Anthropocene." Todd speaks of the notion of white space as a "space in which Indigenous ideas or practices are appropriated, or obscured, by non-Indigenous practitioners." For her, Western terms and theories have a gentrifying effect in how they land, circulate, and begin to organize thought and action. She writes, "Not all humans are equally implicated in the forces that created the disasters driving contemporary human-environmental crises, and I argue that not all humans are equally invited into the conceptual spaces where these disasters are theorized or responses to disaster formulated." She references human geographer Juanita Sundberg's evocation of the Zapatista principle of "walking the world into being" and geographer Sarah Hunt's idea of how dancing at the Potlatch brings Indigenous ontologies into the world. Todd writes, "When discourses and responses to the Anthropocene are being generated within institutions and disciplines which are embedded in broader systems that act as de facto 'white public space,' the academy and its power dynamics must be challenged."[67]

This brings us to the second core problem with invoking the Anthropocene: the word itself mocks difference. All the other contenders might fall prey to the same hubris, except that they are largely conceived of in (usually winking) opposition to Anthropocenic conceits. Any claim to single-determinate causalities or effects of ecological peril is doomed before getting out of the blocks. Anthropocenic discourses of climate change imply that not only are we all to blame, but we are all equally imperiled.[68] But the repercussions of global warming are being experienced profoundly unevenly, and it is hardly any surprise that it is the poorest and least privileged who are being most egregiously affected. It is often said that Africans are bearing the brunt of a warming planet.[69] The leading edges of climatic disruptions are already producing moving disasters across Africa as farmers desperately try to adapt, but many see the writing on the wall and migrate, near and far. The dispossession and displacement that global warming instigates has only just begun, and not only in Africa.

But, of course, not all Africans are imperiled. That argument is itself condescending. There are elites all across the African continent who are and always will be insulated by their wealth and power, just as intense stratification in all societies inures differential exposure to the effects of global warming. Increasingly, even middle classes in every corner of the planet find themselves affected by the precarities of the economic system as a result of rising inequality, which in turn exacerbates climatic disruptions and uncertainties.[70]

Anthropocenic claims perform a double or even triple trick while collapsing all humans into one humanity or human civilization: while cleansing the landscape of difference and wiping the record of responsibility or context, such claims simultaneously reify humans as gods who should accept our elevated place and set ourselves to performing our godlike duties.[71] The trick, of course, is that not all humans are rendered as gods in this story, just an extremely select few, who the rest of us must now entrust to geoengineer the planet. It's an impressive sleight of political hand. As Eileen Crist puts it, the discourses of the Anthropocene present a homogenized protagonist named the *human enterprise*: "Not to put too fine a point on it, the Anthropocene discourse delivers a familiar anthropocentric credo, with requisite judicious warnings thrown into the mix and meekly activated caveats about needed research to precede megatechnical experimentations."[72]

When global warming is subsumed into depoliticized milieus, technocratic solutions emerge not as merely possible, but necessary. And of course, these quickly tend to grandiose geoengineering fantasies, or what some dub the "Good Anthropocene" of benevolent sovereigns.

There is no lack of proposals: Crutzen wants to inject vast amounts of sulfate aerosols (sulfuric acid, hydrogen sulfide, or sulfur dioxide) into the stratosphere via balloons, aircraft, and/or artillery shots to create a "global dimming."[73] Nathan Myhrvold (the former chief technology officer for Microsoft) suggests giant hoses in the sky, carried by balloons, to spray the aerosols more effectively.[74] David Keith wants airplanes flying through the lower stratosphere spraying sulphuric acid.[75] Scottish engineer Stephen Salter—drawing on an idea developed by John Latham at the National Center for Atmospheric Research—wants to outfit 1,500 ships with special propellers that will churn up seawater, spraying it deep into the clouds to make them whiter, and thus reflect more sunlight. Roger Angel, astronomy and optics professor at the University of Arizona, wants to build twenty mile-long electromagnetic guns to each shoot 800,000 dinner-plate-sized ceramic disks every five minutes for ten years into the atmosphere to block and scatter sunlight.[76]

There are many other albedo enhancement (or increasing reflectiveness) proposals drifting around (as it were), plenty of reflector and aerosol distribution plans, and still more suggestions using a mind-boggling array of approaches from carbon capture and sequestration, to ambient air capture, to enhanced weathering, to ocean fertilization, to sun-blocking. Among the problems with all of these schemes is that the general public tends to be suspicious and often interventionist. In his essay "Geoengineering: Why All the Fuss?" Mark Lynas writes about the "rather hush-hush" Stratospheric Particle Injection for Climate Engineering project that is considering building a one-kilometer-high chimney near Cambridge, UK, to spray stuff into the air, but he sneers at what he presumes will be a questioning and critical public reaction: "You can imagine the tabloid headlines."[77]

The perverse arrogance that Lynas so adeptly spews often merges easily into antidemocratic, technocratic, and even quasi-fascistic claims that everyday people are far too ignorant and capricious to be entrusted with such critical questions: this is an emergency, there is no cushion for debate or ponderously slow public conversations, and it is time for the experts to take over. Listen again to James Lovelock who believes that humans are just too stupid to prevent their own demise: "I don't think we're yet evolved to the point where we're clever enough to handle as complex a situation as climate change. The inertia of humans is so huge that you can't really do anything meaningful."[78] Lovelock doesn't then descend into the fatalism or nihilism of a Scranton or a Kingsnorth,[79] he just goes straight to the authoritarianism. He and his enlightened cadre understand the path forward and so he just wants the correct actions implemented, whatever it takes: "Even the best democracies agree that when a major war approaches, democracy must be put on hold for the time being. I have a feeling that climate change may be an issue as severe as a war. It may be necessary to put democracy on hold for a while."[80]

We should fear and revolt against this authoritarian approach. Granted, it is easy to see how Lovelock and others might end up with this position. The sheer frustration, anger, desperation, and even despair of those who can see global warming so clearly but cannot make themselves heard is palpable. The blind greed and awful obfuscations of the fossil fuel industry and the climate change deniers can make anybody feel like choking a Koch brother. We feel that ourselves, and sympathize.[81]

Scientists should be, could be, and often are on the front lines of global warming. Grasping the problem requires as much sophisticated scientific analysis and research as can be mustered. Scientists should be treated with respect, which means subjecting all science and scientists to the same rigorous and recursive questions about their work as anyone else: who funds the work, who is doing it, what is it for, what are the implications of the research, what power flows from the work, what worldviews does the work concretize? All science is political and should be willing to stand up for itself.

We have no doubt that a significant commitment to renewable energy is a critical part of a passably livable future. The question is not whether the technological sophistication currently exists to forge new tools. The problem is the economic and social milieu that privileges certain technologies (say, the G20 countries spending $444 billion USD annually to subsidize fossil fuel industries)[82] and makes other tools prohibitively expensive, unfeasible, marginalized, or swiftly extinct.

The scientific hubris that stands above the messiness of social relationships and imagines itself as beyond reproach, or objective, or apolitical is exactly the hubris that has contributed mightily to global warming. The cheerleaders for geoengineering explicitly want to place the fate of the Earth in an ever-smaller number of hands: a technocratic cadre of superheroes who have unimaginable powers of control and are all that stands between the planet and disaster. Bruno Latour has famously exhorted that "we must embrace our monsters," an allusively malleable claim that he has deployed in a variety of ways.[83] If that means (as Latour occasionally seems to suggest) that all humans must acknowledge the pervasively spectacular impacts of human life on the planet and take responsibility for righting our wrongs, then we are almost in the right territory, especially if that claim is relentlessly politicized.[84]

FORWARD

The major international climate summits that represent peaks in interest in global warming highlight the most pressing of our political contradictions in myriad ways. These convergences generate huge publicity and nurture promises of real change. Global elites engage in high-level and track-two discussions on the future path of global warming mitigations and changing approaches to energy. But who actually participates in such discussions and who is making the decisions? Very powerful interests are determining and limiting what change is possible in the present, while boxing out future transformative possibilities. Entrenched power is always happy to speak seductively about change, while demarcating who and what constitutes that change.

Capital insists on a particular rendition of "growth" coupled simultaneously with an obsessive commitment to destruction. As Joseph Schumpeter famously put it: "Stationary capitalism would be a *contradictio in adjecto* [contradiction in terms]."[85] This relationship between capital and communities not only creates regulatory capture, it also seduces the hearts and minds of people who directly benefit from their relationship to industry. Their sympathies, understandably, end up on the side of capital, especially in the absence of believably affirmative renditions of change beyond disciplinary calls to limits.

Too often and for too long, the most articulate and sophisticated voices of change have been marginalized, buried beneath constructed binaries that force people into ideological echo chambers. Over and over again the air gets squeezed out of conversations about change by ostensibly green authorities. Take Justin Trudeau, for example—who aggressively positions himself (and is positioned) as a reasonable and progressive leader. When he claims that "there isn't a country in the world that would find billions of barrels of oil and leave it in the ground while there is a market for it,"[86] all the possibility for transformative change implodes. We're just as subject to these false choices as anyone, just as curious about routes to ecological futures, and just as frustrated by our consistent inabilities to articulate alternatives. So we sat down again with Leanne Simpson to ask her about land and ecology. We wanted new ways to think about change in the face of such intransigence, and she was the most hopeful person we could think of.

—

MH & AJ   We're interested in new kinds of action, new interventions in the face of global warming and capitalism. In the face of so much confusion and paralysis, how might people act?

LS   I feel like that's something my ancestors had figured out. They knew how to do it. They knew how to live. They had their own economy; they knew how to live in the world without being capitalists. They knew how to organize societies and nations, and how to do international diplomacy. I feel like it's not that far away from me. Another world is possible. I think I've already seen it. I come from that.

My ancestors didn't bank capital as a way of maintaining security, as a way of mitigating fear and anxiety—they banked relationships. My ancestors had very intimate and strong relationships with the land, with plant nations and animal nations and neighboring families and neighboring Indigenous nations. In times of hardships they relied on those relationships. They couldn't bank capital; they couldn't kill 600 moose and have a rainy day fund. They had to rely on a different way of being and that relational way of being creates a different way of being in the world.

It's a different relationship with the world. In Indigenous political structures, you've got systems of governance that mirror how I govern myself in the world. That same system of values and processes governs how you make decisions as a family and then amplifies across scales—that's a much different relationship with the world. It's more difficult for me think about how to transition from a capitalistic-greed-accumulation model based on violence than thinking about regenerating the system of my ancestors. The sites where I see that happening is in families. It's small collectives and these islands of resistance.

Our theory is emergent, it's full body intelligence, it's physical, spiritual, intellectual, and emotional engagement in this process. When you're engaged in this process, the whole is greater than the sum of its parts. My kids are growing up much differently than I grew up. They're growing up much more embedded in the Indigenous systems that I'm talking about, so the questions they're going to ask and the answers they're going to find are different. The idea behind Indigenous resurgence and on-the-land education is that you re-embed people in this system. You grow humans up in this nest of relationships, and then there's a shift that occurs that we can't really predict because of the disconnect created by the violence of colonialism. We can't see it, but we're creating people who can see it. If we start to make it happen on a small scale, it's easier to amplify it on different scales.

MH & AJ   Do you think it is useful to speak of global warming and biocollapses as emergencies?

LS   Recently I was driving down the highway around Oshawa on my way into Toronto. I was wondering if my ancestors would recognize anything. Would my great-grandmother even recognize this as our territory? And I thought they wouldn't.

How would they recognize this as home? Everything they would recognize is gone, the salmon are gone, the eels are gone, the old growth white pine forests are gone. A lot of the sugar bushes are gone. What we have is a nuclear power plant. We do have the lake, and they'd probably recognize the lake but it wouldn't look right. This landscape has been so fundamentally altered and we've seen the extinction of so many species. The destruction of our territories has been incremental and when you no longer have salmon in a huge ecosystem, no eels, or caribou or bison, that's a crisis. That's a continual crisis. It's almost as if my people have lived through local apocalypses.

I'm of two minds—but yeah, it's an emergency. We're quickly approaching the point where we can't go back. Our heads are in the sand and nothing is happening. Our elders have been warning about this for years and decades. Nothing is happening and people are not willing to make real changes. So yeah, it's an emergency but it's always been an emergency.

A lot of that language gets co-opted and used. But I do think it is an emergency, especially given how slowly society has changed. It's a really depressing issue. Global warming is a real white person's issue: if they can't get behind global warming, which profoundly affects them too, they won't get behind Indigenous issues.

I want people to link global warming to accumulation and dispossession. But the opposite of dispossession isn't possession, it's *connection*. Settler-colonialism strangulates my connection to the land, and it has a vested interest in legally dispossessing me from my territory. As long as I'm disconnected from my territory, it doesn't care if I'm displaced or not. I can be assimilated in my territory, dispossessed in Western legal perspective from my land rights, but I can still be in my territory and completely assimilated and that's totally fine. The government's OK with that. I'm no longer a threat.

I become a threat when I'm enacting an Indigenous body that is a political order reproducing itself. That's when women are targeted. The more intimately connected I am to land, to my own people and to how my ancestors lived in the past, then it's easier to understand how my body is a threat to capitalism. So I think in terms of dispossession, then, what I'm trying to do in my work is connect Indigenous people intimately to their territory. You will fight harder if you are in love with the land and in love with your people.

And you will choose not to be displaced. The Mississauga Nishnaabeg Nation is dispossessed but isn't displaced, and we have ways of interacting with the land. We have these strange deals with racist landowners to maintain a connection to our territory even though we're legally dispossessed of the land, but not displaced. There are elders who can get certain medicines because they are able to access private land through relationships they have built and negotiated. The elders know to leave me in the truck because I'm lippy and political. So they have their own means and methods to get to the land. The elder will tell me that the landowner might be a super-hick but he'll let him launch his canoe. Elders have nurtured webs of relationships with people that I would find appalling, but allow them to hunt, fish, gather, and visit ceremonial sites, and thus remain embedded in the land.

I wrote a story about a group of Anishinaabe women who tap maple trees in Peterborough, for example, because that's their sugarbush—we've been dispossessed, but we are not displaced and we are going to do what we can to increase our connection with the land. And that means we're going to tap guerilla-style into these maple trees without permission, boil it in our backyard, and make sugar as a means of increasing connection.

You have to be extremely cognizant and critical of Western legal systems because the processes by which decisions are being made are not Indigenous processes. I don't think the Western legal tradition in my territories is legitimate so I need to not give it power. So I don't like getting caught up in a rights-based discourse because it's been a tool of dispossession.

The early treaties still allowed for Indigenous self-determination: they were political and diplomatic relationships to figure out how to share land while respecting individual jurisdictions. That fundamentally changes as settlers gained more and more power, as Indigenous people got less and less power. By the time you get to the numbered treaties, in the agreements, I can see that our political traditions were encoded in them, Anishinaabe traditions are there, but that's not how they have been written down. Now treaties are almost like contracts for dispossession. That was not the game that we were playing. It was the game we had to play when we lost power.

For global warming we need to build the alternative, real people, on the ground in real time. Pressuring governments and institutions to change seems like a misuse of our power. We just sunk a huge amount of energy into COP21 climate agreement and have a deal that cut Indigenous peoples out, and won't solve the problem. What if all of that energy had gone into building the alternative in local communities? That's how change happens, not the other way around.

MH & AJ   Do you think a critique of development is useful here?

LS   You settlers are so weird! It's so weird to think of development, no? Indigenous people have always thought outside of development. We did rice, we did sugar, we did life. We sunk ourselves in life and relationships. We had a lot more fun. We weren't developing. Development is a very powerful story though—it's like assimilation. Look what happened to participatory development and how that got co-opted. From my perspective, development is totally the wrong paradigm and the wrong question. It's not hard for me to think outside of it. Solar panels and green energy still fits in to some kind of development. In some ways, development is based on exploitation, and it's hard to look past that. Development is based on getting something for nothing. It is based on exploitation. Taking without giving. Rights without responsibility or accountability or consent. Meaningful actualization, both individually and collectively, doesn't work like that.

Development is related to *anxiety* because accumulation is never enough in capitalism. Which ultimately is also about *shame*—this idea that Indigenous peoples and our societies, our knowledge is less developed than Western ideas is a very prevalent, Canadian idea. Economic development and intellectual development, for instance, is used to make Indigenous peoples feel ashamed of our societies and nations. This, combined with an historicization of our nations and the continual erasure of us from contemporary society, places us in this situation that if we want to survive as humans, not even as Indigenous peoples, but as humans, if we want to feed our kids, then we need to get on board, develop, and fully participate in this hyper-exploitation of natural resources, or we won't survive. It is a jobs/environment dichotomy that has been intensified in a settler colonial context.

The shaming part of this is interesting to me because it's also linked to the emotional part of capitalism. Colonialism has always used shame as a weapon. It has the ability to immobilize people really quickly—it's not only saying your *actions* are wrong but that *your way of being* is wrong. Capitalism is offered as a way out of shame—you can buy your way to a better life. You can feel powerful by exploiting. If your community partners with us on this mine, you aren't poor dirty Indians any longer. You are part of the contributing middle class, and you can practice your culture on the weekends.

The violence of colonialism implants shame in us, and then capitalism is presented as the cure, the way out, the fix. Break us down to the point where we no longer have the emotional capital to resist, and then buy us into the process. It's a very old colonial trick—and you see it repeated over and over again from treaties to modern-day land claims to agreements to pipelines.

Let's think about shame though, because without shame, the trick doesn't work. Shame works at an individual level to implant the idea that you are wrong as Indigenous people, by nature. The overwhelming emotional response of shame is very effective in terms of restricting people's ability to mobilize collectively. It is fear and anxiety that forces people to try to buy themselves out of this narrative—i.e., if I can just afford more and feed that egotistical side, and then the more disconnected you are, the more anxiety and shame can take hold.

Shame is a very powerful tool of control in the colonial mentality. And I think gender violence and sexual violence is a lot about implanting that shame. Once you've implanted shame in someone, you have the ability for them to self-regulate and self-control how they are in the world based on that. It's a paralyzing emotion. Shame creates disconnection, and the more shame you have, the more anxiety you have, the more depression you have, the more immobilization you have. And the more that propels capitalism.

—

Leanne's calls to a different way of being in the world sound totally compelling to these settler ears, but how can we make sense of it in the everyday world full of pipelines and highways, rent and jobs? Leanne's traditions are full of hope: her ancestors were living non-capitalist lives long before colonialism. Decolonization, in part, is the political project of reclaiming and building new traditions of re-establishing relationships to land outside of state jurisdiction. It is an assertive claim to make fundamental changes, in order to invigorate certain traditions within the context of new resurgences.

Many of us have too few traditions to trust. The origin myths of colonial societies that were thrust upon us were built on abhorrent lies and violent practices. Most of us *are* alienated from a relationship to land. So much of our histories cannot be relied on to guide us to better lives. New renditions of the good life ask of us to face the demands of *both* tradition and change, to take responsibility for how privilege has been built without becoming mired in self-absorbed guilt. Shame has a relationship to the past, and anxiety has a relationship to the future.[87] As we left Edmonton, heading north on the infamous (and often lovely) Highway 63, we were a little anxious about what the next weeks were going to hold, but also energized. We were driving through land that has been intensely subjected to development, but also land that tells many other stories.

Oops! Did I say "tar sands"?

Never forget: The words you use show what side you're on,

and those won't go over well with the hard-working, hard-playing laborers and engineers cruising Franklin Avenue in "full-size" pickup trucks splattered by honest "on site" mud.

ATHABASCA BUILDING

Imagine

Choices

"Tar sands" is technically inaccurate but favored by environmentalists as an easy swipe at the gooey mess in which the bitumen petroleum found here is locked up.

So Matt Hern, an author-activist, and Am Johal, a media philosopher, both from Vancouver, British Columbia, and I — all of us Proudhon-quoting lefties — have been practicing saying "oil sands" instead.

OIL SANDS.

OIL SANDS.

OIL SANDS.

Though industry itself once tossed about both expressions interchangeably, "oil sands", which emphasizes the desired end product, not its dirty beginning state, is now the officially preferred label for the deposits that make up 97 percent of Canada's massive oil reserves — the third largest in the world.

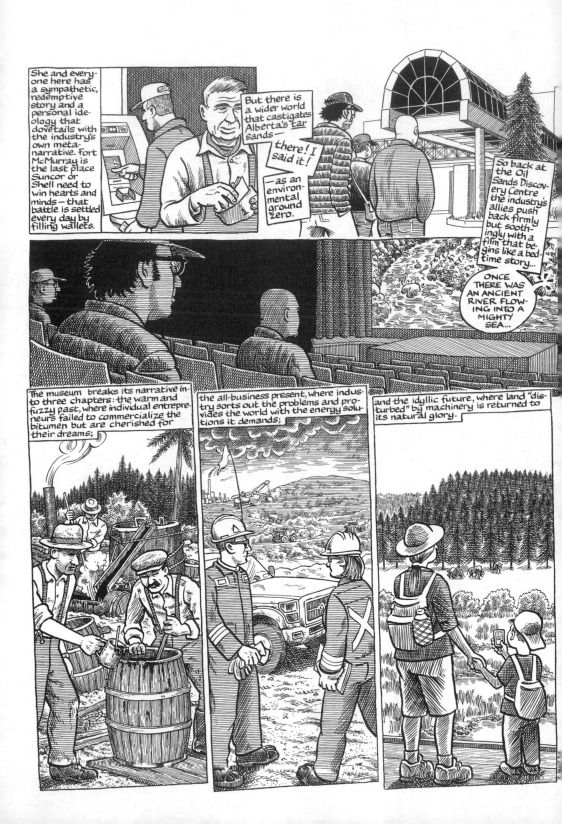

She and everyone here has a sympathetic, redemptive story and a personal ideology that dovetails with the industry's own metanarrative. Fort McMurray is the last place Suncor or Shell need to win hearts and minds – that battle is settled every day by filling wallets.

But there is a wider world that castigates Alberta's tar sands—

there! I said it!

—as an environmental ground zero.

So back at the Oil Sands Discovery Centre the industry's allies push back firmly but soothingly with a film that begins like a bedtime story...

ONCE THERE WAS AN ANCIENT RIVER FLOWING INTO A MIGHTY SEA...

The museum breaks its narrative into three chapters: the warm and fuzzy past, where individual entrepreneurs failed to commercialize the bitumen but are cherished for their dreams;

the all-business present, where industry sorts out the problems and provides the world with the energy solutions it demands;

and the idyllic future, where land "disturbed" by machinery is returned to its natural glory.

Down below we spot bison—the poster child of this redemptive project—who will wait in a holding pen a few years longer until the churned-up ground is restored to the "equivalent land capability" of its original state.

But will trees spaced evenly, a repositioned swampland, and an iconic beast make for a viable ecosystem?

The industry assures us that the future is already as secure as the past is certain, while digging and drilling for the last drop of oil is all but inevitable.

"Shovels and trucks continue to grow," we learned at the Discovery Centre, as if the machinery evolves organically on its own.

And, to be honest, not even we can resist taking pictures of ourselves against the earth-clawing colossi to acknowledge our insignificance by comparison.

Look into the maw of the 2,400-ton bucket-wheel excavator and you know your role is to get out of its way.

4

FORT MCMURRAY

—

Dene, Woodland Cree, and Chipewyan Territories

Arriving in Fort Mac for the first time is strangely anticlimactic. It's just another average-looking, mid-sized resource town. Sure it's an infamous one with a particularly sharp and resonant reputation, but most everything about the place resembles every other blue-collar place you've ever been to. Fast-food outlets, big box stores, oversized trucks, wide streets, functional housing. It does evince a particularly aggressive extractive vibe, though: for miles and miles on the route in it's just huge machines, dirt piles, industriality everywhere with little attempt to hide or pretty anything up. It's also extraordinarily cold for most of the year. We were there for the first time in early May 2015 and there was still snow on the ground and in the air, and the wind ripped into our delicate southern constitutions.

This town has its share of corporate pillagers and sociopaths in suits, but probably no more than anywhere else. Fort Mac, like most places, is essentially populated by good, decent people just trying to earn a living. It is different from most places, though, in that so many people there are sacrificing so heavily to travel from far away, which changes the calculus. Working the tar sands is a siren song for many people trying to figure out how to afford school, bank a little cushion, finance their next move, get out of debt, or incubate some long-held dreams. People from all over Canada work in the patch, most iconically huge numbers of Newfoundlanders, but people from a lot farther afield too: there are over a hundred identifiable ethnic communities in Fort Mac. The total population of the town and region is difficult to pin down because maybe a third of the population (possibly up to 35,000 at any one time) are people working in camps who rarely and only transiently intersect with the actual town. The 2016 census says Fort McMurray has 66,573 people,[1] but every major report claimed that between 80,000 and 90,000 people were evacuated during the massive wildfire that enveloped Northern Alberta in May–June of 2016 (lots more on the fire to come).[2] The area periodically undergoes rhythmic waves of international influxes, and huge numbers of people in the Mac are supporting extended families back home, sending money to far corners of the globe. Not everyone in town has one foot somewhere else, but the dynamic is a foundational one. If it weren't for the spectacular incomes, few people would arrive, or stay.[3]

The Mac provokes a visceral reaction—a muscular piston pumping away in a zombie engine—but it's also just another place, another node in international networks with circuits of capital frantically pushing carbon around the globe. Potentially massive tar sands reserves are waiting to get online in Russia, Kazakhstan, and Venezuela. Enormous shale oil deposits can be found all over the world (the largest known reserves are in the United States), fracking is being ramped up almost everywhere, and who knows how many other unconventional strategies are lurking. And that's not to mention the international centers of finance—London, Dubai, Tokyo, Shanghai, Hong Kong, New York—where all the financing and profits flow to and through. Those places are surely more culpable than anywhere, but happily obscured from the grit and grime. The tar sands are a magnet for vitriol, but how much worse really is oil extraction than, say, uranium or diamond mining, or flying everywhere for work, or shipping stuff to the far corners of the globe, or financing massive data servers? Why does this spot attract so much attention and derision?

It is so common for people—from the oil patch or anywhere else—to feel alienated by and from conversations about global warming. In part, this is because so much of the environmental movement reverts to the language of *education*. That refrain, usually repeated with a sigh, is *We just need more education*, or *We need to educate people about the issues*. This position claims that the real problem is that most people just don't have enough information, or are not sufficiently versed in the issues, which purportedly then explains why social or environmental change is not occurring at a sufficient pace.

The educative stance implies that if everyone knew as much as *we* do, if everyone had read the same books and studies *we* have, then they would think the same as us. It is this condescension that has

FIGURE 4.1
Syncrude plant, the Loop just north of Fort McMurray, summer 2016,
just after the wildfire. Photo by Am Johal.

infiltrated so much leftist thought in particular. The educative stance, with all its tentacular implications, is especially evident in the environmental movement's heavily documented and endemic inability to articulate coherent class politics.

Arguments and debate are the foundation of an agonistic politics and are an entirely different relational proposition from education: they present a position for consideration.[4] This book is an argument, or a series of interlinked arguments, and we certainly lean heavily on theory here—explanatory frameworks for understanding what is in front of us—and we were never shy to talk theory with people in Fort Mac, Janvier, Little Buffalo, or at home. We met (and meet) all kinds of people, from all kinds of positions, who were happy to engage us in theoretical arguments. Essentially everyone has considered and articulated positions on global warming (especially in Alberta!); and on our trip, few people were reticent to tell us about theirs, or to offer counterarguments and countertheories.

Difference is difference, and agonistic politics require an ability to respect and argue with positions that are not one's own. People who are deeply concerned about global warming do not need to find ways to communicate to people; we need to talk with people who occupy all kinds of positions that are not ours, and to listen and argue carefully. We're all implicated in these extractivist ideologies of fossil fuels, biocollapses, and species extinctions: we're all burning most everything we can get our hands on.

EMPIRE STATE OF MIND

Shortly after arriving in town we met our hosts. She was a yoga teacher, nutritionist, and wellness advisor. He was a shy, thoughtful shift-supervisor north of town. They were both friendly and welcoming. They were making very impressive incomes. They were selling their modest suburban-style home for $780,000, and even though by 2015 housing prices in the Mac had just started to plunge, they were confident they were going to get their asking price. They had almost paid off their mortgage, and were going to take their profits, and as much more as they could gather over the next year or two, and open a retreat in Nelson, a blissed-out small town in the southeast of British Columbia. They were so familiar to us: the organic milk, the incense, the array of tea choices, the yoga mats rolled up in the corner.

Their house was a comfortable place to land, but honestly, the whole town felt easily recognizable to us, redolent of so many resource communities we've spent so much time in. We immediately had an intuitive sense of where to eat, where to shop, where to drink— and where to best avoid. But in all kinds of ways, our visits to the Mac were lightened by the fact that we had some friends to meet: that's what made this trip plausible in the first place.

One of Matt's kids had been up to the patch to work the year before, trying to make enough money to pay for nursing school. Ashley has a similar story to so many people we met in town: she's full of energy and ideas without enough money to pay for it all. She didn't have the easiest of upbringings, and when her mother died, she was adopted into Matt and Selena's family as a teenager. After working in bars and restaurants for more than a decade, and at least one previous run at college, Ashley was twenty-seven, and short of the funds needed to cover at least three years of full-time nursing school. She probably didn't *need* to go up there—there's a lot of money to be made in Vancouver—but it seemed probably worth it to get out of town for a few months, get a look at a new place, and make some significant cash.

Heading out into the bush to make bank is a time-honored (and of course highly clichéd) Canadian tradition: tree-planting, fishing, logging, fish canning, forest-fire-fighting, prospecting, bear and beetle-counting, fruit-picking, shake-and-shingle cutting—you can make real money (and realistically save a lot of it) in a relatively short time if you're willing to suffer bodily a little. Ashley got a job at a work camp, staffing the front desk, seventy hours a week, three weeks on, one week off. She made twenty-five dollars an hour for the first thirty-five hours a week, thirty-seven and a half per hour (time-and-a-half) for the second thirty-five hours. Not bad for checking people in, handing them their room keys, informing them it was a dry camp, and letting them know where the cafeteria was. We asked her how it felt when she decided to go up there, if she felt guilty, or ashamed or anything:

Guilt is a strong word. I'd say I had serious reservations. It was conflicting being part of something that I have strong moral opinions about, but it also felt frightening not to be able to afford to live here in Vancouver. There are so few opportunities for good work in the city without a massive amount of education. I felt helpless: even people I know in Vancouver with good paying jobs don't have any money.

I definitely had people go out of their way to tell me they thought what I was doing was lousy. I didn't really make it all that public that I was going to the tar sands. I really only told a few close people. I didn't want to share it with more people than I needed to. So, sure, I guess there was some shame.

It was a mix of people who felt it was necessary to impose their opinion on me about my choices. Some were people who come from well-off families and have always had what they needed, with no idea what debt or student loans feel like. Some people were from more of a grassroots background whose only idea of Fort Mac is oil is the root of all evil. I get it, I know what oil extraction does, but going up there opened my eyes up to how that place has a positive side to it, and how it often betters the lives of however many thousands of people work up there.

For me, I think the shame comes from knowing you are benefiting directly from oil extraction. Of course you can believe in global warming and the bigger picture and still work up there, it's just not worth your while to think about it much, or you'll make yourself mad. There really are positive things there: it's culturally diverse; people sustain themselves in a country that is financially unsustainable, and they are able care for generations of families. There are so many people I know, from Vancouver and from my time there, that found their best lives from working there.

It also helped plenty that a couple of Ashley's oldest and best friends were already in town. Gita had headed up to the Mac in early 2013, Vanessa about eight months after that. They were both looking for the same basic things: some adventure, some new friends, some money, some possibility. And they both found something lasting. While Ashley spent five months working at her camp and came home three times during that stretch, Gita and Vanessa stayed in town, for almost three years each. They both worked in a slick brew pub downtown, made new relationships, and for the most part were thrilled with how things had turned out.

Sitting in her bar late one night after work, Vanessa's position was so clear to us. She is an instinctively likable young woman, warm and thoughtful, with a relentless, dogged cheerfulness. Vanessa gives the impression of being **always ready** to have a good time, and she's exactly the person you are glad to be serving you beer: always ready to playfully chirp you but never willing to take any bullshit. It's no surprise that she made great money working in that pub. You could tell right away how many friends she had working there as she moved from table to table, effortlessly talking gentle trash and laughing loudly enough for you to hear her clear across the room through the rubble of bar noise.

Vanessa had come up to town for all the obvious and defensible reasons. We've all chosen at one time or another to take shitty jobs for shitty institutions: the only thing worse than a lousy job is no job, and Vanessa had reconciled herself to the whole package that comes with working in Fort Mac. She wasn't afraid of our questions, but why the hell should she have to answer them? Sure she's a friend who trusts us, but environmental discourses seem to inevitably back people into untenable positions, eliciting shame and anxiety from and for people who have no business attracting either. There is no reason Vanessa should have to justify her employment choices, and certainly not to us, but somehow, unintentionally, we sort of found ourselves there. As if pulled by a tide, rationalizing the tar sands somehow ended up on her plate. She is sharp and had anticipated the conversational direction (why else would we be there?). She stayed warily articulate, and she wasn't about to take any crap: "Sure I wonder about what's going on, and sure I'm worried about climate change. But how is me working here, or not working here, going to change that?" She meant it rhetorically, but specifically too.

In a lot of ways that's exactly the right question, and one that highlights one of the internal contradictions of environmental discourses. Writing a generation ago, David Harvey put it nicely in one of

FIGURE 4.2
Syncrude plant, winter 2017, just a month before the plant fire.
Photo by Selena Couture.

his seminal essays, first published in 1993 as "The Nature of Environment," when he juxtaposed two quotes, one from Aldo Leopold and one from Karl Marx, noting that not only had there been little "rapprochement between ecological/environmentalist and socialist politics" but that "the two have by and large remained antagonistic to each other."[5] It is a distinctive and well-trod analysis, and a useful one that Harvey deploys here, but one that obscures the problem again even as it reveals it. He suggests that, from a biocentric stance like that of Leopold's,

> Working class politics and its concentration on revolutionising political economic processes comes then to be seen as a perpetuation rather than a resolution of the problem as Leopold defines it. The best that socialist politics can achieve, it is often argued, is an environmental (instrumental and managerial) rather than an ecological politics. At its worst, socialism stoops to so-called "Promethean" projects in which the "domination" of nature is presumed both possible and desirable.[6]

Harvey concludes this bifurcation between biocentric and redistributive politics by noting that he "wants to see if there are ways to bridge this antagonism and turn it into a creative rather than a destructive tension" by inserting an "'ecological' angle" to socialist politics.[7] Harvey hopes to transcend the trope that ecology is all fine and good, but basically a bourgeois affectation that is an impediment to socialist, antipoverty politics. In many ways, Harvey ably describes a fundamental fulcrum in contemporary radical thought, but with decades of perspective and considerable sophisticated thinking on the subject, it has become increasingly clear that anticapitalism is necessary to ecology but not sufficient. Ecology cannot be reduced to a simple additive, a supplementary angle, or a hyphenated prefix to existing socialist thought.

Couched within this conversation is a question that has attracted, plagued, even consumed thinkers for millennia: are humans part of *nature*, or are we something else again, something apart? Dismissing any theistic claims that "man was created by god as sovereign of the earth," it might seem at first glance blatantly obvious—*of course* humans are part of the natural world. Humans are products of evolution and reside within the same biospheric constraints and circumstances as all the rest of the world, subject to the same logics, living and dying just like every other organic species.

Huge swaths of environmental thinking have relied on this argument as a foundational assumption, namely, that humans are a part of nature and that the misapprehension that humans are different, or apart, or better than the rest of the world is at the root of ecological crises. Thus so much green thinking claims to *heal the divide*, put people back into nature, *reassert humanity's place in the biosphere*, or, in Harvey's words, *make the tension creative*. There is some truth here, and it is right to challenge any notions of anthropocentric superiority, but this stance has to clear a number of hurdles.

The first is that if humans are *part of nature*, does that make nuclear weapons, toxic waste, geoengineering and the like *natural* as well?[8] Second, there are a number of supposedly clear differentiations between humans and all other species (symbolic/recursive language, generative computation, institutionalization, cooking, record-keeping), all of which are highly contested. We're not really sure about any of these distinctions, but for our argument here, only one differentiation really matters: (some) humans are the only population on Earth with the collective capacity to destroy all the rest. No other species, or subsection of a species, appears to have anything like that power, and thus nothing like the same burdens and responsibilities.

That differentiation sets humans aside from the rest of evolution, but is that place *within* nature or is it in a special category? Murray Bookchin (among many others) tries to resolve this question by distinguishing between what he calls *first* and *second natures*.[9] The former is what is commonly understood as the other-than-human world; the latter comprises human social relationships including all its technologies and artifacts, a second nature that has emerged

[handwritten margin note: are our inventions the products of evolution?]

from first nature's evolutionary trajectory. Bookchin takes pains to note that first nature is not blind or directionless, but evolves dialectically with a *general directionality* toward increasing interdependence, mutualism, complexity, and complementarity: "We slander the natural world when we deny its activity, striving, creativity, and development as well as its subjectivity."[10]

Bookchin's political philosophy flows easily from this, rectifying what he calls "a steady process of estrangement from nature that has increasingly developed into outright antagonism" which requires a "reentry into natural evolution" that is "no less a humanization of nature than a naturalization of humanity."[11] In his view, a free, ecological society is one that replicates and is grounded in the ethics— the complexity, interdependence, and mutualism—of first nature: "This much is clear: the way we view our position in the natural world is deeply entangled with the way we organize the social world."[12]

For Bookchin, a free society is by definition an ecological society, "overcoming the divorce between nature and society—or between the biological and the cultural" by sharing an ethics and a directionality with first nature, including "a greater diversity in evolution; the wider and more complete participation of all components in a whole."[13] Just as diversity in any ecosystem is necessary for stability and resilience, it can also be understood in the language of human freedom as inculcating and nurturing creativity, self-directedness, and participation. This is absolutely *not* to say that everything we find in first nature is worthy of human social replication—far from it—but that its general thrust toward differentiation and participation can form an ethical basis for thinking about both first and second nature.

This interpretation of first nature, celebrating its subjectivity and creativity, and finding an ethical basis for social organization that strives toward differentiation, reasserts humans as active agents in the biosphere. Humans can and should be actors who behave with all the power of second nature to articulate an ethical place on the planet, but not as dictators, shepherds, gods, or sovereigns.

Working from this understanding of the more-than-human world and humans' relationships to and with it frees us from endlessly recursive and self-referential meanderings about whether *we* are inside or outside of *nature*. It's actually entirely the wrong question: humans are both of those things, and much more as well. First, it's way too reductive to speak just of human relationships with other-than-humans—there are spectacular levels of differentiation within and between humans and within and between the rest of the world. Foregrounding mutualism, complementarity, and differentiation as ethical principles to be invoked in social organization opens up endless amounts of possible political space to redefine ecology as a social question.

Second, this approach provides the basis for ethical relationships with the other-than-human world that are neither dominatory nor passive. Any approaches that see humans as distinctly separate inevitably place humanity at the sovereign apex of evolution. Biocentrism that tries to subsume humans entirely within first nature tends to depoliticize and render mute human agency and responsibility, leaving humanity unable to make real choices or assert ourselves using particular tools. Starting from principles of ethical complementarity means that humans are able to make choices about the ordering of human society and first nature, and ground them in an ethics and politics.

This is to say that of course *nature* is socially constructed. It is such a complicated and complicating idea that it is highly inadvisable to use the words *nature* or *natural* without considerable trepidation. Every linguistic and ideological mechanism we invoke when we claim anything as *nature* is part of human culture and society: there is nothing natural about nature. But the more-than-human world is far more than that and not entirely subsumed within human discourse. It is much more useful to claim that *natures*, both first and second, are emergently produced and co-constructed by both humans *and* all the other-than-human inhabitants of the planet. Acknowledging the endless rationalities and subjectivities in the world means accepting the unique capacities and responsibilities of people, but simultaneously it means accepting the capacities of other species to be and to act in ways that humans are incapable of. As Brian Massumi writes in *What Animals Teach Us about Politics* (here partially responding to and agreeing with a provocation from Judith Butler):

> Do not presume that you have access to a criterion for categorically separating the animal from the human. ... So don't get it into your head that consciousness will provide the dividing line. ... Where the typological thinking of category separation falls apart, there the need—and the opportunity—will be found to undertake the positive project of constructing a logic of differential mutual inclusion of modes of existence, and ages of nature, that is more to the animal-political point.
>
> Where typological thinking falls apart? That would be ... from the beginning, in the end, and most especially in the middle (which it fancies to exclude).
>
> Don't be mistaken into thinking that the more-than-human is outside, surrounding the human, in the environment. The more-than-human is in the very make-up of the human. For the human body is an animal body, and animality is immanent to human life (and vice versa).[14]

This ravaging of the logic of human superiority is exactly the sort of complication we need here. If it is true that nothing in the other-than-human world is free of the taint of human techniques—if there is residue of Chernobyl in caribou across the high arctic, if every creature in the sea is filtering human toxins, and so on—it is equally true that every human is composed of billions of other-than-human entities; the water we drink and the air we breathe has passed through countless other organic bodies. The differentiations between us and them, human and other-than, are very far from clear. Thus the project of constructing an ethical, ecological politics has to be *relational*.

To blur the human/other-than lines is to say that we are bound up in this together, but highly differentially, with highly variegated sets of powers and responsibilities and accountabilities. Opening up space for nondominatory, nonexploitative politics has to mean a nondominatory, nonexploitative sensibility. As soon as claims for inherent human superiority are in play—via reason, or brute power, symbolic language, or whatever criteria you want to invoke—politics gets lost down dominatory dead-ends. An ecological politics, the politics required to answer global warming, must acknowledge that the domination of other-than-humans and the land is made permissible by the domination of humans by humans.

Toward this project, we also find it fruitful to employ something akin to what Bookchin called *dialectical naturalism*. This is a dialectics that reworks Hegelian and Marxist renditions and mirrors the other-than-human world—a constant unfolding, striving toward differentiation and complexity, a vision of history that has no end, no heaven.

Dialectics is a tremendously valuable, possibly indispensable way to conceive of the world, at least in part because of its insistence on constant change, contradictions, tensions, and unfolding (becoming). It is wholly possible to appreciate both idealist and materialist renditions without accepting any insistence on finalities. As in Adorno's negative dialectics, we cannot believe any inherent force is pushing dialectics forward to an inevitable end. The directionality may well be backward, sideways, multiple, simultaneous, indiscernible, indecipherable, and multiple other directions as well. Becoming is an end that has no end, aside from a general tendency toward more complexity, a differentiation that is more generous and mutualistic, but in no way assured. That end is no End, and will never be reached. As Bookchin puts it: "Dialectical naturalism thus does not terminate in a Hegelian Absolute at the end of a cosmic developmental path, but rather advances the vision of an ever-increasing wholeness, fullness, and richness of differentiation and subjectivity."[15]

BUFFALO SOLDIERS

One afternoon, Vanessa took the afternoon off to drive around with us. She was a little dubious: there isn't much sightseeing to be done in or around Fort Mac. We headed north of town to drive the infamous Loop, a ten-kilometer hang-noose-shaped stretch of road that takes you right past the iconic Suncor and Syncrude plants, some oceanic tailings ponds, spooky reclamation areas, and a weird open-air museum called The Giants of Mining that is particularly baffling. The Giants of Mining or GoM is on a modest little crescent just off the road, backing up onto a major tailings pond, and sitting across from a steaming, humming upgrading plant that looks like a movie-set archetype for an oil industry facility: acres of wires and filthy buildings, gas flares bursting regularly from the tops of chimneys, and perfect factory aesthetics. The GoM has a bunch of jumbo-sized retired mining equipment to gawk at, some informational displays about the historical evolution of tar sands extraction, a couple of port-o-potties, and inexplicably, a sign inviting you to camp there.

The Loop also gets you right to the poster children for Fort McMurray's public relations efforts: buffalo. The whole district that Fort Mac[16] sits within is called The Regional Municipality of Wood Buffalo—for the massive herds of wood bison (or wood buffalo, the names are basically interchangeable) that once populated the area before settlers arrived. Largely slaughtered across North America, buffalo are making a moderate comeback in small artisanal herds, some farms, and zoo-like facilities, and there are now approximately 7,000 wood bison (as differentiated from the smaller-sized plains bison) living "wild" in carefully managed and monitored herds. The wood bison was once thought to be extinct, but in 1957 a small herd of about 200 animals was discovered in Alberta. Since then that one herd has been carefully nurtured back to about 2,500, but the species is still listed as threatened.

In 1993, Syncrude moved thirty of the animals onto five hundred hectares of reclaimed tar-sand-mined land in an attempt to burnish their image and demonstrate that the industry's claims to rehabilitate land post-extraction were viable. Since then the herd has grown to 300, and these beasts are deployed extremely strategically and energetically by both state and capital as the centerpiece of promotional and advertising efforts.

FIGURE 4.3
Matt and Vanessa overlooking tailings ponds. Photo by Am Johal.

The Fort Mac buffalo herd shows up on pamphlets and websites, posters and sculptures all over town. The bison are referenced constantly as living, breathing evidence of the industry's environmental responsibility, their willingness to consult with Indigenous people, and the regenerative capacities of the land. We'd been at the Oil Sands Discovery Centre the day before, a slick (if apparently severely undervisited) museum and welcome center run by the province but sponsored by major industry players, with Syncrude and Suncor stickers slapped everywhere.[17] The center has legions of fun exhibits, demonstrations, videos, displays, and all the accoutrements of contemporary museums, and is occasionally rather frank in accounting for the environmental damages of the work. The narrative spins just enough to leave even the most credulous visitors assured that once operations in any area are ceased, everything will be put back back just the way they found it. The companies claim that they replant the forest extensively, regenerate the local ecosytems and quietly exit out the side door—no harm, no foul. The Syncrude buffaloes are repeatedly invoked as snorting, steaming evidence of reclamation and regeneration.

So of course we wanted to see these majestically bovine rockstar bison. It was a little harder to find the herd than we had first thought, given the sheer volume of acclaim these *Bison bison athabascae* attract, and few people in town seemed to even know what we were talking about. We eventually located the Bison Viewpoint after a couple of drive-bys: a marginally marked entrance just off the northern reaches of the Loop.

The site itself is pretty underwhelming. It's a scrubby little hill with a strange assortment of flags flapping in the cold wind at its peak: two Canadian, two Albertan, one District of Wood Buffalo, and one Syncrude (!) flag. There is a quick little turn-around, a few educational efforts displayed on historical-marker-style pedestals, and not much else. The fabled *b.b.a.* were nowhere to be seen. The fence of their paddock was right there, but evidently they were in a distant part of their pasture, although a couple of us thought we saw some black lumps in the far distance that might have been moving.

The location of the viewpoint, however, is spectacular. From the slightly elevated vantage point you can see massively scaled industrial facilities in several directions, smoke and flares billowing impressively out of huge smokestacks. The little hill we were on looks like a desert isle with enormous tailings ponds all around, striated at the edges with rows and rows of virulent-looking effluent trenches. The formal name of the place is the Beaver Creek Wood Buffalo Ranch Viewpoint, but there sure aren't any fucking beavers damming those tailings ponds down below.

Even in May 2015, it was freezing cold with treacherous patches of lingering ice on the ground and snow in the air—which took us a moment to realize wasn't snow at all but a sooty-white-charcoaly

FIGURE 4.4

The authors looking authorial, posing in front of various flags, at the Beaver Creek Wood Buffalo Ranch Viewpoint. Photo by Vanessa Elie.

residue that smeared on your jacket when you wiped at it. The stink in the air reminded us of pulp-and-paper mill towns, a smell that didn't exactly nauseate, but left a weird slimy visage across our consciousness and got us wondering what we were breathing. Every few seconds, cannons echoed back and forth across the vista, designed to scare any ducks or wild birds from landing on any of the vast tailings ponds around us. The water kills them en masse.

The cracking of these cannons incrementally and sort of stealthily accumulates so that over time they really get on your nerves. They're not *that* loud (at least from the places we heard them), but they come from multiple directions and are relentless, going off somewhere within hearing distance every twenty seconds or so, and eventually jangle your attention in a subtle way. The cannons are legally required because the sheer toxicity of the ponds kills birds off, but also because the residual bitumen and chemical brew in the ponds gets on their feathers, weighing them down so that they are unable to fly. Every mining operation is required to set up dense systems of cannons, noisemakers, scarecrows, and various other ingenious techniques designed to scare away waterfowl and migratory birds.

Sometimes, though—because of a variety of factors—all these systems fail. Typically, it is storms or wind or dense fog that forces the birds to land, and over time the birds just get inured to the noise and land anyways.[18] In 2008, for example, a spring storm forced thousands of migratory birds down onto ponds and 1,600 died. Syncrude paid a $3 million fine for that one. In 2010, 550 more birds had to be destroyed when they landed on Syncrude and Suncor ponds. No fine was apparently levied then.[19] Smaller incidents occur every year despite the intensive infrastructures designed to prevent any migratory bird contact, but it's hard to imagine how they could be fully prevented—northern Alberta is on the path of scores of critical migratory routes, and the tailings ponds are just immense (having more than doubled in size since 2008).

The whole sensory experience—the smell, the distantly powing cannons, the post-apocalyptic scenery, the cold—the whole deal fulfilled all our worst eco-porn nightmares. We goofed around for a bit, wandered around the viewpoint shivering and chucking snow, took a bunch of photos, read all the information, attempted bison mating calls in a failed bid to lure some animals close, then quickly piled back into our vehicles. We felt dispirited, terrified, shocked, and all that, but also smugly gratified in that it substantiated some of our worst prejudices about the place.

WHERE THERE'S SMOKE

We didn't know it then (obviously) but almost exactly a year after that first visit, in May 2016, a massive fire—the largest and most expensive natural disaster in Canadian history—would tear through town. The fire caused the mass evacuation of nearly 90,000 people, with 2,400 structures (10 percent of the town) and at least 600 work camp units destroyed, and at least $3.6 billion in insurable losses. The fire started just south of town (sparked by unknown human causes, probably a spark from a four-wheeler catching a dried-out bush) and quickly grew into what became known as The Beast. The fire was an international story for its sheer size (at its peak more than 500,000 hectares, spread all across northern Alberta and into Saskatchewan), its ferocity (it took over a month to get it substantially controlled), and the stark ironies (the fact that the fire's spread was attributed to global warming-induced drought and record-setting Alberta temperatures was not lost on commentators when tar sands production was shut down for most of a month).

The damage wasn't just to the residential town, of course, as essentially every tar sands operator in the area had to stop work and evacuate all employees. The repercussions were immense and immediate. By the time workers started trickling back into camps and operations slowly started back up after approximately a month in stasis, an estimated 40 million barrels of oil production had been lost and vast amounts of infrastructure needed replacing.

Amazingly, there were no direct human fatalities from the fire (although two people died in a car crash en route out of town) and no major injuries to the almost 2,500 firefighters who rotated in and out of battling the blaze. The incredible size and speed of the fire combined with the scope of the evacuation made it near-inconceivable that there could be no loss of human life, but somehow there was none. The bison, however, were left behind to fend for themselves: "Syncrude has left as much food and water as possible," said spokesman Leithan Slade.[20] The herd's area is built largely on recovered mines, and when the fire started the animals were pushed into a northern pasture with a large buffer zone from the boreal forest, enough hopefully to protect them from the fires. Greg Fuhr, vice president of mining and extraction with Syncrude Canada, flew in and out regularly to check on the bison, and said, "Wood bison are 'adaptable' creatures and the smoke hasn't bothered them. ... Actually, one of the interesting things about the smoky conditions is that the number of insects that would typically irritate them are not around."[21]

The next day we spent two hundred dollars for an hour-and-a-half flight over the area. It was easier and cheaper than we expected—approximately as difficult to organize as hailing a cab. We made a quick call, drove to the edge of town, dropped the cash, and wandered out onto the tarmac to meet Bruno, our congenial pilot. He jammed the three of us into his tiny plane, hooked us up with headsets so we could talk to one another, and happily narrated the sights as we flew up the Athabasca River, over multiple processing plants and mining ops, circled above camps and tailings ponds, and then turned back for some beautiful views of the town. The ride was very pleasant actually, and added perspective to what we had seen from the ground. The scale of the tar sands is staggering. The patterns and repetitions are beautiful, the ambition and arrogance breathtaking. Bruno swooped down at every request, so we could get better looks at the trucks and quarries, and then back up so we could see a stretch of the river. He answered every question with straightforward, chill replies that betrayed no opinions at all. It is commonplace to hear the tar sands described as *Mordor*, and that's not far off, if a little theatrical.[22] The tailings ponds really are immense (small lakes, really), the strip-mining looks like the whole of northern Alberta has been pummeled with meteors, the destruction comprehensive for as far as the eye can see, even from the air: everything is on a scale multiple times vaster than what we expected, even after preparing ourselves. The *biggest industrial project in human history*? Sure seems plausible.

We landed around lunch time and headed off to meet Reinalie Jorolan at a local Filipino-owned café. Reinalie is an activist in town who had arrived as a domestic worker ten years previously and settled down. She works multiple jobs and still sends plenty of money back home, and is very content to stay in the Mac. Actually she is a lot more than just content; she really loves the place and is an energetic booster. At several points in our conversation she emphasized to us: "This isn't a boomtown, it's a *hometown*." Reinalie is pretty

FIGURE 4.5
Matt at the Oil Sands Discovery Centre's Industrial Equipment Garden
and Bucketwheel Exhibit. Photo by Am Johal.

energetic about everything, though. She has a testy style, and struck us as someone who knows how to handle herself in a scrap. And she, like everyone else we talked to in town, was keenly alert to all the subtexts and subtleties of our conversations. Everyone knew what we were there for, and were trying to read us, get a sense of our commitments. Reinalie articulated counterarguments—one after the other, lined up like a well-prepped legal brief and without prompting—to the objections she presumed we had to the tar sands, beating us to punches we weren't even about to throw.

As quickly as Reinalie jumps to extoll the virtues of Fort Mac, she isn't naive. She spent a good hour telling us about the indignities and suffering that so many imported domestic workers face, a huge percentage of them Filipina. Plenty of families in town hire nannies

and cleaners and then violate the terms of the agreement extrava-
gantly: working "the help" far too hard, denying them days off, short-
ing them pay, providing substandard accommodations, and sometimes
subjecting them to harassment and violence, sexual and otherwise.
There are also plenty of wonderful families and employers in town, but
Renalie had been shocked enough upon arrival to start organizing almost immediately. While we were there, two separate grassroots organizations were trying to ameliorate conditions and create networks so
that homecare workers wouldn't be so isolated and vulnerable.

Later on that on that same night we met up with Gita. Matt has
known her and her family for many years. Gita has a similar feisty
energy to Reinalie, ready to drop the gloves over most any insult,
perceived or overt. She rarely hesitates to let you know what she's
thinking and is not overly concerned about your feelings. It's a
charming set of traits, and one of the reasons we like her so much,
even if it turns on you now and then. Gita is a lot more than just that,
of course—she has a wealth of stories and attitudes—but her com-
bativeness is probably a big part of why she feels so comfortable in
Fort Mac. Women in resource towns pretty much have to be fierce:
the gender imbalances, the mercenary vibe, the macho workplaces,
the hostility to regulation, the general roughness—resource towns
often deserve their reputations as dangerous places for women, who
face violence and harassment.

For a long time, Fort Mac has cleaved closely to that stereotype. For
years, its crime statistics across the board reflected boomtown pathologies of drugs and violence, assault and alcohol. The stories get
amplified and exaggerated for more genteel ears down south, but the
reality was (and in many ways still is) that the tar sands are a tough
place to earn a living, and especially so for women. The violence in the
Wood Buffalo region peaked in 2008, though, and through 2015 declined on almost all counts, reflecting comprehensive policing and
policy efforts. Starting in 2015, and hardly surprisingly mirroring the
downturn in oil prices, violence statistics started to turn upward
again. In 2015, Fort McMurray's score on Statistics Canada's Crime

Severity Index rose by more than 2.5 percent, erasing seven years of steady safety gains, "but with a rating of 94.54 incidents per 100,000 people in the urban area, it's a long way from the high of 207.73 recorded in 2008."[23] Disaggregating the statistics reveals that drug arrests remain high, as do sexual assaults (about two-and-a-half times the national average), and in the small (largely Indigenous) towns surrounding the Mac, the crime severity numbers are almost four times higher.

There is significant body of feminist scholarship related to gender in resource towns that can be very helpful in understanding a place like Fort McMurray. Sara O'Shaughnessy writes that "frontier masculinity creates three particular subject positions for women which reinforce beliefs about women's perceived dependency and anomalousness on the frontier: gold diggers, devoted mothers and lady truck drivers."[24] However, O'Shaughnessy's research reveals that narratives are much more complex and contradictory. Elsewhere, writing with Goze Dogu, she remarks, "where ... are the opportunities to reflect upon the necessity of, or the alternatives to, the oil-driven economy, its colonial foundations, or its hegemonic masculinity?"[25] As Sheena Wilson, a petro-feminism scholar and director of the short film *Petro-Mama: Mothering in a Crude World*, writes, "Rather than succumb to the fears of what the end of cheap oil might mean for the future in general, or for feminism in particular, it may be more productive to reevaluate current discourses around oil and alternative energy sources for their potential to disrupt rather than to simply reproduce intersectional social inequalities."[26]

The same volatility that is shot through oil economics keeps showing up repeatedly, inscribed on the climate, social relations, politics, everyday lives. We're not much interested in fetishizing stability or calm, but the careening feeling that many people articulate when speaking of global warming gets invoked repeatedly in the tar sands, if in slightly different ways: everybody's just hanging on for the ride. But that too, like so much of Fort Mac, defies easy characterization.

The tremendous diversity of Fort Mac is for real, and it intersectionally inflects the everyday experience of all women and all genders there. Vanessa said once that Fort McMurray was the first place she had lived where she wasn't thinking about her skin color all the time. We were told there is an openly LGBTQ2+ community in town that no one seems to pay much ill attention to, a claim often cited as evidence of Fort Mac's underappreciated progressive milieu. Such facts complicate any easy narratives, but let's not wax rhapsodic about the situation: any town with sexual assault rates 2.5 times the national average has nothing to boast about, and nothing should obscure that.

We spent a lot of time at the bar downtown where Gita and Vanessa both worked, meeting coworkers, drinking, watching sports. We met so many people, almost all of them thrilled with the money they were making, a huge percentage with families and partners in other parts of the province or country. So many people from Canada's Maritimes—Newfoundland and Cape Breton especially—were there paying off huge student loans, or had been laid off elsewhere, or just were depressed at the job prospects in their hometowns. Gita was straight gold one night, standing up to leave and telling us, "Look, coming here is the best thing that's ever happened to me," daring us to challenge her. No one did. How could we?

She had found great-paying work, a partner and a family, and stability, and she wasn't going to take any shit for it. In her words: "No one has ever said anything disparaging to me. Not directly. I have never felt guilty or ashamed to be working here. Everyone is really proud of me. People are so supportive—they thought it is brave of me to come here. Even people I wouldn't have expected to be so supportive. The scale of pollution and environmental issues are so huge, how can that be my responsibility, or my fault? No one ever once made me feel bad personally for working in Ft. McMurray." It is impossible not to feel proud of Gita and Vanessa and Ashley, of their toughness and grit and resilience.

We have no intention of making anyone feel bad for working in the tar sands. What purpose would that serve? But global warming is still real and accelerating. So we're back to the same impasses of action and culpability. It's easy to sit in Vancouver or Portland and say that the tar sands have to be shut down, but it's a lot harder to say when you're sitting on Franklin Avenue having a beer with people whose lives would be catastrophically affected. Ecology has to be able to look Fort Mac in the eye and say: "Leave 85 percent of it in the ground," and be ready to answer when people ask, "OK, then what?"

Because Reinalie is right: Fort Mac is a hometown, a family town, and a town full of resources. You don't have to go any farther than the colossal recreation center—MacDonald Island Park, or Mac Island—which is "Canada's largest community recreational, leisure, and social centre" to grasp this.[27] Mac Island is like a megamall with pretty much every sporting and recreational facility imaginable—a library, rock climbing, four ice sheets, indoor turf field, pools and water-slides, curling sheets, giant dance and fitness studios, a major gym, a childcare center, conference facilities, indoor playgrounds, and more. It's just endless: outside there is a baseball stadium with four diamonds, a 240-acre eighteen-hole golf course, a full-size stadium with a 20,000 capacity—you get the picture. Of course, all of it has been heavily sponsored and in many cases totally paid for by oil and energy giants. Mac Island is saturated with signs and plaques congratulating corporate generosity: the Shell Place (the stadium), the Suncor Community Leisure Centre, the Nexen CNOOC stage, the Syncrude Aquatic Centre, the Canadian Natural Resources Arena, the Total Fitness Center, and lots else.

Oil companies have every reason to pour money into this facility. The winters are something ugly in the Mac (for five months a year the average temperature stays well below zero), and if the town is going to stabilize, employers need people to have something to do other than get right-gooned every night. The companies have a vested interest in the culture of the town shifting away from the wild-west madness of years past when drug and alcohol abuse were rampant, and legions of workers were falling prey to addiction and violence.

Hang around Mac Island for a few hours and you'll see rivers of families pouring in and out. Mothers in hijabs shepherding rambunctious kids to their swim lessons. Latinx families chatting away

FIGURE 4.6
Joe staring down a historical bucketwheel at the Industrial Equipment
Garden and Bucketwheel Exhibit. Photo by Am Johal.

in Spanish as they head to the library. East African teenagers carrying hockey bags. All happy vignettes of Canadian immigration and diversity. One relative newcomer to town, Ana Maria Mendez, had originally been a curator in Peru before landing in Fort Mac with her husband, where she was now working as Manager of Arts and Culture at Mac Island. Her infectious personality gave her a real advantage as she worked with others to skillfully repurpose an empty hallway in the cavernous rec center into an art gallery and exhibition space. Focusing mostly on local artists, the gallery also has a deeply international orientation given the diverse global makeup of the town. She has overseen over seventy art exhibitions and countless public events, administers a dance program, and is involved in other public art projects in town. She has done all this having only immigrated to Canada in 2009.

It's not just Mac Island; the whole town defies easy portraits. It really is a family town, and a young, prosperous family town at that. Sixty-nine percent of people in town are married (compared to 47 percent nationally). Only 12 percent of the town is over fifty-five years old. Almost 40 percent of households have kids under the age of six. And more than 70 percent of households make $150,000 or more.[28] These stats are a bit of a distortion because huge numbers of workers fly straight into the camps and straight out, barely registering on any census data or local population surveys. Those folks bring their bodies in and take their commitments out with them when they leave, invisible to the town's deeper workings; but left behind are a significant number of people, maybe even a majority, who are not planning on going anywhere anytime soon.

Declarations of love and fidelity to the town are easy enough when times are bumping. But these stats we just cited are from late 2014 and early 2015, when everything was humming along. We were first there just as the real oil slump was starting, and while we could sense a lot of latent fear and anxiety then, most of it was still speculative, a lot of "Ha ha—yeah, holy shit, it's not good, but it'll pop right back up" sentiments. But prices kept dropping through 2015 and stayed volatile and low through 2016 and 2017. The cheerfulness of the town turned resentful and bitter as layoffs started coming, overtime dried up, debts started piling up, and marriages showed cracks. As Bernard the Roughneck, a patch worker who has emerged as a pseudo-grassroots public booster of pipelines, put it: "Alberta—we feel like that guy that always buys a round at the bar for everyone, and the one time we don't have that cash, no one is willing to buy us a round."[29]

We have no better idea than anyone else: maybe 2018, or 2019, or maybe further down the road, oil prices will leap back up and all will be forgiven. Maybe they'll plunge right down to $10 a barrel. Or maybe, perhaps even probably, we have entered into long period of volatility. Long-range investors, such as managers of pension funds, are no longer viewing oil and gas as a stable investment. Major foundations like Rockefeller and many others are actively divesting from fossil fuels and establishing fossil-free funds as investment vehicles.[30] The continuum of volatility is built into the DNA of capitalism, and creative destruction is part and parcel of its operating principle. Capitalism attempts to absorb the extreme swings of global warming into its own logic as a justification for its own repetition. Capitalism reproduces volatility in the climate just as much as in markets.

Through 2016 and early 2017 the world was awash in oil. Production and consumption continued to plow along at spectacular levels, in part owing to OPEC's willingness to open the taps and let their members produce as much as possible, and with any luck push the extreme or unconventional producers—the shale, the tar sands, the frackers of the world—out of business. It was an old-school price war, and OPEC (led by Saudi Arabia) was hoping that by flooding the market with cheap oil, they would be able to capture enough market share to suppress competitors sufficiently to keep them under control. This strategy is so effective because OPEC, and particularly Saudi oil, can be produced so much more cheaply than unconventional sources.[31]

Eventually, prices have to head back up. At least, that's what we heard one night at the bar when a petroleum engineer convinced us that all would be well soon. We had been spending a lot of time at that bar in downtown Fort Mac and we got introduced to a youngish guy who worked for Suncor.

He was generous with his time, and we really appreciated his willingness to talk with us. Let's call him Brad. He looked the part: twenty-eight years old, but could have passed for forty-five. Pastel polo shirt. Stylish hair. Very happy to trade golf tips back and forth with Joe. Finished his engineering degree in 2010, looked around for a while in Ontario, couldn't find anything; so he made his way to Alberta and quickly found himself in the Mac. He intimated that he was making piles of cash, but never said how much, and we never asked. The man was thrilled, *ebullient* about how things had worked out for him (especially financially), and he was eager to share his investing strategy: "Invest everything, like all of it, like *every* last bit, in oil." He had paid off his house and was taking all the surplus capital he could find and was reinvesting it back in the industry. Prices were low, so all the better, he reasoned. "Q2 2016, it is going to be right back up again to $80. Just watch." We took some careful notes.

We probed him about global warming and the kaleidoscopic environmental and social reverberations of the tar sands. Brad is a smooth one. He said all the right things: "Sure it's an issue, but the Alberta tar sands are rigorously regulated by multiple layers of government. And we welcome that regulation because we want to be as conscious and environmentally sensitive as possible." His logic was straightforward: Foreign oil is dirty and unmonitored and supports authoritarian governments. Coal is worse for the environment. And really, if you look at it, the tar sands, even at their worst, are just a drop in the bucket. He easily answered all our questions, happily untroubled by much doubt.

Honestly, it was hard not to believe him. The three of us left that conversation thinking Brad had performed brilliantly in his able defense of his industry and adopted hometown. He had painted a picture of oil powering our world for generations, with a mostly benevolent, or at least willingly regulated, industry that would continuously improve safety and emission standards while Canadian liberal tolerance would lead the way. And every major political actor, provincially or nationally, across the ideological spectrum, agrees with Brad. As he said: the oil is there; it must be taken out for our collective economic well-being. Recently elected Canadian governments— Rachel Notley's NDP in the province of Alberta and Justin Trudeau's Liberal majority running Canada—are seemingly progressive and yet both leaders and parties are entirely behind the oil industry— lobbying hard for pipeline building and fossil fuel export expansionism (while at the same time ushering in tepid but well-marketed climate-change policies). The state is very firmly on Brad's side. The state sure isn't going to leave those barrels of oil in the ground.

The Canadian economy is so deeply wedded to the oil industry that the routes to disentanglement are bewildering: The energy sector makes up roughly 10 percent of Canadian gross domestic product.[32] Energy accounts for roughly one-quarter of Canada's exports.[33] It's a

PLATE 1

Highway 63 Bitumen Slick. Dënesųłiné translation: Tulu k'é 63 t'á tłes tué boret'į. Cree translation: 63 mēskanaw ēkwa askiy-pimiy ē-pimicowahk. A huge "sail" of residual bitumen seems to tower over a bus on Highway 63, carrying workers at the end of their work shift from Syncrude's Mildred Lake upgrading refinery. To support Fort McMurray as a community, Syncrude's policy is that all employees must live in Fort McMurray. Coordinates: +57° 1′ 9.82″, –111° 34′ 47.97″. Nearest geographical reference: Syncrude Mildred Lake, Alberta, Canada. Photo credit: Louis Helbig, beautifuldestruction.ca.

Slag Piles and Bulldozer. Dënesųłiné translation: K'aıgú chu tłes narı̨k'ą ts'ı̨ t'es. Cree translation: namōya ē-āpacihtāhk asiskiy ēkwa asiskiy-kāskahikēs. Slag piles—each a massive dump truck load—of various shades of coke ash, a by-product of the upgrading process that is used to generate some of the energy for converting bitumen into synthetic crude oil. The ash is being covered by light brown sand and gravel by a bulldozer. Coordinates: +57° 20′ 39.24″, –111° 30′ 34.17″. Nearest geographical reference: Syncrude Aurora North, Alberta, Canada. Photo credit: Louis Helbig, beautifuldestruction.ca.

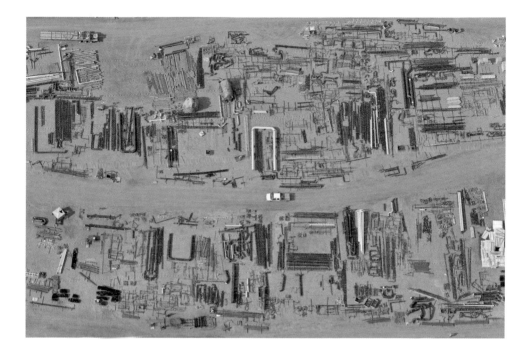

PLATE 3

Meccano Set. Dënesųłiné translation: Są ha ʔasí ʔ︁ëłk'elyé ha są yué. Cree translation: Meccano kā mãmawi ayāk. Reminiscent of a Meccano toy set, complex pipes, couplers, and other fittings for ConocoPhillips Surmont 2 SAGD expansion. Coordinates: +56° 10′ 53.99″, –110° 55′ 36.69″. Nearest geographical reference: Anzac, Alberta, Canada. Photo credit: Louis Helbig, beautifuldestruction.ca.

PLATE 4

Mildred Lake Extension. Dënesųłiné translation: Mıldred tué t'ok'é lak'e nunįdhér.
Cree translation: Mildred sākahikan kāyahkisihtahk. Forest-clearing, as part
of a process known as overburden removal, in preparation for the expansion

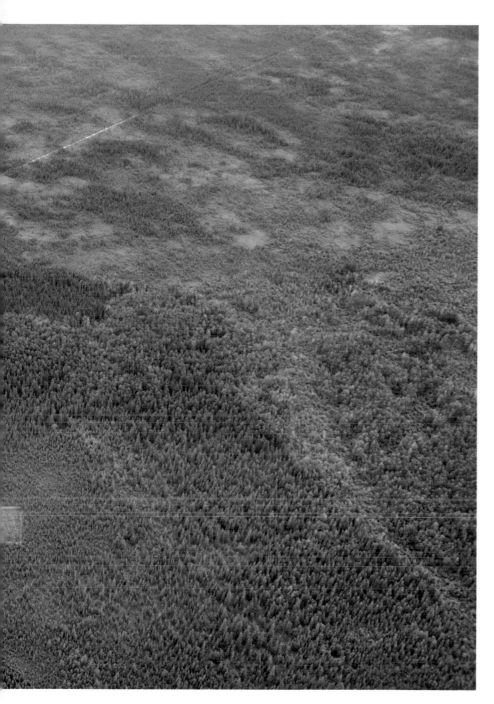

of Syncrude's North Mine. A further mine expansion is planned for 2018 and will include mining west of the Fort McKay River. Coordinates: +57° 8′ 0.83″, –111° 40′ 24.57″. Nearest geographical reference: Fort McKay, Alberta, Canada. Photo credit: Louis Helbig, beautifuldestruction.ca.

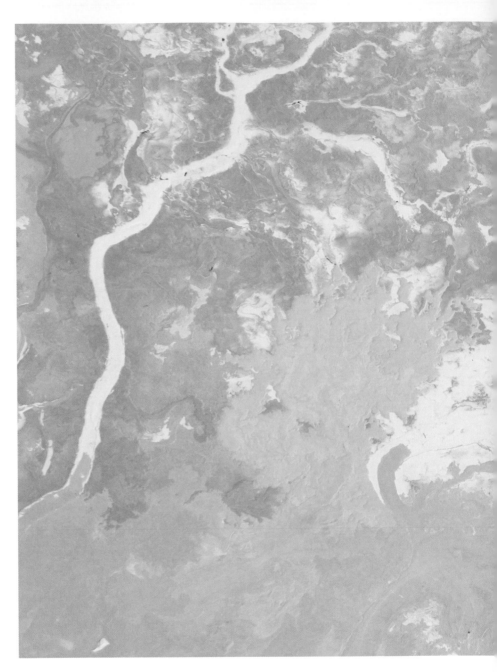

PLATE 5

Sulfur and Snow. Dënesųłiné translation: Dok'ą tthé chu yath. Cree translation: kā matspakwahk ekwa kona. Bitumen, a low-grade or heavy oil, contains about 5 percent sulfur, which is removed as part of the upgrading process to create synthetic crude oil. This image shows details of one of the massive sulfur piles on which sulfur, a by-product of the bitumen upgrading process, is dispersed in

liquid suspension. The liquid is contained by walls resembling concrete formers (commonly seen on construction sites), creating a clean division between fresh dispersal areas and those covered by drifting snow. Coordinates: +57° 2′ 32.78″, –111° 39′ 57.33″. Nearest geographical reference: Syncrude Mildred Lake, Alberta, Canada. Photo credit: Louis Helbig, beautifuldestruction.ca.

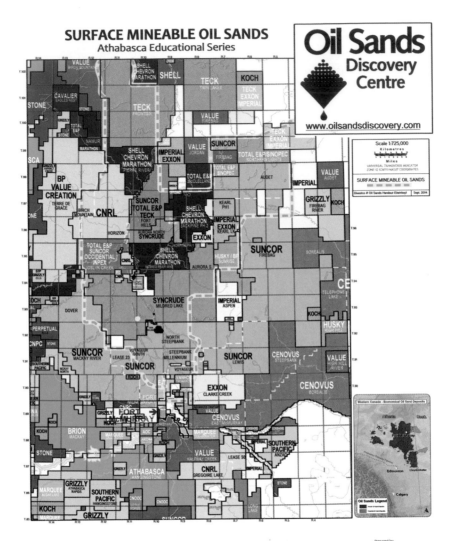

To learn more about Divestco's Oil Sands products and services, please visit www. Divestco.com or call (403) 537-9898

PLATE 6

Surface mineable oil sands: Athabasca Educational Series. The town of Fort Mac is visible in the middle of this map, about four-fifths of the way down. Map by Terry Steinkey, 2016. Courtesy of Divestco Geomatics.

lot more pronounced than that in Alberta, where "the energy sector makes up nearly 30 per cent of the Alberta economy. Direct revenues from energy royalties account for more than 20 per cent of the provincial government's revenue base—and that's before we even get started on the big slice of the corporate and personal income tax pie that the sector delivers."[34] Even those estimations don't reveal the full depth of the extractive sector's direct and indirect economic influences: "One-third of all Toronto Stock Exchange-listed companies are resource related, and another third are financial with heavy exposure to the resource sector."[35] Virtually *everything* is directly or indirectly (via transportation or plastics or whatever) bound up with extractive fuels, and this is true in every part of the globe, to greater or lesser extents.[36]

So is it true, as Brad says, that we have no choice? Is the only option just to double and triple down on oil and gas and hope for the best, because there really are no alternatives, or the alternatives are basically unthinkable? That's exactly the language politicians the world over use, because the (short-term) consequences of anything else are considered to be too brutal.

Maybe those choices are being made for us by the erratic economics of oil. The volatility of the Canadian dollar is largely attributed to the oil and gas sector. When oil prices are high, the dollar becomes artificially inflated and negatively impacts manufacturing and tourism. When oil prices are low, the dollar crashes. And when prices stay low, the oil and gas industry sheds workers across the world at a startling rate. Stories blanket the media landscape of layoffs from North Dakota to Alaska, Russia, Venezuela, Alberta, and everywhere in between. Economic projections in every jurisdiction are repeatedly battered by cheap oil. Industry is spinning hard, hoping that the new realities of extractive economics are somehow positive, giving us a chance to tighten belts, increase competitiveness, redouble R&D. Governments chirp about how economies now have an opportunity to rebalance and rebrand, to shift to more stable and dependable revenue sources, that global warming is really a great opportunity for capital.

This brings us back to the relationship between tradition and change, and the proposition that *this changes everything*. What has to change is the incipient, roiling, twitching anxiety that informs our colonial relationships with development and progress, locking us all into highly limited sets of possibilities. Affirmative routes forward cannot simply resist and ultimately mirror extractivist ideologies; they must articulate and construct something new, something else. Those visions have to be able to speak directly to the hundreds of thousands of employees

FIGURE 4.7
Illustration by Joe Sacco.

who are dislocated by oil sector shocks, and everyone who is thrown back and forth by the capriciousness of global capital: rolling in cash now, scrambling and buried in debt tomorrow. Alternatives to development cannot be nostalgic; they have to be able to overcome corporate promises of yet another F350 truck, one more casino-themed vacation, and a house that's just a little bit bigger.

Those affirmative visions have to surpass the dispiriting, constant hustle for more and *still more*, with compelling renditions of resurgent

social relations. An ecological future has to answer the seductive promises of capital, to imagine our lives and land beyond profit, beyond
domination. If we can find ways to relate with the other-than-human
world that are not saturated with exploitation, then new articulations
of sovereignty and alternatives to sovereignty start presenting themselves, and new forms of life become believable. That sounded right to
us, but we needed to see and smell and taste that more clearly. How
can that vision be forged into a believable argument, an argument that
a tar-sands worker with a shitty mortgage, a family, and no job back
home might take seriously? How can land rematriation be articulated
as a fulcrum for a better world for all of us? We needed to get out of the
Mac to clear our heads, to look for other ways of thinking about these
questions. So we clambered back into our dusty, mud-ravaged SUV and
headed west across the province, aiming for Lubicon Territory.

5
LITTLE BUFFALO

—

Lubicon Territory

The relief was palpable in the car that first time we left Fort Mac. But we felt a little disappointment, too. Or ennui. Or despondency. Or something. Maybe a combination of all those, plus some unmoored bundles of emotions we couldn't quite find the right words for. There is a heaviness to the tar sands that wears on you. Being there makes for a strange, unnerving experience, one we strangely enjoyed and reveled in, and more so on each subsequent trip back. We all developed a genuine and unapologetic fondness for the place. It feels so familiar and yet so astonishing. Its chain food aesthetics, rough industriality, and banal civic accoutrements were so predictable—and yet *that* bland little spot is the place that's tipping the whole globe into climate doom?

Hitting the road again after our first encounter with the tar sands felt like a long exhale. We were heading for Lubicon Territory, specifically the town of Little Buffalo, which is about 250 kilometers due west of the Mac, but to get there you have to head southwest about halfway back to Edmonton and then scoop up northwest again. It's about an eight-hour drive, and as we pulled farther and farther away from Fort Mac the intensity of industrial development gradually receded in our rearview mirror. Soon we were cruising along a standard-fare North American highway, and we all started relaxing, or unclenching, in an undefined but giddy way. As we turned back north we were singing, telling stories, and chirping each other as the latent tension drained away. We barreled along small provincial highways, through one indistinguishable town after the other, and what felt like mile after mile of unfettered forest. Northern Alberta is really not the loveliest part of the world at the best of times, but, all that scrubby, late-spring boreal muskegy forest felt fecund and teeming with life and color after the tar sands.

Our illusions were slightly deflated sometime after Slave Lake on Highway 88. Along the route we had come to notice a steady rhythm of unobtrusive driveways marked only with small white signs, each sporting a long series of numbers as identification. We were pretty far from any town by then, and traffic was minimal; we hadn't really paid those driveways much attention. Somewhere up near Loon Lake, still forty minutes from Little Buffalo, we pulled over and turned into one of these little dirt roads. As we all tumbled out of the car we noticed a gentle humming sound. A quick investigation revealed a pump jack about twenty yards down the trail, hidden behind a veil of trees, peacefully nodding away.

We were a bit chagrined that we hadn't guessed that each of these turn-offs was actually an oil and/or gas operation. We had seen scores of them all along the highway. We poked around this one for a few minutes, circumnavigating the pump which was maybe thirty or forty feet high with the footprint of maybe a mid-sized house, and then scrambled back to the car when a friendly looking black bear poked its nose out of the bush. There was no one around, and no evidence of any regular supervision, although it had a very solid fence topped with razor wire and several high-end surveillance cameras. For the next couple hours, we intermittently checked out a few more

FIGURE 5.1
Illustration by Joe Sacco.

of these turnoffs, and they were all the same: humming little jacks, nodding up and down smoothly, efficient little operations going about their business, sucking away. Pretty much the whole of the drive was punctuated by a metronomic cadence of these driveways, and that was just along the main highway.

The Lubicon's territory covers a significant piece of north-central Alberta, land they have never surrendered. Approximately five hundred Lubicon still live on their land, and they have proven a relentless, sophisticated, and determined opponent to both the petro-state and capital since oil was discovered on their territory in the early 1950s. The area was so isolated that it was essentially overlooked by the Indian Agents who came through in the late 1800s and early 1900s, and thus the Lubicon were never signatories to Treaty 8, which covers all the area surrounding their land. Since then, both federal and provincial governments have enacted a series of juridical, administrative, police, and economic maneuvers to dislodge them, without success: the Lubicon are still there, and still fiercely resistant.

That resistance is being sorely tested by aggressively expanding extractivism. In 1971, when the Lubicon were still mainly traveling by horse-drawn wagons and dog teams, the Alberta government started building an all-weather road through the area, and after various legal contortions to fend off Lubicon court challenges, they completed it in 1979. Oil and gas exploration and construction broke out almost immediately in every corner of the territory, and the Lubicon have been scrambling ever since. They continue to file grievances, complaints, legal motions, and appeals and have undertaken a raft of subsequent court actions, but at every step, the collusions of industrial interests, officially and unofficially sanctioned capital, and the Canadian and Albertan governments have manipulated processes, stymied action, and ignored repeated rulings.

The province of Alberta has now licensed more than 2,600 oil and gas wells on the Lubicon's traditional hunting, fishing, and trapping territory: more than five wells for every Lubicon person. As of 2015, more than 2,400 kilometers of oil and gas pipelines crisscross their land.[1] As Melina Laboucan-Massimo explains, "The traditional territory of my ancestors and my Nation of the Lubicon Cree covers approximately 10,000 square kilometres of low-lying trees, forests, rivers, plains, and wetlands—what we call muskeg—in northern Alberta. For three decades, our territory has undergone massive oil and gas development without the consent of the people and without recognition of our treaty & Indigenous rights, which are protected under Section 35 of the Canadian Constitution. ... Currently there are more than 2,600 oil and gas wells in our traditional territories. Over 1,400 square kilometres of leases have been granted for tar sands development in Lubicon territory, and almost 70 per cent of the remaining land has been leased for future development."[2]

The Canadian state's ongoing intransigence has meant that the Lubicon have consistently sought assistance wherever they can find it, and have often developed creative resistance strategies, including soliciting international solidarity. Canada has been repeatedly cited and disciplined by international bodies for ongoing human rights violations with regard to the Lubicon, to very little effect.

In 1983, the World Council of Churches visited and concluded that "government and multinational oil companies have taken actions that could have genocidal consequences."[3] In 1986, the Lubicon instigated an international boycott of the 1988 Calgary Winter Olympics, trying to draw attention to "that small group of wealthy and powerful interests in Alberta who are trying to wipe us out."[4] In 1987, after a three-year investigation following a formal complaint filed by the Lubicon, a UN Human Rights Committee came to the conclusion that "historical inequities ... and more recent developments threaten the way of life and culture of the Lubicon people and constitute a violation of Article 27 so long as they continue." The UNHRC agreed to hear the complaint and instructed the Canadian government to "take interim measures of protection to avoid irreparable damage"[5] pending a hearing of human rights violations. Canada ignored the instructions, doubled down on their legal strategies, and continued to grant oil and gas licenses in the territory.

In 1988, the Lubicon withdrew from the formal land negotiations that had been dragging on for fourteen years, declared sovereignty over their territory and blockaded the road, stalling all extractionist activity for six days. Alberta responded swiftly, bringing in overwhelming force and arresting twenty-seven Lubicon and four supporters; but the action prompted the premier of the province to meet with the Lubicon, which produced the Grimshaw Accord, a temporary agreement granting them a reserve of 79 square miles (204 square kilometers)—just a sliver of their territory, some of which the government would retain subsurface rights for. The understanding was that both parties would eventually return to land negotiations, but this sliver is the de facto reserve where the Lubicon still reside.

At the time, some believed that it might be the start of something new, that the accord might signal a commitment to resolution, but the charade has just kept dragging on. The subsequent decades have seen few substantive changes or ameliorations. In 1990, the United Nations charged Canada with human rights violations under the International Covenant on Civil and Political Rights, stating that "recent developments threaten the way of life and culture of the Lubicon Lake Cree" and called on Canada to take "immediate action,"[6] a call they repeated in 2003 and 2006, with no response. The land claim is still outstanding: it's hard to imagine what pressures might now force a just resolution.

Both sides continue to maneuver—the Lubicon staying with the land-claim process and deploying every possible legal tactic and strategic political maneuver, while the Canadian and Albertan governments continue to stall, obfuscate, deny, discipline, and control. Incensed observers have written books and articles; Amnesty International, the UN, Greenpeace, and many other large non-profits and NGOs continue to produce condemning reports. In 2007, UN Special Rapporteur on the Right to Adequate Housing Miloon Kothari visited and called for a moratorium on oil and gas development in Lubicon Territory. Investigative reporters continue to find the same appalling conditions on the reserve: most of the houses have no running water and no indoor plumbing, the levels of poverty and unemployment are alarming, and the social pathologies that arise in any isolated impoverished community are stark: "While over $14 billion in oil and gas revenues have been taken from our traditional territory, our community lives in extreme poverty and still lacks basic medical services and running water."[7] And seeping through everything is the incredible toxicity of the oil and gas industry, and pollution continues to be a major threat. In 1986, for example, there were twenty-one Lubicon pregnancies, nineteen of which resulted in stillbirths or miscarriages.[8] There have been repeated major spills and constant violations of basic environmental standards. Trap lines, fish lakes, and hunting grounds are disrupted, and the air and water quality are consistently compromised.

We've traced only a little of the history here; a thorough recounting involves one travesty after another, and so much of that recent history is a battle against unwanted and unasked-for development. The cold reality is that this story describes the ontology of capitalism and development perfectly. Lubicon Territory is riddled with tar sands: a significant and potentially monstrous amount of oil saturates their land, and only a small number of people live there. It is a simple calculus: a huge amount of money is just sitting there for the taking, with a trifling population in the way. And they are Indigenous people, whose very existence challenges not just the Canadian state but something far more essential than that: they will always be in the way of development.[9]

This story would be an isolated awful situation if the Lubicon were the only Indigenous nation under assault. The reality, though, is that Indigenous people across Alberta and Canada, throughout the Americas, anywhere and everywhere on the globe, are fighting tooth-and-nail for their land and existence. On every continent we hear distinct but similar stories: the Tuareg of Sahara and Sahel, Mapuche in Chile, Nivkh in Russia, Cham in Vietnam, Sami in Scandinavia, Maori in New Zealand—just to pick a few among scores of others—are battling for their land.

There are currently around 370 million Indigenous people in the world, something like 6 percent of the world's population, comprising at least 5,000 distinct groups, and so many are under consistent assault: their unique ways of life, cosmologies, and landed rationalities threatened by dams, mines, oil and gas, logging and industrial-scale extractivist development: "It is no coincidence that when the World Wildlife Fund listed the top 200 areas with the highest and most threatened biodiversity, they found that 95 percent are on Indigenous territories."[10]

The two dominant metanarratives of our time—capitalism and colonialism—each articulate themselves materially through the languages of development: progress and rationality, growth and acceleration. Development is so entwined with capitalism and colonialism as to be nearly indistinguishable from them. As the British Conservative Party's 2009 Policy Green Paper no. 11, *One World Conservatism: A Conservative Agenda for International Development*, puts it: "Capitalism and development was Britain's gift to the world." An ecological society requires a thorough renovation of our white-knuckled attachment to development. It's confounding, though: development rationalities are so deeply embedded that even post-development claims tend to run aground on similar ideological and discursive rocks.[11] What are the alternatives to development?

If development is commonly understood as "a process of incremental, managed change toward a final state," then more "developed" areas can be distinguished from the less so by the degree, speed, and extent of "their progress from traditional to the modern."[12] Thus development rationalities presume that all societies are converging on the same ultimate goals. This is not an observation, of course, but a disciplinary performance, a "way of organizing power in a society, and of simultaneously concealing this power arrangement—more accurately, of concealing that it *is* a power arrangement."[13] In response, Mario Blaser has suggested *life projects* as a descriptor of something beyond development narratives: "Life projects ... encompass visions of the world and the future that are distinct from those embedded in projects promoted by state and markets. Life projects diverge from development in their attention to the uniqueness of people's experiences of place and self and their rejections of visions that claim to be universal."[14]

Development is an extrapolated expression of exploitation, a gaze that sees everything as a natural resource: land, human bodies, animal bodies, plants, dirt, water. Once the whole of the natural world is cast as resource, all kinds of contortions can be undertaken to justify extraction. Even claiming that there might be something else, something beyond development, immediately becomes a treacherous and fraught exercise, one that has to be approached with considerable care. In a time so beset with such spectacular inequalities, critiques of development can immediately sound like bourgeois romanticizing for premodern times.

The question here, though, is whether the discourses of development contain within them possibilities for genuine, and genuinely distributed, wealth, and ultimately ecological societies. Given the demonstrable reduction in absolute poverty globally,[15] there are substantive reasons to argue for holding the current course, but lurking throughout any discussions of poverty are deep-rooted, compelling reasons to distrust any narrative that relies on *development* as a construct.

MOTHERLANDS TO MOTHERBOARDS*

The end of the Second World War launched the development era, the starter's pistol going off with Harry Truman's 1949 inaugural address. Emboldened by the reconstructive success of the Marshall Plan, Truman declared that no longer would international dealing between the Global North and South be articulated by crass colonialism and outright pillage, but would be characterized by "fair dealing"

*A blatant shout-out to the (great) Doomtree song "Final Boss." Thanks Mike! https://www.youtube.com/watch?v=xDx40dshmUQ.

with all "peace-loving nations." He noted that more than half the world's population was living in poverty: their "economic life is primitive and stagnant," and the solution was "reducing the barriers to world trade and increasing its volume [because] economic recovery and peace itself depend on increased world trade."[16]

Truman committed the United States and its allies to a program that would "provide military advice and equipment to free nations which will cooperate with us in the maintenance of peace and security ... [and] embark on a bold new program for making the benefits of our scientific advances and industrial progress available for the improvement and growth of underdeveloped areas." He was unequivocal that capitalist production was the only route forward, not just as an antidote to communist expansionism, but because "all countries, including our own, will greatly benefit from a constructive program for the better use of the world's human and natural resources. Experience shows that our commerce with other countries expands as they progress industrially and economically. Greater production is the key to prosperity and peace. And the key to greater production is a wider and more vigorous application of modern scientific and technical knowledge."[17]

Thus the development agenda set its resolve that primitive, backward areas of the world cannot simply be disciplined militarily; they have to be nurtured, brought into the flows of world commerce. Their perceived stagnancy is attributed to the insufficiency of their social and cultural pillars, and thus they have to be taught how to build an economy and all the institutional apparatuses that grease the wheels of international trade. The languages, institutions, cultural practices, worldviews, and ways of being that cannot support this project thus have to be displaced, disrupted, adapted, or at best, marginalized and constrained. Development starts with a presumption of backwardness; then all the solutions fall easily into place, rightfully delivered by legions of professionals, experts who are convinced that the restructuring they are prescribing is for these poor peoples' own good.

FIGURE 5.2
The kind of unobtrusive pipeline infrastructure that perforates
the landscape all over Lubicon Territory (and throughout Northern Alberta).
Photo by Am Johal.

Perhaps the single most pervasive and emblematic artifact of the development project is the gross domestic product (GDP), the one number to rule them all. The GDP has emerged in close relationship with development, mimicking its trajectory, and has become so deeply entwined that it is nearly impossible to disentangle. It was conceived in the United States during the Depression and was first presented in 1934 by economist Simon Kuznets under the title *National Income* as a methodological route to quantifying what was happening to the country. His was a comprehensive but straightforward formulation that was quickly used during World War II to provide a massively inclusive, quantitative, and documentable assessment of the country's productive capacity. For many observers, this ability was an unheralded key to the Allied/American victory, and after the war the GDP was eagerly deployed to take on other tasks, with the 1944 Bretton Woods system enthusiastically adopting it as the standardized tool for measuring national economies.

It is a deceptively simple formula: GDP = consumer spending (C) + government spending (G) + total investments (I) + net exports (NX). There are three (slightly contentious routes) for measuring each of these, but all three approaches technically should end up with roughly the same number, which defines a country's annual (or quarterly) productive capacity. Since 1944, this number has become fetishized to a spectacular degree, emerging as the single number with which economies can be assessed, monitored, and ranked against one another. It has become *the* hegemonic contemporary measure of collective wealth.

Its dominance is relentlessly enforced discursively (via global rankings, measures of poverty, tracking movement up or down) but also materially and institutionally via international loan agencies like the World Bank, the European Investment Bank, the Asian Development Bank, bond markets, and every global financial agency that assesses countries' loan capacities. Governments everywhere use it to budget, create monetary policy, and assess and guide social policy. A standardized measure, it can be applied anywhere and comparatively over time, making it extremely useful in tracking performance and gauging reactions to specific policies.

The GDP *is* a useful tool, but it is explicitly limited in that it measures only a small sliver of human life—monetized expenditures that flow through the market—and nothing else. In measuring that activity, it is highly successful, but it is a disaster when that measure becomes synonymous with wealth, well-being, flourishing, health, or success or failure. In a neoliberal era, the GDP has emerged as an extremely adept disciplinary tool for enforcing development while simultaneously defining the limits of what development might possibly mean.

The clear danger of fetishizing the GDP was recognized immediately by Kuznets himself, who warned that "economic welfare cannot be adequately measured unless the personal distribution of income is known. And no income measurement undertakes to estimate the reverse side of income, that is, the intensity and unpleasantness of effort going into the earning of income. The welfare of a nation can, therefore, scarcely be inferred from a measurement of national income as defined above."[18] He cautioned that if his simple measure was extrapolated further than intended, real damage would be done. His warning went unheeded, and since then the GDP has faced a steady drumbeat of opposition, critiques, and outright revolt, all of which has failed to dislodge it from its centrality to economic measurement.[19]

The GDP is an additive measure, so it notes expenditures and investments but fails to adequately incorporate ills or negative externalities such as, say, environmental damage. It cannot distinguish between harmful expenditures (e.g., car accidents, oil spills, or weapons) and valuable expenditures. More: it fails to recognize any non-market labor, says nothing about the distribution of wealth, ignores anything (e.g., food) that is grown and consumed by the same person or household, and cannot account for any household or nonmarket activities. It says nothing about health or education, levels of poverty, or well-being. In emerging as a proxy for the economy and more, for the success or failure of a nation, the GDP effectively collapses political and policy discourses into a zombie pursuit of a very specific, limited, and suspect rendition of "growth."

Amazingly, almost everyone agrees with this assessment. Start looking and you will soon be overwhelmed with critiques and condemnations of the GDP from all sides, many from economists but hardly exclusively. Herman Daly says it treats the Earth like "a business in liquidation";[20] Vandana Shiva says the GDP creates an "artificial and fictitious boundary, assuming that if you produce what you consume, you do not produce. In effect, 'growth' measures the conversion of nature into cash, and commons into commodities."[21] Marilyn Waring, detailing in *If Women Counted* how the GDP formalizes the banishment of so-called women's work from official records, writes, "Walk into a pool of clear water. Look *at* the water. It has value. Now look *into* the water. The woman we see there counts for something."[22]

And it's not just dissenting radicals who are critical of the GDP. For fifty-plus years, concerted and often extremely well-resourced attempts have come from multiple ideological directions to replace the GDP with a more effective and justifiable index. There are scores of contenders, generated by think-tanks, governments, and international organizations, many extremely comprehensive and piling up into a dismaying alphabet soup of acronyms. Herman Daly and John Cobb proposed ISEW (index of sustainable economic welfare) in 1989; the HDI (human development index) was created in 1990 at the UN's behest by Mahbub Al Haq and Amartya Sen (among others); in 1995, the Redefining Progress project launched the GPI (genuine progress indicator); in 2010, Bhutan launched its GNH (gross national happiness) index to quantify its long-standing national focus on happiness; in 2004, China attempted to replace the GDP with a "green GDP" that accounted for environmental damage, but the results were so startling that in 2007 they abandoned the effort; in 2008, Nicolas Sarkozy (of all people) commissioned a major report on replacing the GDP authored by Joseph Stiglitz, Amartya Sen, and Jean-Paul Fitoussi, published in 2008 and emerging in book form as *Mismeasuring Our Lives: Why GDP Doesn't Add Up.*

Running alongside attempts to create alternative indexes have been simultaneous efforts to nuance, ameliorate, and/or contextualize the GDP. Virtually every economic entity that measures and charts economic "progress," from national governments, to the OECD, to the UN, tries to blunt the GDP's force with additive+ measures like millennium development goals (MDGs), health and welfare statistics, initiatives like the UK happiness/wellbeing index, and insistences that the GDP is not all there is. Many of these attempts to either replace or cushion the GDP are laudable, but all fundamentally miss the point.

Despite remarkable unanimity about the failings and repercussions of the GDP's iron grip on economic rationalities, its gravitational pull is undiminished. In part, the reasons for this are obvious: adhering to this specific definition of economic growth substantiates the ideologies and practices of neoliberalism that are yielding unimaginable profits for a select few. Very significant and powerful interests rely on this rendition of growth. At another level, though, the logic of the GDP is intimately bound up with deeper allegiances to the development era. The two have emerged in close concert, each buttressing the other, and each relying on the same assumptions. And each fails in precisely the same way—by collapsing the full range of human endeavors, creativities, and subjectivities into one crass measure of success.

For generations now, good-hearted thinkers and activists have grappled with the blatant contradictions and pathologies inhered in development discourses. Just as there have been scores of attempts to replace the GDP, there have been equal numbers of thoughtful attempts to displace what is sometimes called "Big-D" Development (or the most crudely manipulative modernizing, industrializing versions of development) with less imperial, more sensitive versions: sustainable development, green, alternative, local, participatory, and so on.

Development discourses, like those of the GDP, collapse difference into universalizing narratives; trying to replace one with another fails to escape the logic's velocity and ultimately sets newer, maybe "nicer" disciplinary limits that are prescribed, contained, and policed. Development shuts down the infinite number of possible views of the future, closing off every imaginative alternative that is outside market logics. Lots of good people want to argue that *development* should not be abandoned—the word and idea just need to be reimagined, restructured, and recovered. We are sympathetic to these arguments, but we respectfully disagree and depart: the foundation of the ideology is too damaged and beyond renovation. The movement has to be in the opposite direction: toward modernities that are multiple, constantly driving toward differentiation and complexity. We need *alternatives to* development.

Poverty has to be front and center: any alternatives to development must have at their core the alleviation of material deprivation, but also must include multiple interpretations of poverty. The production of poverty requires us to think about it critically, to think about distribution, to think about reparations and rematriation, to think about every measure of wealth possible, and to acknowledge that these definitions will always be incommensurable. Alternatives to development, or routes to alternate modernities cannot be romantically local or parochial, nostalgic or antimodern or antiscience, or anything like that. Alternatives require sophisticated, technologically adept, and extrovertedly collaborative strategies. As Arturo Escobar writes in *Territories of Difference*, based on his work with Afro-Colombian activists of Colombia's Pacific rainforest region, the Proceso de Comunidades Negras (PCN):

> The meaning, for me, of alternatives to modernity or transmodernity is a discursive space in which the idea of a single modernity has been suspended at an ontological level; in which Europe has been provincialized, that is, displaced from the center of the historical and epistemic imagination; and in which the examination of concrete modernities, symmetrical projects, and decolonial processes can be started in earnest from a deessentialized perspective. This leaves one with a view of multiple modernities or multiple MCDs [modernities/colonialities/decolonialities] as coexisting theoretical possibilities to be maintained in tension.[23]

This gets us back to global warming. If ecology is defined both by and as constant differentiation and complexity, then it also has to think through and beyond the reductionist and essentializing discourses of development. Which is to say: ecology has to be, at heart, decolonizing.

Colonialism is not the only power relation in the world today; many other subalternizing, suppressive, violent, oppressive and marginalizing forces are at work. But colonialism articulates a fundamental set of relationships to land, territoriality, and sovereignty: a politics and ethics of domination. It is not by accident that 95 percent of the world's most threatened areas are Indigenous land.[24] If an ecological future requires mutualistic biological complexity, it also requires equally interdependent and differentiating subjectivities, languages, worldviews, and cosmologies.

So much of contemporary leftist thought turns away from that project. The left, especially in North America and Europe, consistently uses terms that mirror dominant capitalist and colonialist projects. The left is habitually on the run, responding to capital's depredations, trying to recover, always susceptible to sentimentality and calcification. In a Global North bathed in cynicism and neoliberalism, affirmatively energetic visions of a different world often seem just so chimeric. One antidote is to look to social, ecological, and Indigenous movements in Latin America, to look far beyond the *marea rosa* (pink tide) that has seen progressive and even radical—at least for a while—governments elected in Bolivia, Ecuador, Venezuela, Paraguay, Nicaragua, and other countries. Beyond the (often compelling) electoral politics are a number of movements—instigated primarily by ecological and Indigenous battles—that can be considered through the concepts of *buen vivir* and *sumak kawsay*.

The two names are not so much titles as designators of sets of ideas, worldviews, and philosophical orientations, but they are also more than that. Nor are they easily taxonomized or delineated, but are entangled and emergent concepts, bound up with a constellation of other ideas and orientations. Loosely speaking, both mean *the good life, good living, or right living*, but these are not nuanced translations, as they miss the collectivity, the responsibility, and the social embeddedness implied by both. As scholar and activist Eduardo Gudynas puts it, English translations tend to refer to individualist, Western notions of well-being or quality of life, but "these are not equivalents at all. With *Buen vivir*, the subject of wellbeing is not [about the] individual, but the individual in the social context of their community and in a unique environmental situation."[25] Sometimes the words *harmony*, *wholeness*, or *fullness* are used, and while pointing in the right direction, these don't quite capture the full force of the concepts.

We must understand both notions, as well as many similar ones, in the context of development and resistance to it. As Gudynas writes:

> In the early 2000s, it was clear that instrumental fixes or economic compensation to balance the negative effects of current development strategies, were inadequate, and the classical development idea had to be abandoned. ...
>
> Approaches to *Buen vivir* ... have emerged as expressions of decolonial efforts, attempts to strengthen cultural identities. Nevertheless, *Buen vivir* should not be understood as a return to a distant Andean past, pre-colonial times. It is not a static concept, but an idea that is continually being created. ...
>
> *Buen vivir* should not be conceived as a position limited to non-Western knowledge, but as a useful concept that can support and enhance critical traditions looking for alternatives to development.[26]

Buen vivir is a malleable umbrella term that is used to describe a number of plural worldviews and philosophies, throughout Latin America, in formal and informal, institutional and vernacular settings, and no single variant is the standard referent. *Sumak kawsay* is among the best-known and most widely discussed of these approaches. It is a Quechua/kichwa phrase that is a central and guiding feature of the 2008 Ecuadorian constitution, and unlike the Bolivian constitution of 2009 where *buen vivir* is an ethical principle, *sumak kawsay* in this context specifically enshrines a series of rights in the constitution, including rights to housing, food, and security, but also same-sex marriage, sexual orientation, gender identity, and most famously, the rights of nature.[27] These rights exist within an "economic,

worldview
cosmology

social and political system oriented towards the realization of good living. ... The Constitution is the result of long historical processes of indigenous mobilization to demand the recognition of their specific cosmovision and the inseparability of humans from nature."[28]

The wide assemblages of approaches that *buen vivir* refers to are often conflated—but are more often delineated, contested, and parsed over—and share a number of key elements. These include (but are far from limited to) an overtly decolonizing politics, a sensibility that actively departs from Euro-centrist modernities, a rejection of Cartesian dualisms between culture and nature, and sophisticated critiques of development. *Buen vivir* also articulates multiple interpretations of coexistence that are not multicultural but plural and intercultural. But it's also more than that, and more than the sum of those parts:

> In its most general sense, *Buen vivir* denotes, organizes, and constructs a system of knowledge and living based on the communion of humans and nature and on the spatial temporal harmonious totality of existence. That is, on the necessary interrelation of beings, knowledges, logics, and rationalities of thought, action, existence, and living. This notion is part and parcel of the cosmovision, cosmology, or philosophy of the indigenous peoples of Abya Yala but also, and in a somewhat different way, of the descendants of the African Diaspora.[29]

The past two decades have seen a tremendous flourishing across Latin America of broader political, activist, and intellectual interest in and around *buen vivir*. Some of it has been highly critical, from multiple directions. Proponents have been accused of venerating a premodern, antiscience, and conservatively romantic worldview. They have been derided for ostensibly propagating an austere vision that has no antipoverty program and no material basis. Others have tried to delineate certain articulations as regressive and others as more worthy. And that's from the Latin American progressive left. The pro-development, neoliberal critiques have been much less gentle.

All kinds of threads have been drawn into the churn, driven by Indigenous, ecological, and autonomous movements, but were propelled into international spotlights by the electoral victories of Rafael Correa in Ecuador and Evo Morales in Bolivia. Each arrived with spectacular promises of social transformation and with new constitutions that were established in 2008 and 2009 respectively and approved by popular referenda. Each of these constitutions reads almost unbelievably to North American eyes, rife with radical language and revolutionary promises. The cold reality of both regimes, however, has been decidedly more mixed. To various degrees, both Bolivian and Ecuadorean governments have backtracked on many of their most fundamental commitments, and both have embarked on aggressive extractivist development agendas, often in explicit contravention of their own promises. As *buen vivir* scholar Catherine Walsh has put it:

> The problem and concern emerges when *Buen vivir* begins to be signified and applied in government policy as "development." … *Buen vivir* and development are used as interchangeable terms which is problematic (particularly since the word "development" does not exist in Andean indigenous cosmologies or languages). But of even more concern is the association of both with the State; *Buen vivir* as development is the State, signified in technocratic, economistic, and humanistic terms.[30]

Both governments have come under considerable fire for their apparent eagerness to fund themselves via expansionist extractivism and particularly for their approval of several huge mining projects on Indigenous and/or ecologically sensitive land. The collapse of the vaunted Yasuni-ITT Initiative has been an especially bitter pill to swallow,[31] and "particularly since 2009, the relationship between the Correa government and the indigenous movement has been hostile."[32] In

Bolivia, Morales has come under equal fire for an apparent collapse of his incredibly eloquent evocations of *buen vivir* and is now eagerly pursuing several controversial pipeline and mining initiatives.[33]

It is not our goal (or place) here to wade into the incredible range of conversations careening around the philosophies and expressions of *buen vivir*, *sumak kawsay*, and multiple other renditions. But we do want to be alert to how any ideas are being invoked, by whom and on what grounds, and for what purposes.[34] Our point here is that *these conversations are happening*. It is popular, sophisticated, and legitimate at multiple levels in Latin America to speak nakedly and hopefully of alternatives to development in ways that are currently unimaginable in North America and Europe. Popular public discourse as well as academic and intellectual conversations are openly evoking visions of a radically different future, and while clearly the distance is significant between ideals and application, between realization and co-optation, notions of *buen vivir* fundamentally shift the grounds of the debate.

Or at least they do in contemporary Latin America. But can the specific situation of the Lubicon be extrapolated to larger Indigenous struggles, or the reverse? Do Indigenous battles around the globe reveal anything about the particularities of Indigenous decolonial efforts in northern Alberta? The same might be asked of Fort McMurray. Can we generalize from the particularities of that one boomtown to other resource communities across the planet? The answers are, of course, both yes and no. Little Buffalo, just as much as Fort Mac, contains multitudes, unique contours and histories and genealogies that defy easy generalizations. In the face of hegemonic development discourses, where the same universalized answers are presumed to be applicable everywhere, it is the very uniqueness of each place that is so welcome. *Buen vivir* has so much generalizable value *because* of its specificity.

It may be that so many powerful radical movements have emerged across modern Latin America in part because so many countries there were subject to the most vicious forms of neoliberal domination via the Washington Consensus policies.[35] Since the 1970s, countries across South and Central America have seen their economies pillaged by colonialism, then repressed by US-led military regimes, and then restructured by the IMF and Eurospheric lending organizations, all within a generation and often in combination and collusion. That experience has a way of sharpening analytical clarity, and it makes sense that countermovements would flourish. But *buen vivir* precedes neoliberal restructuring, and is not defined as its antipode.

Those same possibilities for resistance are available everywhere. Alternative worldviews are all around us, often articulated by Indigenous and ecological movements, but in perhaps more unexpected places as well. It is the incommensurableness of those forms of life that resist domination by their very existence.

DIRT ROADS, PUMP JACKS, AND SOLAR PANELS

We drove past one pump jack after another, a thousand perforations in the northern Alberta muskeg. So much of the official conversation now around global warming is about adaptation, about mitigation, about transition. Listening to the current climate consensus makes it evident that dominant interests are spinning a happy new narrative: a story of global convergence to collectively transition away from fossil fuels. Suncor and Syncrude are right in there, along with every other big player in the oil and gas industry. State and capital are trying to get out in front of it, to show some accountability to communities and reap the obvious downstream public relations benefits—but mainly to ensure their hegemony isn't threatened. Extractivist capital is happy to transition, and even willing to lead the change to other forms of energy, but it wants to manage the pace and form of change, so that in effect nothing really changes. This question of change is important: there is a distinction between true change and false change as it relates to energy transition. Solar power funded by industry is one transition with a certain set of purposes; it's a different thing altogether if transitions to solar power are owned and operated cooperatively by communities themselves.

It is not enough to constantly speak of the future—this papers over the reality that people are being severely affected across the globe right now. The languages that commandeer timelines and assemble strategies for decades down the road are the province of privilege, and no one knows this better than the Lubicon. Extractivism is not an abstract threat there; it is as here-and-now as it gets. We knew about the big spills. We knew that in 2006 the Rainbow Pipeline burst and spewed out a million liters of oil on Lubicon Territory. We read about the same pipeline rupturing in 2011 and spilling 4.5 million liters (one of the biggest spills in Alberta's history), soaking into the forest and muskeg. We knew that each of these spills correlated with a bevy of health problems on the reserve, especially among pregnant women and children. But we didn't know much about all the other spills, the mid-sized and smaller breaks, the mistakes, the human error, the seepage, the minimal reporting. It was only when we saw it, and smelled it, and tasted it up close that we actually got it.

Soon after we arrived in Little Buffalo, we visited with Lubicon writer and organizer Melina Laboucan-Massimo's Auntie Lillian, who told us about the long history of her community and family's struggle. She showed us around her new house which had running water, unlike so many others in town. She was optimistic about the Lubicon's future, but kept returning to all the damage done to the land: "How can we live on our land when the air and water are so polluted?" She sent us over to meet with Melina's cousin Veronica, who lived just down the road with her family. We sat and talked in her living room for a while, listening as her kids ran in and out of the small house, while she told us about the fear in the community about air quality, how people are afraid of the fumes, of whether the wild game is safe to eat.

Soon after we met with a paramedic friend who welcomed us into his office and patiently answered scores of our questions. As we sat there drinking coffee, he noted that most of the structures on reserve, including his office, do not have indoor plumbing. We used the wooden outhouse out back, wondering what it must feel like in the cold of the northern Alberta winter.

The longer we talked with people, the more the full scope of the conflict became clear. The Lubicon are under extreme pressure: the brutal poverty on reserve; the duplicity of the successive provincial and federal governments; the endlessly recursive and dispiriting legal battles. The Canadian and Albertan governments are relentless—they keep harassing the Lubicon from every conceivable angle, using every dirty trick and every Machiavellian strategy—and they hold all the cards. The situation feels unimaginable, and it's a struggle to name it anything but genocidal.

Perhaps most blatantly, though, it is the oil and gas industry that is exerting direct pressure on the Lubicon. Even to say *the industry* makes it more abstract than it feels. It's the actual, corporeal, right-there extraction that haunts the Lubicon. They face regular spills, the constant looming threat of pollution and poisoning, and drinking water that has to be purchased and trucked in. The relentless slow constriction of the industry is squeezing their lives, disrupting

FIGURE 5.3
Driving through Lubicon Territory. Photo by Am Johal.

and displacing the traditional hunting and trapping patterns so essential to their way of being. The industrial wealth is so close—an unasked-for, unwanted neighbor, right there across the road from everyday economic deprivation.

We spent a couple of days hanging out, talking with folks, driving around, looking at buffalo, drinking tea. Probably what surprised us most was just how close everything was. Northern Alberta is a vast area and the Lubicon's traditional territory is sizable, and we assumed that the oil and gas operations would be out in the field, somewhere away from the community. Instead, every direction we turned we saw evidence of industry, infiltrating everything. The pump jacks are sitting right there, all over the land. There are also these weird little configurations of pipes and gauges and valves scattered randomly, beside roads, in small clearings, sometimes encircled by fencing, sometimes not, looking unobtrusively malevolent, but each of them sucking up sour gas and feeding it into pipelines that paralleled the dirt roads we were driving along. We hadn't noticed any of this, of course, until our friend showed us the flagging tape and long, uniform strips welling up alongside the roads. Decommissioned pump jacks and sour gas units habitually leave small spills of oil and various chemicals that wildlife are drawn to and then get sick from licking. He pointed out all the evidence of various animals visiting the old spots we stopped to check out, drily noting the effects on different species.

It didn't take long to understand just how flagrantly hostile the extractivist presence is there. The industry is just so plainly, so swaggeringly disrespectful. The Lubicon have been violently contained in a reserve that is a tiny fraction of their lands, and yet the oil and gas infrastructure can't even respect *that*, edging right up against the houses and water and land, spewing contaminants, spilling toxicity everywhere. It was the sheer aggressiveness of it all that shook us, the starkness of the violence. When we got out of the truck to look at the gas-processing plant that was right up against the reserve line, our host pointedly slung his rifle off his shoulder and cradled it, indicating the surveillance cameras aimed our way, and noting wryly that they would be keeping a close eye on us.

As we wandered around town, we saw the damage everywhere. Much more than that, though, and as in so many Indigenous communities we've been in, the life and energy was impossible to miss. Kids were everywhere, teenagers ripping around on four-wheelers, scores of horses, a huge outdoor ball hockey tournament, people walking, smiling, and waving at every truck that rolled past. We saw herds of buffalo the Lubicon steward down by the lake, the huge animals resignedly turning away from us whenever we approached and ambling into the bush.

Listening to the Lubicon is critical, not to fetishize or romanticize their lives, but as possibly articulating routes to a better, more ecological world, in times that are desperate for a narrative other than inevitable environmental calamity. The Lubicon are just one example among thousands in a universe of worldviews and ways of being. That difference is not passive or constrained by tradition. Despite everything, the Lubicon are known for struggle and resistance, and also for new tools. In 2015, they had eighty solar panels installed in the community, generating 20.8 kilowatts of power, enough to run their health center while still adding power to the grid. More are planned. Melina Laboucan-Massimo, the driving force behind the initiative, sees a close connection between control of energy and control of the land:

> We have a false economy that's dependent on resource extraction, but that's not the only possible form of economic development. ... That's why we're putting up the Lubicon solar panels. These are actually creating jobs for people that currently work in the oil patch. Construction, engineering, electricians and trades. The skills of tar sands workers are transferable to renewable energy sources.
>
> I'm working on solar in part just to show people that it is possible. It's not a technology of the future—we can use it now.

FIGURE 5.4
Buffalo declining comment. Photo by Am Johal.

The price of solar panels have gone down by 99 percent. We can utilize this part of technology today.

Our community is still propane dependent. Energy dependency resulted from colonial policies—renewable sources show local communities that it is possible and is more in line with Indigenous values and worldviews. Since that time that we put up solar panels, we actually haven't gotten an electricity bill. These types of technologies can save communities.

My community's been living in energy poverty. Putting up solar panels helps them in a very tangible way. Our fight is ongoing and will continue to be ongoing. We need viable alternatives. This is part of the Lubicon Nation. This is the way to lead change in our communities. We need energy sovereignty, but our communities won't be sovereign unless we produce our own food and energy. We can transform ourselves.[36]

In a time so barren of prefigurative alternatives, of dual power, this has to be the right place to start. Leanne Simpson keeps insisting to us that the rematriation of Indigenous land is not just an ethical demand but an irreplaceable political life raft for non-Indigenous folks: a chance to see the world and particularly human/nonhuman intersections in a new light. It is a chance to see the world around us not as a resource, but as a vast constellation of relations. Melina echoed this idea to us:

> *Development* is a loaded term. What we are doing is *not* development in many ways. We have become dependent on external food and energy sources. We were zero-waste communities before there were zero-waste communities. That way of living is closer to Indigenous values. Ideas of development and progress are antithetical to what real life looks like for us. What would be great to see is an ushering in of Indigenous economies. For families destroyed by colonialism, what we'd like to see are renewable forms of energies and becoming food secure. There is a link between the future and the past and where it comes from.[37]

And this brings us back to the tar sands. Thinking through global warming has to be a lever for something far beyond just *transitions* or *renewables*. It has to be able to speak directly to the experiences of marginalized people from across the globe, including those who are drawn to the sweet-paying jobs in places like Fort Mac. Challenging development has to hate poverty. But it also has to hate those renditions of wealth that are chewing up the other-than-human world and are genocidal to every other divergent worldview.

The Lubicon's plight needs to be addressed sincerely, directly, and immediately. More than that: the Lubicon deserve an accounting for the circumstances and worldview that make their situation not only thinkable, but also so predictable. The exploitative relationships between the colonial state and Indigenous people, between development and the land, is replicated in every corner of the planet, and global warming is only one of the consequences.

6

FORT MCMURRAY
AND JANVIER

—

Dene, Woodland Cree, and Chipewyan Territories;
East Vancouver: səlil'wətaɬ (Tsleil-Waututh), Sḵwx̱wú7mesh (Squamish),
and xʷməθkʷəy̓əm (Musqueam) Territories

In the weeks and months after each visit to northern Alberta we kept chewing over the trip, trying to make sense of what we had seen: trying to think through global warming and the sweetness of life, not in the abstract, but with Fort Mac and Little Buffalo and Vancouver directly in our view. One of the central tropes we keep returning to repeatedly is the problem of scale and the relationship between change and the state. We keep yearning for a politics that is not just critical but constructive.

Just as Fordist modes of production gave birth to Fordist modes of centralized opposition and resistance, new shape-shifting forms of capital solicit new modes of organizing and opposition. The left has to articulate new visions that are not returns to stagnant or nostalgic ways of thinking. We love that prescription, but are highly skeptical that it means that a reconstituted left should be striving to control *the state* for progressive ends. That strikes us as unnecessarily unimaginative. We tend to diverge from people like Christian Parenti, who has considerable faith in the state as a site of critical possibility, especially for confronting ecological conundrums; but we're listening when he argues that "young activists should be approaching the climate crisis the way the left approached the economic crisis during the Great Depression. We need to drastically restructure the state. We need it mobilized and able to transform the economy."[1]

We believe that dominant political scholarship has made a critical error over the last several decades in describing neoliberal hegemony as only the withdrawal and constriction of the state in favor of market mechanisms. This description has become entirely taken for granted—neoliberalism is widely understood as an ideological package built on deregulation, lower taxes, privatization, and free trade. This is true in many ways, but there is a lot more to it. Neoliberalism uses particular trajectories of withdrawal to deepen disciplinary state commitments and investments that are masked and obscured by the rhetoric of small government. The mythology of neoliberal freedom is consistently propagated by the right, and the rest of us faithfully mimic it.

This conception of neoliberalism is also a beautifully designed discursive and political trap. Neoliberal regimes—which are essentially planetary and all-encompassing now—are not about, and have *never* been entirely about, the withdrawal or reduction of the state. Neoliberalism loves Reaganesque tropes of rugged individualism and "getting government off our backs" while playing to narratives of personal responsibility and liberty, but ever since its inception, neoliberalism has been equally about the *roll out* of policy, of the expansion and deepening of the state—just in different ways than the traditional left has hoped for. Instead of a comprehensive welfare state, neoliberalism calls for an aggressively pervasive militarism, a massive police and correctional state, a stringent monitoring and disciplining of bodies (especially Black, brown, and women's bodies) and regimes of governance that privilege corporatism and the accumulation of private wealth. All of these neoliberal strategies require heavy state interventionism and a constantly vigilant governmental apparatus.

Despite all evidence to the contrary, neoliberal ideologues are still permitted to masquerade as fiscally conservative and interested in transferring wealth to everyday individuals. This mischaracterization of neoliberalism has reduced the left to calls for more state power, for saving the remnants of social programs that have been gutted, for a return to the golden era of the New Deal. Thus, in the face of neoliberal planetary hegemony, the left's dominant political vision has been "recapturing the state," clinging to "the assumption that effective social change can only be achieved simultaneously and *en masse*, across an entire national or supranational space."[2]

We concur with Alain Badiou who claims that to be a political subject today, you have to be *outside* the state, outside the state's desire to place a movement or an organized opposition under its duress. That's not to say that any given movement doesn't interact with the state; his argument is that you have to be firmly planted on the outside to construct a new political possibility. He talks about the crisis of negativity of the left, and suggests that in some sense, emancipatory politics today is what comes *after* the exhaustion of the possibility of the political party. This is getting closer to where our analyses of land, power, and capital point us, echoing Mann and Wainwright's claim that for any responses to global warming to be just, "there can be nothing left of sovereignty."[3]

In the wake of the failures and atrocities of Leninist, Maoist, and other authoritarian state forms of socialism, Badiou theorizes that a politics without a party should be the new way to construct a communism in the present—communist in the sense of advocating equality for all as an emancipatory political project. We bring Badiou to ecological questions because his ideas about change are particularly relevant. For Badiou, ecology is a "rupture with the modern world and a rupture with the revolutionary tradition."[4] Capitalism's vision is one of destruction and change via accumulation—a vision of change that works against the collective organization of human life.

A revolutionary tradition is also an old idea of change—the idea that the old world must be destroyed. The Western Enlightenment presented history as a struggle against the other-than-human world, and by extension as a struggle that, in a colonial sense, destroys civilizations, languages, species, and geographies that are on the side of tradition. We propose that change has a necessary relationship to equality, not only for human life, but for the other-than-human world as well. We are interested in change that is moving toward ever-more differentiation and complexity—and this change, by definition, cannot be dominatory, but must be relational and durational. It also ought to be functioning on a temporal horizon at the scale of the problem. For Badiou, ecology is a movement not from the past to the present, but from the present to the future. It is "an attempt to create a future which is not the continuation of pure change, of destructive change."[5]

Badiou is not an environmental philosopher, but he is a major thinker on political change. On this basis, we feel his work needs to be brought more forcefully in to ecological questions because they are ultimately and increasingly about radical political change. Reinforcing the other-than-human world's repetition is a new form of a traditional idea of change.[*] Ecology is a human construction that attempts to think through the problem of the relationship between humanity and the other-than-human world, through a subject. This is precisely why the task of ecology must be "to organize inside the subject the struggle against false change or bad change."[6] This is not a passive or static operation, but an active one—the act of creating and maintaining some traditions as a form of ecological evolution. In this sense, an ecological vision of the world is simultaneously an attempt to preserve future traditions that are materially taking place in the present. This calls for a mutual entanglement between history and the other-than-human world: a modern tradition in ecology that

---

[*]Our use of the term *repetition* here is referencing the dialectical relationship between tradition and change. In the movement from the present to the future, tradition demands a certain type of repetition of the world as it is. Change attempts to organize a new type of repetition—to enforce different tempos of living—that overwrite the old.

creates "the possibility of a future which is not only composed of change but also of continuity and repetition."[7]

Global warming is often framed as a monstrously-scaled crisis, one which transcends all traditions, ruptures existing tensions between tradition and change and enforces new kinds of repetitions. One of the problems with calling something a crisis is that it tends to benefit those on the inside of power. A consistently confounding obstacle to change is the problem of determining what is inside and what is outside the repetition of power that keeps the capitalist world going on as it is. True change is always possible through political organization and mobilization, particularly if affirmative political power is located outside the state form. In Badiou's notion of affirmative dialectics, something of the future precedes the present, and an "emancipatory politics must at least be equal to the challenge of capital."[8]

When confronted with powerful progressive politics, the state tends to reveal its repressive tendencies, its excess of power.[9] The state has a desire for certain forms of repetition that work against the repetition of an ecological vision of the world. States want to keep doing what they are doing and manage *acceptable* change within this idea of state power. Acceptable change tends to change very little. For Badiou, true democracy only exists from time to time, outside of state democratic structures. Today, to be inside the state is also to be inside of capital. Nowhere is that clearer than in the tar sands, where state and capital walk hand in hand.

Leanne Simpson, in talking about restoring Indigenous nationhood, argues for building new sovereignties outside of the desire for recognition by the settler state or Western-based legal systems.[10] The state has to be engaged in a certain sense, but one's politics does not, cannot, should never *need* to be defined in its shadow. Politics must be defined by its own demands. It's a powerful idea that she articulates which echoes Malcolm X's notion that you should never negotiate by begging on your hands and knees. You ought to stand on your own two feet and push back on your own terms—it's the basis of an affirmative negotiation even if the state refuses to acknowledge you.

We want to stake out a nonstate position, but not dogmatically: what we are talking about is building social power. It often seems to us that questions of scale, especially confrontations between proponents of state versus nonstate, are more abstracted than they need be. A game that gets played out so often in leftist circles tends to adhere loosely to anarchist versus socialist dogmas: anarchist types rail against the state, while socialists argue for it. Mostly these ideological binaries serve only to manipulate us into believing that we have to choose a team and then defend its castle against attack.

In reality, questions of state versus nonstate organizing are always intensely complex and contingent. It always depends: what state are we talking about, where in the world do we mean, what are the alternatives, what nonstate actors are we lionizing? The binaries required to make this argument work (from either side) necessitate such contortions that they don't reflect or inform any of our lived experiences of the world. Clinging to the state/nonstate binary is useful only if our goal is to sabotage routes to lasting action. This is where thinkers like Simpson (and so many others), working in very distinct ways and operating from different worldviews, are able to articulate theoretical positions that are simultaneously strategic, tactical, and intensely hopeful.

We are constantly suspicious of, and typically overtly hostile to, the neoliberal state and all its apparatuses of colonial biopower and dominatory tendencies. But we're also antagonistic to populist anti-state positions that fall so easily into rationalities of individualism, parochialism, and bigotry. Dogmatism plays into the hands of existing power.

So, rather than spiraling down into abstracted questions of scale, we need emergent and adaptable commitments that are constantly flexing and reconfiguring. The drive to simplify political situations is a real barrier to navigating a constantly surprising and serendipitous world: change always shows up in spontaneous and unpredictable formations and arrangements, and our politics should be agile, flexible, and generous enough to be able to construct new dynamics of power. What should be defended and fought for, which coalitions should be hazarded, which projects should be built: such questions are always contingent and dependent, but they can be solid if they rest on political fidelities.

There is a dangerously flammable idea in broad circulation today that the only reasonable path to the future is a reconstituted capitalism. We've seen capital's unapologetic, triumphalist acceleration— it is swaggering around with an attitude that we've seen all too often, or worse, have never seen like this. What is different today from, say, the 1980s is that it's now a truly integrated global structure. It is a planetary-level hegemon that has few countervailing forces. State democracy is just one possible element of a capitalist structure, but it is neither a necessary nor contingent one. You can do pretty well in global capitalism without any real relationship to democracy.

FIGURE 6.1
Post-fire detritus, August 2017. Photo by Matt Hern.

Reengaging the state in some sort of ecologically animated New Deal-esque intervention is not the worst way of looking at things, but the social power has to live fundamentally *outside* the state. In this context, *the outside* has to be something far deeper than just a reactivated civic sphere or robust social movements; it has to be a trickle-up or bottom-up politics with an independent and polyphonic vitality and trajectory *beyond* the state. The state is not the right vehicle to organize our dreams around, but a reflexively dogmatic anti-statism is of little value.

Contemporary state and capital are united in a symbiotic front, functioning to enact closures by marginalizing any other responses as insignificant and naive. One of Giorgio Agamben's key concepts is the *apparatus*, which he defines as "anything that has in some way the capacity to capture, orient, determine, intercept, model, control, or secure the gestures, behaviors, opinions, or discourses of living beings."[11] For Agamben, a subject is that which results from the fight between living beings and these structures—"the everyday hand-to-hand combat with apparatuses."[12]

As with Badiou, we are interested in bringing Agamben's work to bear on ecological questions as a way to reestablish a political potency when the very idea of politics and change have become *captured*.[13] One of the dominant apparatuses of our time is the machine of capital, which captures resistance and results in what Agamben calls *the eclipse of politics*[14]—where the very stage of politics is overtaken by capital and turned in to a pantomime. Global warming is a new type of apparatus that disorients our relationships to time and existence in fundamentally new ways. The consequences of what happens today with greenhouse gas emissions last longer than a human lifetime, so the effects feel vague and distant rather than immediate. This dislocation tends to result in a collective failure to act.

This temporal and spatial distance and the distributed unfolding effects of global warming are thus presented by authorities and experts as such a densely complex political issue that most of us presume we cannot really understand the issues, that they are bigger than us and our actions. Timothy Morton calls these problems of vast spatial and temporal dimensions *hyperobjects*.[15] Global warming gets presented as a hyperobject so complex that everyday people are told that they cannot understand the way out of the impasse—only highly sophisticated scientific, bureaucratic, and political elites can solve it. But in a very basic way, global warming (at least in its rough outlines) is actually just not that complex. A broad and wide understanding of the issues is available, including the requisite ameliorations, the timelines, and the potential consequences. We know *exactly* how much global warming is tolerable and have very clear information about the egregious consequences that will ensue beyond 1.5 degrees of warming, but that information is constantly evolving because the planet is in such uncharted territory. New phenomena beget new scenarios immediately demanding new study.

One of the more alarming branches of global warming science, for example, is the status of glaciers. For hundreds of thousands of years, snow and precipitation has been accruing in glacial deposits, the most important of which are the polar icecaps and glaciers covering the Arctic, Greenland, and Antarctica. Currently, just under 70 percent of the world's freshwater is held in glaciers, but that number is rapidly diminishing as billions of tons of water annually flow out from glaciers and into the sea. Glaciers melt unpredictably, sometimes cleaving off huge chunks without much warning. While those thousands of miles of compact snow look impenetrable and indestructible, it may well be that they are in the midst of a catastrophic melt that is difficult to fathom.[16]

The problem is one of Bergsonian *duration*.[17] New techniques for measurement and prediction are emerging in situ: we are watching glaciers disappear around us while scrambling to count the losses. It's not just glaciers, obviously; it's whole watersheds, forests, species, languages disappearing while we scramble to document the disappearances. Brilliant minds devise ever more inventive ways to tabulate and catalog that which will never be again—at least in the span of imaginable human history.

This is part of how global warming confuses traditional political action and theory. The dislocation and distances, both spatial and temporal, are confounding. Actions of today and the recent past (primarily the burning of life forms who died millions of years ago) are having profound impacts far into the future. Those consequences are not necessarily felt directly here, or anywhere, but are diffuse and dispersed. Calling for urgent action on global warming tries to compel people to care about places far removed, to take immediate action for the distant future. This disorientation fuels a sense of impotence, both specifically and generally, and tends to make people feel politically useless.

Uselessness, however, can be tremendously powerful. Uselessness can become a politicized and active humility if it refuses to default to the state or capital or apathy. Agamben claims that humans are born useless and without work: the desire to work is a desire to fill that lack. For Agamben, merely existing outside of work becomes a form of justice and resistance. But today, even inoperativeness (not being productive) or withdrawal can be accommodated by power. Thus preserving the good life has to be considered an *act* of volition and material production, rather than a static or symbolic gesture in respect for tradition. Driving through the tar sands, we kept thinking about how to act, and we kept agreeing with Agamben when he echoes Foucault: "What is at stake today is life."[18]

One way to see the task today is as one of reclaiming the uselessness of the human. After all, we're the only species that doesn't have a biologically interlinked purpose on the planet—everything else has a reason to be. When Agamben claims that humans are animals that have no job, biological task, or even function, he means that humans can do almost anything but don't *have* to do anything, and thus we are forced to justify our existence.[19]

Uselessness becomes meaningful when it insists on ethical action rendered as a form of humility. Once humans' essential purposelessness is affirmed, it becomes liberating. We are not sovereigns of the Earth, we are not residing at the apex of evolution, we are not called upon to steward the planet. Humans are entangled with the rest of the world in every fiber, and an ecological future requires a commitment to an unfolding diversity, differentiation, and complexity, as much social as ecological. Human agency and action is required and demands responsibility—but difference demands humility. Uselessness is only useless if it retreats into passivity.

THE BEAST

We drove back into Fort Mac in August 2016, three and half months after the massive forest fire that came within a hair's breadth of destroying the entire town and devastated the region. We were a little on edge. The past two years had not been kind to the Mac. The city had been buffeted by extreme volatility in oil prices and by layoffs and downsizing across all layers of industry. The Beast had forced the entire population to evacuate as it torched whole neighborhoods. And then, at the end of July, just a couple of weeks before we arrived, heavy rains had caused severe flooding in several parts of town. We had seen very recent pictures of people canoeing and jet skiing down Gregoire Drive.[20] It all had a biblical tenor to it, like judgment had arrived.

Driving into town, we braced ourselves for the devastation. But the landscapes of destruction never really came. A couple of hundred kilometers out we noted how alive the scenery was, fecund and humming with greenery in the late summer heat. The slate-gray industrialized topography was muted. We kept up a countdown: 250 kilometers out, 200, 100, still no devastation. Only a few months earlier, the Beast had been the lead item on news sites and televisions across the world: the maelstrom of fire and its metaphorical implications ruthlessly documented. We had studied maps and watched hours of coverage, sketching out which neighborhoods had been hit hardest, which areas had escaped. But as we hammered down Highway 63 toward town, the scenery wasn't what we expected. We did come across some stretches of charred forest, but

FIGURE 6.2
The Gregoire Neighbourhood, Fort Mac, August 2017. Photo by Am Johal.

then the green would return, with little rhyme or reason, at least to our eyes.

The same anomalous destruction marked the city. This time we were staying in a tight little suburban pocket, hastily built within the past five years. It was a tidy cluster of short cul-de-sac spurs branching off a humble collector street, with perfectly organized, closely bunched, two-story townhouses lined up with F-150s, four-wheelers, and snowmobiles shining in the driveways. None of the houses were marked by fire; all the turf lawns were bright green, flower baskets hanging on porches, tasteful arrangements on every second door. And then boom! Two adjacent houses, right there in the row, burned to a crisp, looking like morning remnants of a campfire. Not just blackened or charred, but reduced to bright white rubble and exoskeleton. The houses on either side of these two were seemingly untouched, as if someone had cast a curse on just those two homes.

Looking out our bedroom window, just across a little creek, the forest behind the house was scorched and desiccated. And then, if we turned forty-five degrees to the right, the forest there was lush with life. We walked along the creek, following the back fences of the houses. The creek was happily burbling along, and on the far bank, maybe fifty feet away, the forest was thoroughly torched, the trees naked and blackened. The suburban-style privacy-fences on our side of the creek ran in one long, curving wall, unbroken and unmarked for hundreds of feet—except just one small section, marking off a backyard that had apparently caught a tinder. That chunk of wall had been kicked down from the inside and was left crumbling and charred on the path, but all the rest of the fences were left absolved, standing solidly on guard.

The same pattern held at the next scale up. As we explored town, most everything seemed unperturbed, perfectly in place. And then all of a sudden we'd run into a whole neighborhood that had burned to the ground, reduced to a series of ghostly white, eviscerated carcasses of rubble. Most of these areas were inaccessible, blocked off by battalions of police and security equipment, but the areas we could get up close to were genuinely shocking. We had not been around major fires before, forest or otherwise, and the devastation was stunning, quieting us into silence. We stared osteologically down streets with every house reduced to its bare bones: white foundations, the frameworks of white vehicles in every driveway, and little else aside from bleached tree trunks.

The whole town was like this at both micro- and macrolevels. It looked normal, nothing amiss, and then we'd run into ribbons, patches, small pools of devastation. Surely some logic had guided what got saved and what didn't, how the fire had moved and its patterns of destruction, but we couldn't discern it. The whole thing seemed incomprehensible and disorienting; it was unbelievable that so much of the town had been spared.[21]

Down south, people spoke of Fort Mac in the past tense, calling it a ghost town or a dying town. But after all it had been through—the layoffs, the fires, the evacuation, the floods—Fort Mac didn't seem to us like a traumatized place that summer. We wandered around visiting old friends, hitting old haunts, drinking beer. Everyone had stories of escape, often epically surreal stories of fire and smoke, but the dominant and recurring stories were of a shared suffering that had bonded people together.

As happens so often in the wake of disasters, the fire had a community-building effect, one that reinforced its collective outsider identity. Fort Mac is so used to being isolated, insulted, and impugned that people love mythologizing the place with us-against-the-world narratives. The last year had reinforced the town's sense of shared struggle, of defiance and resilience, but it seemed softer this time, more vulnerable. The downtown core was clearly trying hard. Civically deployed flower pots could be found on almost every lamppost and median, Mac Island was bursting with upcoming events, screens everywhere blared national pride from the Rio Olympics, bars were full of happy spending; we couldn't see any evidence that this was a town in its death throes. Billboards scattered around town warmly welcomed people home, and the *Ft. Mac Strong* affirmation was plastered on every available surface.

Beneath all the exhortations to normalcy, though, the rest of the story was never far from the surface. Oil economics remained volatile and projections grim. The panorama of environmental degradation was still extraordinary: that had also emerged from the fires wholly intact. We drove north of town in another failed attempt to commune with the Beaver Creek bison, and gaped once again the giant scale of everything: the supersized industry, the tailings ponds, the cannons, the machines—it's all astonishing. But when you're in town, it's easy to forget all that. It's easy to forget about global warming.

We hung out for a few hours with Reinalie Jorolan again. She had gone through a brutal evacuation, had lost all her possessions, and had been exiled to Calgary. She had been unsure if it would ever make sense to return, but now she was absolutely thrilled to be back in the Mac. The experience of fleeing and returning that she shared

FIGURE 6.3
Illustration by Joe Sacco.

with 90,000 other residents had left her feeling deeply grateful—she talked of people's amazing generosity, their politeness and caring, and the solidarity she'd felt in fleeing the Beast. The fire had burned through any feelings of alienation she'd had for Fort Mac and left her convinced that she was part of something bigger than herself. She and a collective of women artists had founded a brand new art space/ gallery/coworking facility hosting several small businesses, including Reinalie's art therapy and bodywork salon. She showed us around the current show in the gallery: it featured work by (almost all) women artists responding to their experience of catastrophe.

We kept hearing people talk about similar experiences of collective emergency: how disaster and solidarity had become entangled. Magnolia is another young woman who lived in Matt's house when she was a teenager and has remained part of his extended family. Tired from years of activist and herbalist work, she had been looking for properly paid labor and found a job restoring historical machinery at the heritage park in Fort Mac, showing up for work a week before the fire. One Friday night, sitting in a quiet little Somali restaurant on a back street in town, it took a full hour and a half for her to tell us her whole epic story of escaping with newly met colleagues, driving at a crawl for twenty-six hours straight through dense smoke and heavy traffic, with little clue where to go or what was happening.

Maggie spoke of her struggles post-fire—the trouble she had sleeping, seeing the fire every time she closed her eyes, her PTSD, the waiting to come back to work, the frustrating stasis, the unfocused anger. She kept emphasizing how badly she had wanted to return to town. Her work was repetitive and demanding, the money good but not spectacular. The job was a job like any other, but she was thrilled to return to it. That night, in a packed bar watching the unforgettable McGregor versus Diaz UFC card with her and her crew, the warmth and camaraderie in the bar was unmistakable.

The solidarity the fire forged is no marketing jingle: it has become essential to Ft. Mac's identity. Most of Maggie's colleagues were like her, people from down south who had made their way to Fort Mac only reluctantly. Almost to a person, their pre-fire prejudices against the town and residents had been eroded. In their escape from the fire, somewhere down Highway 63, battered and exhausted, their crew had encountered a family who had pulled over on the side of the road with a flatbed truck, handing out food and water to cars inching along in the smoke and shouting encouragement. As her buddy said, recounting that story, "I'll never talk shit on Albertans again."

UNDER PRESSURE*

The next day we met Melissa Herman. Melissa is a remarkable Dene organizer who seemingly holds thirty-five separate jobs in town, although it's probably only a half-dozen or so. She is constantly on the move, working at the homeless shelter, connecting people to the Salvation Army, feeding elders at the Friendship Centre, taking care of her daughter, and mediating a swarm of community issues, some minor, many not.

A lot of Melissa's time and energy is devoted to Janvier, the reserve about 120 kilometers southeast of town where much of her extended family lives. One Saturday we drove out with Melissa and her Auntie Diane. About halfway out we encountered two young moose right in the middle of the highway. We were moving at a good clip and Melissa had to jam on the brakes and fishtail onto the shoulder to avoid them. The two animals leapt in opposite directions, charging into the bush on either side of the road, all gangly legs, fat noses, and stomping hooves, disappearing in seconds. Melissa was jacked about it. She hadn't seen a moose that season, and her family had yet to shoot one, an absence they were starting to get anxious about. She leapt out of the car and got on her phone immediately, regretting she didn't have a gun with her, amazed at what had happened, laughing and hooting.

*Our regards to Queen and David Bowie, but not Vanilla Ice, at all.

We spent a full day in Janvier, and it was easily our favorite day of that trip. Melissa had really wanted us to meet her Uncle Dennis, but he was hardly the only one at home. We arrived to the warmest welcome possible, and settled in to smoking and drinking coffee in the kitchen, cracking jokes and telling stories. Kids and cousins, aunts and sisters kept rolling through the little house, happily greeting us and making us feel at home. Dennis talked about the season's hunting, showed us photos, and told us about their family.

Soon we were in his truck, bouncing through dirt bush roads, with Auntie Diane, Melissa, and the kids in lawn chairs in the back. Dennis drove, pointing out important spots on their land, showing us eagles, bear and wolf tracks, and taking us past camps and fishing spots, traplines and cabins. We stopped several times to pick buckets

FIGURE 6.4
Dennis Herman, Ja-Nene Janvier, Matt, Renee Herman,
Melissa Marie Herman, and Diane Herman on their front porch
in Janvier. Photo by Am Johal.

of wild blueberries. We'd be driving along and Dennis would pull up suddenly and point at the undergrowth. We didn't see much, but in minutes we were all fanned out, kneeling and squatting, clutching yoghurt containers and trying not to eat more than we collected. At three or four places we parked and gathered around for Dennis to show us pools of clear, fresh water, bubbling up in covert spots, filtered through the muskeg. We dipped cups into the little oases, feeling like we'd shared in a secret, and the water tasted earthily clean, like moss and bush.

After a long, slow, frequently pausing drive, we stopped beside a lake: perfect and peaceful, white pelicans floating offshore, fish jumping, and the fire pit already prepped. We cooked steaks and baked potatoes, and rolled on the grass after stuffing ourselves with

FIGURE 6.5
Dennis and his kids showing us how to find muskeg water.
Photo by Am Johal.

too much food. An uncle walked over from a cabin downshore and regaled us with expansive stories of his love life. All the while Dennis talked to us about the land. He kept repeating how lucky he was to live this life. He spends as much time on the land as possible, hunting and fishing, gathering blueberries and medicinal herbs, and it is all around him, right outside his door. He remarked to us several times how richly satisfied he felt.

It was impossible to listen to Dennis and not think about the other parts of our drive to the lake. Because it wasn't just berries and muskeg water we had stopped to look at—it was also pipelines, signs of pipelines to come, pipeline detritus, bush roughly cleared for pipelines, working and abandoned pipeline equipment, pipeline garbage—remnants and reminders everywhere of the oil and gas industry. The carelessness, the intrusiveness, the virulence was grossly redolent of Lubicon Territory. We saw so many pipelines around Janvier—running beside the road, one after another crossing our path, markers locating buried lines. Everywhere we drove—far off the reserve and deep into the bush—still the presence of industry was everywhere, it just never stopped. Oil dominates everything in northern Alberta and capital cannot, will not leave anywhere alone, especially when it is Indigenous land.

When Dennis and Melissa spoke about industry, they were by turns sanguine, infuriated, and resigned, and mostly all those things and a whole lot more. Dennis kept wondering, "When is enough enough?" Later in the afternoon, talking about a set of signs we had seen that promised more pipelines to come, he looked across the fire and said, "They're getting ready to make us nothing—why not just bomb us now and get it over with?"

We asked Melissa whether she thought much about development, and she replied: "That's not a word we use. When I see a word like *development* being used, it's exclusively talking about industry." Melissa, in so many ways, lives the tensions that lurk throughout this book. She told us that people don't like to hear her talk about global warming in Fort Mac; they immediately position her as biased against

FIGURE 6.6
Semidiscarded pipeline garbage near Janvier. Photo by Am Johal.

industry. They ask her: "Whose side are you on, anyway?" Melissa lives in town, but gets challenged when she tries to balance her life in Fort Mac with her life on the reserve; people mock her desires to share a traditional life with her family and daughter. For Melissa, carrying on traditions like picking berries and hunting moose is part of thinking long term. She says she can talk about sustainability with industry, but what difference will that make to her relatives in Janvier? Who in industry is willing to talk about decolonization? "When I go north of town, I find myself physically and emotionally drained when I see the effects of industry on the land ... I'm more interested in preserving a traditional way of living."

ANXIOUS DEBT

In the late summer of 2016, we met up with Vanessa again, this time back in Vancouver. She had been home for a while, getting out well before the fires. She was working two restaurant jobs, learning how to box, hanging out with her friends and sister, and generally seemed delighted to be back in the city. She had no regrets about her time in Fort Mac: "Yeah, the money *really was* that good." But it wasn't that good forever. By early 2016, collapsing oil prices had taken a toll on the town; fewer people were coming into her bar and the tips were meager. As always, calamity was felt hardest at the bottom layers of the socioeconomic scale, and as Vanessa watched friends get their shifts shortened, laid off, or leave town, she saw the writing on the wall.

We asked her about how she felt about her time there, given all that had happened. "It was an important time in my life. I really had a lot of fun, made a lot of money. I'm glad it's over, but I'd do it again." We talked about our writing project, and how she felt about ecological questions, about global warming. She wasn't shy or evasive, and wasn't wringing her hands: "I'm not ashamed of my time there. Not at all. I guess I drank the Kool-Aid a little bit—I believed what companies were saying, that they were taking all the right precautions, in part because I didn't want to hear anything else. But everyone there is so hyperaware of the environment and so hyperaware of being judged, you form a bubble around yourself. I feel fine about it. If I wasn't there, someone else would have taken that job."

Gita had another experience. After a few years she had stopped working and was taking care of the kids full time. The downturn started affecting her family and her partner was laid off, but he found more work right away. They had always talked about leaving town to be closer to family, but then the fires bumped that timeline up dramatically. Now she was back in Vancouver, training to be a carpenter and working at a restaurant, with no plans to go back to Fort Mac. But maybe. "Never say never. I really miss it there." We talked about ecology for a bit and she concluded, "Look, I know there's a problem, but the problem isn't the people working there."

In a lot of ways *debt* is a particularly useful analytical vehicle for thinking about the tar sands. Over and over again we met people in town who are doing a stint in the patch to pay off student or truck loans. Or are trying to cover mortgages. Or bemoan the credit card debt they couldn't think of any other way to get out from under. Or have declared bankruptcy. Or are just trying to keep afloat. Access to credit has been the primary driving force behind capitalist growth, but the logic of this is nearing exhaustion. The obligations of debt condemn the future to economic and ecological choices made today. Indentured relationships to both debt and creditors coerce us into an apparatus of control that sabotage our capacities to conceive of the good life at individual and social scales. Howard Caygill's book *On Resistance* spends a lot of time on the idea of the very *capacity to resist*. Debt, and the obligations surrounding it, undermine the democratic idea of this capacity to resist.

This gets us back to development, via anxiety and debt. We are intensely interested in a large constellation of ideas swirling around debt, not the least because we have been in debt for so long. Huge parts of our lives have been predicated on debt: we have gone to school, gone traveling, floated our lifestyles on the back of debt. Like so many others, we're middle-aged still dealing with student loans and credit card debt, and yet none of us owns very much of anything. Debt is a persistent narrative of our personal lives, and without a doubt it induces rather piercing forms of anxiety.

Essentially every country in the world is profoundly in debt,[22] and most of us in the Global North are deeply personally indebted as well.[23] Debt is implicated—in a very material way—in almost everything about the modern world. Debt is only partially about the present: it always has a far more sophisticated relationship with the future. Taking on a debt speaks to what you think the future will hold, but it also sutures dreams of the future to the present, and emerges as an articulated expression of anxiety. Debt creates collective and individual regulating narratives that reference obligation, shame, morality, power, and ordering. Environmental degradation is debt materialized, justified with a faith that the future will make up the balance.

Contemporary willingness to flaunt biocollapses creates governing relationships that capture and enforce certain regimes deep into the future. As the cliché goes, future generations will be cleaning up our messes for dozens, scores, hundreds of years. Present whims are being funded with resources from the future—resources that may or may not exist but that the future will have to provide. Debt-resistance projects like Rolling Jubilee, Strike Debt, and the Debtor's Union are doing brilliant work in the face of foreclosures, student debt, and credit card debt.[24] We like to think that the same organizing logic could be used to think about our ecological debts.

As Maurizio Lazzarato writes: "It is debt and the creditor-debtor relationship that make up the subjective paradigm of modern-day capitalism. ... [Today] 'production' is inseparable from 'destruction.'"[25] In Deleuzean terms, capitalist "growth" is antiproduction in that it is constantly creating debts that necessitate creditor-debtor relationships of repayment: policing, discipline, austerity, and privation.[26] Just as debtor nations are being made and remade via disciplinary capital, we are told we must accept disciplinary policing and restructuring in the face of our climate debts, while simultaneously doubling and tripling down on development. Global warming is just one debt coming due. As Lazzarato puts it: "The debt economy is an economy that requires a subject capable of accounting for himself as a future subject, a subject capable of promising and keeping a promise, a subject that works on the self."[27]

The calculus of neoliberalism demands immense and cascading debt-loads—financial, social, and ecological. Huge expenditures (personal and collective) are justified by the argument that future earnings will cover what cannot be afforded now. *Development* posits that immense damage to the world is justifiable today because the rewards accrued will be able to pay for the ameliorations. The huge investments in the tar sands propel development forward: capital is in too deep, and it has too many debts to stop now. This is exactly the language of global warming adaptation and resilience.

The question of *who owes what* is typically viewed through a legalist, rights-based lens, which immediately runs aground theoretically as much as practically. It strikes us that, rather than rights, a renovated definition of ecology offers far greater possibility for understanding debts and obligations. Rather than a disciplinary performance of maintaining and policing dominance, debt has to be understood within a relational fabric. Just as debt resisters, debtor's unions, and debt jubilees insist on foregrounding the social context of debt, we are seeking imaginative space to move forward, to think affirmatively, to believe in the future. Thinking through and past debts, and toward reparations and rematriation, is a move to freedom—not a simple freedom *from*, but a freedom *to*, an affirmative freedom.

Consider again the Yasuni-ITT initiative (see chapter 5). The 2007 offer to the international community was that if $3.6 billion could be raised (half of the estimated oil revenues then available from the region) Ecuador would suspend oil extraction in the Yasuni National Park, one of the most biologically diverse areas on earth. The money was to be put into job creation schemes in sustainable energy and the protection of Indigenous lands. The initiative failed after less than $200 million was raised, but the proposition was visionary. It was a generously creative proposal that both acknowledged responsibility for global warming and spoke to dislocated workers. Despite the initiative's collapse, we consider it a specific, tangible intervention that can be built on and adapted elsewhere. We remain intrigued by the initiative, so we called up Alberto Acosta to ask him about it, but also to speak with him about *buen vivir* as a larger political rationality.[28]

Alberto is an Ecuadorian economist who was the country's Minister of Energy and Mining in the first Rafael Correa government of 2007. He was the President of the Constituent Assembly from 2007 to 2008, which created the transformative Montecristi Constitution that enshrined the "rights of nature" among many other groundbreaking elements. He was also the driving force behind the Yasuni-ITT initiative, but has now split from the ruling party and is a vocal critic of the Correa administration while working as a researcher at FLASCO-Ecuador (the Latin America Social Sciences Institute). We had so much to talk with him about but constrained ourselves to asking about state versus nonstate change in the context of global warming. We were particularly interested in how *buen vivir* animates his political thinking.

—

MH & AJ   You were a very prominent member of the Correa government, but are now an equally prominent critic. In this book we are interested (in part) in the relationship between state and nonstate responses to global warming and ecological imperatives. Given your experience inside and outside government do you now have faith in the State to drive ecological change, or does that momentum have to be generated from outside?

AA   Ecuadorian experience in this area is very enlightening. Let's look at the case of the Yasuni ITT Initiative.

We must bear in mind that the Ecuadorian Amazon has been affected for decades by oil activity. As a result, Indigenous peoples have removed themselves from the areas of exploitation and currently find themselves in the last remaining forested areas. In an ever-shrinking area, which has lost its true wealth—biodiversity—at an alarming rate, there are now increasingly larger concentrations of Indigenous people who oppose oil activity. They are supported by groups and movements in Ecuador and the rest of the world.

Coming from this complex reality, the Yasuni ITT Initiative, born of civil society much earlier than the current Ecuadorian government of 2007, was based on four pillars: (1) protect the territory and with it the lives of Indigenous peoples in voluntary isolation; (2) conserve a biodiversity that is unequaled anywhere on the planet; (3) take care of the global climate by keeping a significant amount of oil underground, thus avoiding the emission of 410 million tons of CO_2;

and (4) take a first step in Ecuador toward a post-oil transition, which would have profound effects elsewhere.

But there's more. As a fifth pillar we could look at the possibility of collectively—as humanity—finding concrete answers to the serious world problems derived from climate change caused by human beings and exacerbated by this latest phase of the global expansion of capital.

As compensation, Ecuador was expecting a financial contribution from the international community, who should assume their shared responsibility, although distinguishing the many layers of environmental destruction provoked by diverse societies on this planet, particularly the most opulent ones. It wasn't about a vulgar compensation in order to keep pushing economic development policies, as was interpreted by the Ecuadorian government. Rather, the initiative was framed by *buen vivir* or *sumak kawsay* as an alternative to development in order to stop and reverse the serious imbalances provoked by extractionism and economic growth.

Currently, this initiative has failed, because the rich countries did not take on their responsibilities, and above all because the Ecuadorian government was not up to the revolutionary challenge proposed by civil society. But this is where the great lesson can be learned: it was not enough for civil society, from whom this proposal emerged, to leave it to the state to continue with the initiative. Civil society should have continued driving this revolutionary proposal directly and actively, both in and out of the country. This task was taken on by the YASunidos Collective in August 2013, when the Correa government recognized that this initiative had been too much for it to tackle.

In summary, the state is neither the only nor the main actor in making structural changes. Not only that, the state, the way it is currently conceived, reproduces and strengthens the structures of domination.

MH & AJ   With eight years' distance now, how do you feel about the 2008 Ecuadorian Constitution? It still reads as a revolutionary document, but in your opinion has it fundamentally changed Ecuadorean discourses?

AA The Montecristi Constitution is a potent document, despite being systemically violated by Correa's government and society not using it as a tool to democratically transform the structures of a colonial and oligarchical state. In it you will not only find advances in the areas of rights and guarantees for individuals and Ecuador's institutions, but also a series of ideas that open possibilities for a civilizing transformation.

Let's look at the Rights of Mother Nature. Its implementation would contribute to overcoming the current anthropocentric civilization in order to move toward a biocentric one. The Rights of Mother Nature would form one of the pillars for a "great transformation," as laid out by Karl Polanyi, a transition toward a civilization that presumes that all living beings in our environment hold their own value, independent of human interests and uses. And from there would come the need to demarketize nature, a point that is specifically made in the Montecristi Constitution, where it is stated that water is a fundamental human right that cannot be privatized. This mission has not been carried out by the Correa government.

Let's analyze what the Rights of Mother Nature represent in regard to citizenship. In the Ecuadorian Constitution, individual rights are stipulated and consolidated—they could be referred to as liberal rights—but collective rights are also consecrated and broadened, opening the door to the recovery and reinforcement of that which is community. The goal would be to take steps toward an ecological citizenship.

The Montecristi Constitution is a proposal that transcends Ecuadorian borders. And it is still a revolutionary document, despite the government (who stated that this constitution would last three hundred years and that it was a song to life) constantly disrespecting it.

MH & AJ Do you think *buen vivir* and/or *sumak kawsay* are the right narratives to think through ecology and social transformation, in Ecuador or elsewhere?

AA They are narratives that come out of determined contexts, in this case of Andean and Amazonian indigenous communities. They are not answers born out of academia or political parties. They represent narratives of existing lives. They encapsulate values, experiences, and a lot of practices. The important point here is that they do not represent a global mandate, like the idea of development does.

—

Our conversation with Alberto was tremendously heartening. Not because Ecuador is a paragon of ecological successes or transformative movement on global warming (it is not), but because so much of his work is so material and practical. The steps required to confront global warming are not magic, ephemeral, or beyond imagining.

Alberto's work speaks to shared obligation and confronting poverty without reverting to callow narratives of development. Responses to global warming that are focused on reducing poverty are just as available in the tar sands of Alberta as anywhere else. We can talk about keeping Fort Mac's oil in the ground just as readily as Amazonian oil. We are obviously intrigued by the parallels between Alberta and Ecuador. Why can't a similarly structured proposal buy out the tar sands, return land to the Lubicon and other Indigenous nations, and build sustainable energy jobs? What would happen if the millions and millions of dollars of oil corporation subsidies were redirected to build energy sovereignty in communities across Alberta?[29] That's why the Ecuadorean experience seems so critical to learn from and why Alberto is such an indispensable thinker as we struggle with ecology.

If land is at the center of any new definitions of ecology, then the impasses surrounding global warming begin to dissolve. Good relations with humans and the other-than-human world cannot be exploitive; they have to be built on other rationalities. If we redefine ecology this way, routes to real action, like the Yasuni-ITT Initiative, emerge easily. Instead of wringing our hands and imagining that global warming is a monstrous threat that surpasses our reaches, we can see the possibility and promise of everyday actions materialize.

A sweetness of life has to stare down capital and be able to articulate real alternatives. The energy to confront global warming has to come from outside the state, from everyday people everywhere, from popular and grassroots movements, and our contention is that they will be most successful when land politics are always front and center. These arguments have to be able to speak directly to workers in Fort Mac. Ecology cannot rest on shame and discipline; it has to offer an affirmative vision of change and a future that is material. A sweetness of life has to present itself as a living alternative to those who are being buffeted by incredible anxiety, volatility, and debt. Supporting Indigenous land struggles and land justice movements is not just a question of justice; it opens up space for all of us to imagine a different way of being in the world. All of us, maybe even especially resource workers, need a revived ecological politics. Capital views labor in exactly the same way it views the other-than-human world: as one more extractive resource. New possibilities for life emerge only when the cloud of originary land-thefts lifts, and we can conceive of how to live an affirmatively ecological future beyond exploitation. Better relationships with land and with each other become available to all of us only when we renounce colonial domination.

CERAMIC SUNSET*

Ecology, not just the present articulations of global warming, requires thinking through and beyond development, through and beyond antiproduction in a way that, as Deleuze says, can create "new possibilities of life."[30] Capitalism requires a nihilistic antiproduction, a desultory and endlessly predictable growth that articulates itself in constant destruction. By contrast, searching for the sweetness of life rests on a faith in both the present and the future, and in fact, requires a new *form of life*. If exploitation and domination, are the antipode of good relations—a desubjectification that precedes and

---

*Another shoutout to Doomtree, this time to their song "Heavy Rescue." See https://www.youtube.com/watch?v=DC3LH-mkM-4.

frames all others as potential resources—then ecology demands we remake all our relationships.

Leanne speaks of respectful relations between humans and "animal and plant nations," a phrasing that sounds unfamiliar to us but reveals a comportment toward other-than-human entities that refuses to be reduced to exploitation. Relational politics defies the supposition that land and other-than-humans are valuable only within the context of human purposes.

This has to be where a sweetness of life can be found: where relationships are predicated on fidelity, not domination; on generosity, not exploitation. That strikes us as the foundation for an ecological future. Glen Coulthard has a clear argument for thinking about relationships with other-than-humans that surpasses extractivist and capitalist logics:

> The concept of development comes with a host of baggage, at least from the Enlightenment onward. Most development ideologies, I think, are incredibly problematic and I try not to use *development* or *rights* in the normative sense.
>
> There are stories from before the Dene were the people. We were relatives of and related to animal life—we were the caribou, they were our kin. We were like a steward, in a trust-like relationship. These stories really break down the developmentalist historical teleology because we have responsibilities both to others who have yet to be born, and ancestors that have come before. When you take a life like a caribou, these are the things you're considering with a long-term, nonlinear understanding of what you have obligations to. They have to be stripped of their normative meaning, reading it through a *more than human* register.[31]

Ideologies of development, capitalist and otherwise, are predicated on scarcity. Extractivism cannot stop because it has no other mode to default to. It has no other frames with which to view other humans or other-than-humans, beyond raw material, and thus we are faced with massive levels of surplus overproduction: humans keep producing material that is of no use or allocative value.

But scarcity is no fiction for huge numbers of people across the globe. Poverty and deprivation are everyday evils that exist in the shadow of profligate overproduction and overconsumption. Anxiety is not an unwarranted psychological condition—people everywhere are anxious because they face pernicious bodily threats every day, and their future, both immediate and longer-term, is in danger. That's why a *sweetness of life* cannot be reduced to an individual endeavor: it has to be understood as the social freedom of time and space. Good relationships are predicated on a resistance to domination.

Ultimately, we want to speak frankly of *love*: loving the land, not just the spectacular, but the humble spaces we spend our days on. Love is not a word that enters easily into most politics, but it is the right one here. We're not talking about a sentimental love, but one expressed by actionable, everyday fidelities. Love is not love without a willingness to defend it, and a resistance to those who do it violence. As Coulthard says:

> Land is where anticapitalism comes from. As Indigenous people, we don't just love this place: it's an affirmation of who we are. It is part of a love for self. But love can be used in a lot of ways. Love requires a critical affirmation of hatred, anger, resentment because anything that violates love is going to provoke a response: "I fucking hate the people who are destroying my family, this place, this neighborhood." Certain forms of activism that are animated by hate or anger are often discredited, but we have to understand them as part and parcel of love. Anger and love are part of the same response to violation or exploitation or being subjected to unjust and arbitrary action.[32]

The constant anxiety and fearfulness infused in capitalist markets forces us to constantly reorder all our lives. Sometimes the response is stressing constantly, hustling every angle, working multiple jobs, and cutting every corner just to make exorbitant rent. Sometimes it means taking jobs you loathe, or are ashamed of. Sometimes it means taking on tremendous indebtedness in an attempt to ward off insecurity, suturing yourself to creditor–debtor relations that smother imaginative possibilities, including resistance. But that is far from all of it.

Every rendition of the sweetness of life is predicated on having both the time and place to articulate it. The sweetness of life invokes a particular tempo of living: an adaptability, a flexibility, and a generosity with time. The sweet life has to be unbound from the restless, anxious dissatisfaction that drives capitalism. As Leanne says: "My ancestors didn't bank capital as a way of maintaining security, as a way of mitigating fear and anxiety—they banked relationships."

Global warming demands that we cultivate new relationships, including a fidelity to the land we live on. It is impossible to love the land while dominating and exploiting it, just as it is impossible to treat others with respect while dominating and exploiting them. Loving the land is predicated on both anticapitalism and decolonization. Ecology cannot speak of humans, other-than-humans, or land as a resource rich with materials to be extracted; instead, it must articulate an ongoing set of relations where we can find what the sweetness of life might mean. This project cannot be seen as work—by necessity, it must be a love affair.

NOTES

—

CHAPTER 1

1. Michi Saagiig Nishnaabeg (sometimes written as Mississauga-Anishnaabe) territory is in present-day Ontario, Canada.

2. This is the officially reported number, but former Vancouver City Manager Penny Ballem disagreed, and in her presentation to Vancouver City Council after the spill, she quoted officials saying that figure was incorrect and the real volume was likely in the range of 3,000–5,000 liters spilled. The confusion remained and was never cleared up (as it were). See Lisa Johnson, "Vancouver Oil Spill Was Small but 'Nasty' and Spread Quickly," CBC News, April 14, 2015, http://www.cbc.ca/news/canada/british-columbia/vancouver-oil-spill-was-small-but-nasty-and-spread-quickly-1.3032385.

The Canadian Coast Guard Independent Review implies that more than 2,800 liters were spilled, since approximately 2,800 liters *remained* during this observation: "Several aerial overflights were conducted throughout the day on April 9, including a National Aerial Surveillance Program (NASP) flight at 12:20h that estimated that there remained approximately 2800L of intermediate fuel oil on the water; however, this estimate did not include any recovered fuel oil from the previous night" (Canadian Coast Guard, "Independent Review of the *M/V Marathassa* Fuel Oil Spill Environmental Response Operation," *Canadian Coast Guard*, July 19, 2015, http://www.ccg-gcc.gc.ca/independent-review-Marathassa-oil-spill-ER-operation).

3. The City of Vancouver tweeted: "Please don't touch oil or try to clean it up yourself. It's toxic w/ health risks! Just report oil on shore to 604-873-7000. #VanFuelSpill." City of Vancouver Twitter post, April 10, 2015, 3:37 p.m., https://twitter.com/CityofVancouver/status/586659324115742720.

4. As of the 2016 Canadian Census, 989,540 immigrants lived in Metro Vancouver, accounting for 40.8 percent of the total population. This is up only very slightly from 2011 (40.0%) and 2006 (39.6%). ("Focus on Geography Series, 2016 Census," Statistics Canada 2016, http://www12.statcan.gc.ca/census-recensement/2016/as-sa/fogs-spg/desc/Facts-desc-imm-eto.cfm?LANG=Eng&GK=CMA&GC=933&TOPIC=7&#fd1_2).

5. KPMG, *Competitive Alternatives: KPMG's guide to international business location costs, 2016 Edition* (Toronto: KPMG, 2016), 3. See: https://www.competitive alternatives.com/reports/compalt2016_report_vol1_en.pdf.

6. Vancouver Fraser Port Authority, *Financial Report 2015* (Vancouver, 2015), http://www.portvancouver.com/wp-content/uploads/2015/11/2015-Financial -Report-final-WEB.pdf. According to the most recent data released, the port handles 19 percent of Canada's total trade in goods (by value): a total of 138 million metric tons of cargo in 2015 valued at $200 billion, including 3.1 million TEU (20-foot equivalent unit) of container volume. Then there's the cruise ship industry. Vancouver is a hub here too, primarily for the West Coast–Alaska runs, at last count serving 805, 400 passengers via 228 sailings per year.

7. Port Metro Vancouver, "Frequently Asked Questions: Tanker Safety," http://www.portvancouver.com/wp-content/uploads/2015/03/tanker-safety-and -navigation-faq.pdf.

8. *State of the Climate in 2016*, American Meteorological Society, Special supplement to the *Bulletin of the AMS* 98, no. 8 (August 2017), http://www .ametsoc.net/sotc2016/StateoftheClimate2016_lowres.pdf.

9. Ibid.

10. We are hardly alone in our preference for the term *global warming* over *climate change*. This is how Timothy Morton describes his rationale for using the term:

> Whatever the scientific and social reasons for the predominance of "climate change" over "global warming" for naming this particular hyperobject, the effect in social and political discourse is plain enough. There has been a decrease in appropriate levels of concern. Indeed, denialism is able to claim that "climate change" is merely the rebranding of a fabrication, nay evidence of this fabrication in flagrante delicto. ... "Climate change" as substitute enables cynical reason (both right wing and left) to say that "climate has always been changing," which to my ears sounds like "people have always been killing one another" as a fatuous reason not to control the sale of machine guns. (Timothy Morton, "Why I Don't Call It Climate Change and Never Shall," *Ecology without Nature*, Jan. 20,

2013, http://ecologywithoutnature.blogspot.ca/2013/01/why-i-dont-call -it-climate-change-and.html)

11. Tzeporah Berman, "The Oil Sands Are Now the Single Largest and Most Destructive Industrial Project on Earth," *Now Magazine*, April 10, 2014, https:// nowtoronto.com/news/the-oil-sands-are-now-the-single-largest-and-most -destructive-industrial-project-on-earth/.

12. Alberta Energy: Facts and Statistics, http://www.energy.alberta.ca/oilsands /791.asp.

13. Alberta Energy Regulator, "Pipelines," https://www.aer.ca/rules-and -regulations/by-topic/pipelines (numbers updated via phone Jan. 3, 2017).

14. "Prime Minister Justin Trudeau's Pipeline Announcement," http://pm .gc.ca/eng/news/2016/11/30/prime-minister-justin-trudeaus-pipeline -announcement.

15. CBC News, "Port Metro Vancouver Fire Was Accidental Investigation Finds: Four-Alarm Chemical Fire on March 4 Triggered Partial Evacuation in Vancouver," April 23, 2015, http://www.cbc.ca/news/canada/british-columbia /port-metro-vancouver-fire-was-accidental-investigation-finds-1.3045165.

16. As per Vancouver's now-omnipresent Greenest City Action Plan: "The Greenest City Action Plan is a strategy for staying on the leading edge of urban sustainability. ... Through a set of measurable and attainable targets, we are putting Vancouver on the path to becoming the greenest city in the world" (http://vancouver.ca/green-vancouver/greenest-city-action-plan.aspx).

17. CBC News, "Port Metro Vancouver Chemical Fire Tested City's Emergency Response," March 5, 2015, http://www.cbc.ca/news/canada/british-columbia /port-metro-vancouver-chemical-fire-tested-city-s-emergency-reponse -1.2983308.

18. Oxford Dictionaries, https://en.oxforddictionaries.com/definition/ecology.

19. Paolo Palladin, "Defining Ecology: Ecological Theories, Mathematical Models, and Applied Biology in the 1960s and 1970's," *Journal of the History of Biology* 24, no. 2 (summer 1991): 223–243. See also Joel Hagen, "Research Perspectives and the Anomalous Status of Modern Ecology," *Biology and Philosophy* 4 (1989): 433–455.

20. Michel Serres, *The Natural Contract* (Ann Arbor: University of Michigan Press, 1995), 86.

21. Ibid., 4.

22. Richard Gove, *Ecology, Climate and Empire: Colonialism and Global Environmental History, 1400–1900* (Cambridge: White Horse Press, 1997).

23. Personal interview with Leanne Simpson, April 9, 2015.

24. She's written stories and academic essays, poems and spoken word pieces, and edited and authored books, all of which keep coming back to the idea of land, to the centrality of land, to relationships with land. Our favorite pieces by Leanne include the book of short stories called *Islands of Decolonial Love*, a collection of essays titled *Dancing on Our Turtle's Back*, and the edited collections *This Is an Honor Song* (with Kiera Ladner) and *The Winter We Danced: Voices from the Past, the Future and the Idle No More Movement* (edited by the Kino-nda-niimi Collective).

25. Leanne Simpson, "Land as Pedagogy: Nishnaabeg Intelligence and Rebellious Transformation," *Decolonization: Indigeneity, Education & Society* 3, no. 3 (2014): 1–25.

26. Leanne Simpson, *Dancing on Our Turtles Back* (Winnipeg: ARP Books, 2011), 17.

27. Audra Simpson, *Mohawk Interruptus: Political Life across the Borders of Settler States* (Durham: Duke University Press, 2014), 33.

28. Glen Coulthard, *Red Skin, White Masks: Rejecting the Colonial Politics of Recognition* (Minneapolis: University of Minnesota Press, 2014).

29. American Studies Association, General Meeting, Oct. 8, 2015, "The Misery of Settler Colonialism: Roundtable on Glen Coulthard's Red Skin, White Masks and Audra Simpson's Mohawk Interruptus," https://www.leannesimpson.ca /writings/the-misery-of-settler-colonialism-roundtable-on-glen-coulthards -red-skin-white-masks-and-audra-simpsons-mohawk-interruptus.

30. There are currently two First Nations who have signed contemporary treaties in British Columbia: the Nisga'a (whose land now covers 800 square miles, signed in 1998) and the Tsawwassen (whose treaty covers 1.1 square miles, signed in 2007). Several other nations are deep in the treaty process and are close to ratifying treaties as of 2017. As well, there are also the Douglas Treaties, a series of agreements signed from 1850 to 1854 covering 3 percent of Southern Vancouver Island, and Treaty 8 (signed in 1899) which was signed in Alberta but covers a portion of northeastern British Columbia. On top of these agreements, there is a certain amount fluidity with regard to several other nations. Perhaps most prominent are the Tsilhqot'in, who won a critical 2014 Supreme Court of Canada decision confirming their title to a major swath of land. What the Tsilhqot'in decision (and several others like it) ultimately means on the ground is still emerging. It is true to say that almost all of British Columbia

is untreated with several important exceptions, and that a number of other nations are at various points in legalistic negotiations to recover their territory.

31. This distinction between treaty and nontreaty lands is often described as a ceded/unceded dichotomy, which is problematic in itself. As Khelsilem writes: "There is a misconception that BC is mostly *unceded* due to a lack of treaties— which implies those in areas with treaties are what? Ceded territories? That is not always the case and that assumed distinction is wrong." Khelsilem, "Khelsilem's Tips for Acknowledging Territory, 1.0," *Liberated Yet?*, http:// memorialparkvignettes.tumblr.com/post/106252238178/khelsilems-tips-for -acknowledging-territory-10.We think it is useful to speak of ceded/unceded only to a very limited extent, to note the state/legal apparatus that defines, constrains, and manipulates relations with land. The fact that a treaty was signed in no way assumes the Indigenous signatories ever meant that they were "giving up" their land or anything similar. Calling land "unceded" should draw attention to the total lack of an agreement without suggesting that "ceded" is a legal or ethical framework for a relationship.

32. Leanne Simpson, Lecture at SFU Woodward's, "Restoring Nationhood: Addressing Land Dispossession in the Canadian Reconciliation Discourse," November 13, 2013, https://www.youtube.com/watch?v=SGUcWih74Ic.

33. Keith Thor Carlson, "Introduction," *A Stó:lō-Coast Salish Historical Atlas*, ed. Keith Thor Carlson (Vancouver: Douglas & McIntyre; Seattle: University of Washington Press; Chilliwack: Stó:lō Heritage Trust, 2001), 2.

34. To this day, even when Am's hailing a cab in New Orleans from Pakistani Punjabis, he can still communicate with them in the mother tongue and usually gets a free cab ride. While traveling in Kosovo, a group of Punjabi-speaking Pakistani peacekeepers even insisted on getting a photo with him and called him brother.

35. See Gavin Hayman and Steve Trent of the Environmental Investigation Agency, "New Challenges to Montreal Protocol," http://www.unesco.org /education/educprog/ste/newsletter/eng_n2/newchall.html.

36. But conversely, a thoroughly socialized and equally devastating tar sands is equally imaginable. There is no reason to think that any socialist oil sands developments would take on ecological characteristics that are not available via capitalist production. It takes only a brief glance at some of the most progressive (or at least that were once very progressive) political regimes of our time, especially in South America, say Ecuador, or Venezuela to see the results. Or maybe better, look to Evo Morales's Bolivia with its inspiring record of "Indigenous socialism," its energetic and eloquent ecological principles and overtly anticapitalist politics. And note that Morales's government has aggressively opened up constitutionally protected national parks (many titled to Indigenous groups) to oil and gas

exploration in conjunction with multinationals and violently suppressed local resistance to expansive extractivism. When confronted on this, Morales famously retorted that antipoverty programs need funds and that his Bolivia was not going to play "park ranger" for the Global North. Rosalba O'Brien, "Bolivia's Morales, Once Leftist Climate Pact Foe, Turns Pragmatic," *Reuters*, Nov. 25, 2015, http://www.reuters.com/article/us-climatechange-summit-bolivia-idUSK BN0TE2H620151125.

37. From Giuseppe Di Lampedusa, *The Leopard*, trans. Archibald Colquhoun (New York: Pantheon, 1960), 214.

38. Ann Ehrlich and Paul Ehrlich with John Holdren, *Ecoscience* (San Francisco: W. H. Freeman, 1977): 942–943. Cited in Joel Wainwright and Geoff Mann, "Climate Leviathan," *Antipode*, 45 (2013): 1–22.

39. It should be noted that many fascist regimes throughout modernity have often been explicitly "green." The German Nazi Party under Hitler enacted strong animal protection, reforestation, air pollution, and conservationist laws, typically framed under the "Blood and Soil" claims that the German people were connected to the land and natural world in ways that other ethnicities could never grasp. See, e.g., Janet Biehl and Peter Staudenmeier's *Ecofascism: Lessons from the German Experience* (Oakland, CA: AK Press, 1995). That legacy is carried on by many contemporary fascist strains, such as Golden Dawn in Greece who echo much of the Nazi green program.

40. Quoted in Leo Hickman, "James Lovelock: Humans Are Too Stupid to Prevent Climate Change," *Guardian*, Mar. 29, 2010, https://www.theguardian .com/environment/blog/2010/mar/29/james-lovelock.

41. Southern Poverty Law Center, Extremist Files: Garrett Hardin, https:// www.splcenter.org/fighting-hate/extremist-files/individual/garrett-hardin.

42. "In democratic countries the destruction of nature and sum of ecological disasters has accumulated most. … Our only hope lies in strong central government and uncompromising [*sic*] control of the individual citizen" (http://www .penttilinkola.com/pentti_linkola/ecofascism/).

43. Mark Beeson, "The Coming of Environmental Authoritarianism," *Environmental Politics* 19 (2010): 276–294.

44. Cited in Nico Stehr, "Exceptional Circumstances: Does Climate Change Trump Democracy?" *Issues in Science and Technology* 32, no. 2 (winter 2016), http://issues.org/32-2/exceptional-circumstances-does-climate-change-trump -democracy/.

45. For his use of "a new modern tradition," see Alain Badiou's *The Subject of Change: Lessons from the European Graduate School*, ed. Duane Rousselle (New

York: Atropos Press, 2013), 5. (Bear in mind, though, this note from Alain Badiou in the book's preface: "This text … reflects an oral contribution, with degree of improvisation, and does not correspond to any text. … Consequently any use or quotation of this text will have to be accompanied with a precise indication of its origin, so that nobody could think that I have either written or proof-read it.")

46. Quoted in Genoa Mungin with contributions from Jesse Allen Sawyer, "A Short Chat with Alain Badiou," http://www.indigestmag.com/badiou.htm.

47. Ibid.

48. Badiou, *The Subject of Change*, 3–4.

49. Eve Tuck and C. Wayne Yang, "Decolonization Is Not a Metaphor," *Decolonization: Indigeneity, Education & Society* 1, no. 1 (2012): 21.

50. Tuck and Wang, "Decolonization Is Not a Metaphor," 7.

51. Walter Benjamin, "Capitalism as Religion," in *Selected Writings*, vol. 1: *1913–26*, ed. Marcus Bullock and Michael W. Jennings (Cambridge, MA: Harvard University Press, 2004), 289.

52. Personal interview with the authors, October 8, 2016.

53. Ibid.

54. Giorgio Agamben, "The "Latin Empire' Should Strike Back," *Vox Europ*, Mar. 26, 2013, http://www.voxeurop.eu/en/content/article/3593961-latin-empire-should-strike-back.

55. Quoted in Verso Blog, "The Endless Crisis as an Instrument of Power: In Conversation with Giorgio Agamben," June 4, 2013, http://www.versobooks.com/blogs/1318-the-endless-crisis-as-an-instrument-of-power-in-conversation-with-giorgio-agamben.

56. When we talk about a sweetness of living, or the good life, we are also talking about a *mode de vie*—a way of life or form of life—just three among many, many other possible formulations or articulations. More on this to come.

57. As Fanon wrote, "Independence is not a magic ritual but an indispensable condition for men and women to live in true liberation, in other words to master all the material resources necessary for a radical transformation of society." Franz Fanon, *Wretched of the Earth* (New York: Grove Press, 2005), 144.

58. Matthew Wildcat, Mandee McDonald, Stephanie Irlbacher-Fox, and Glen Coulthard, "Learning from the Land: Indigenous Land Based Pedagogy and Decolonization," *Decolonization: Indigeneity, Education & Society* 2, no. 3 (2014), http://decolonization.org/index.php/des/article/view/22248.

CHAPTER 2

1. These are all constantly evolving and emerging numbers. As of 2015, it was estimated that Venezuela (with 298 billion barrels untapped) had passed Saudi Arabia (268 billion) for the biggest reserves in the world. Canada was next (with almost all of its reserves locked in the oil sands), followed by Iran (158 billion), Iraq (144 billion), and Kuwait (104 billion) (data from the US Energy Information Administration, https://www.eia.gov/cfapps/ipdbproject/IEDIndex3.cfm ?tid=5&pid=57&aid=6). These are generally agreed-upon rankings by most mainstream multinational and national estimates (with slight variations in numbers based on a variety of factors).

In 2016 and 2017, however, a series of reports emerged suggesting that, given the new technological capacities to access shale and other unconventional sources, America has greater reserves than any country in the world. This is not a widely accepted fact, nor is it an apolitical assertion, but it also plausibly true. Many sources claim that numerous (maybe all) countries misrepresent their reserves and habitually overreport, and that if all supplies are accurately measured, taking into account all the nonconventional sources and new technologies existing and expected to be online shortly, then the United States and Russia have the world's largest supplies. Suffice to say, though, Canada and the tar sands are a significant source of oil, and remain in the very upper echelon of national reserves. See Magnus Nysveen, "United States Now Holds More Recoverable Oil Than Saudi Arabia," *Rystad Energy*, Jul. 4, 2016, https://www .rystadenergy.com/NewsEvents/PressReleases/united-states-now-holds-more -oil-reserves-than-saudi-arabia.

2. That was the widely reported 2015 number. See, e.g., https://www.thestar. com/news/atkinsonseries/2015/09/04/temporary-foreign-workers-help -drive-fort-mcmurrays-24-7-economy.html. Throughout, all dollars are CAD unless otherwise noted.

3. Gillian Steward, "Alberta's Oilsands Trade-Off," *Toronto Star*, Aug. 28, 2015, https://www.thestar.com/news/atkinsonseries/2015/08/28/albertas-oilsands -trade-off.html.

4. Naomi Klein and Bill McKibben in the preface to Steve D'arcy, *A Line in the Tar Sands* (Toronto: Between the Lines, 2014).

5. The production of the book fell into place pretty easily. Am and Matt did all the writing, Joe did all the drawing and cartooning (thankfully). All of the book is built on conversations in Vancouver, Portland, Edmonton, Fort McMurray, Grimshaw, Janvier, and Little Buffalo over four separate trips to the tar sands, barreling around Northern Alberta, debating global warming in a long series of bars, fast food outlets, low-end grocery stores, and sleeping bags spread out on basement floors.

6. See, e.g., Andrew Nikiforuk, *Tar Sands, Dirty Oil and the Future of a Continent* (Vancouver: Greystone Books, 2010); Samuel Avery, *The Pipeline and the Paradigm: Keystone XL, Tar Sands and the Battle to Defuse the Carbon Bomb* (Washington, DC: Ruka Press, 2013); Tony Clarke *Tar Sands Showdown: Canada and the New Politics of Oil in an Age of Climate Change* (Toronto: Lorimer Press, 2008); William Marsden *Stupid to the Last Drop: How Alberta Is Bringing Environmental Armageddon to Canada (and Doesn't Seem to Care)* (Toronto: Vintage Canada, 2008).

7. Postmedia News, *Financial Post*, "Oil Sands Pollution Linked to Higher Cancer Rates in Fort Chipewyan for the First Time: Study," July 8, 2014, http://business.financialpost.com/news/oil-sands-pollution-linked-to-higher-cancer-rates-in-fort-chipewyan-study-finds. The full report from the researcher featured in the article is: Stéphane M. McLachlan, *"Water Is a Living Thing": Environmental and Human Health Implications of the Athabasca Oil Sands for the Mikisew Cree First Nation and Athabasca Chipewyan First Nation in Alberta* (Winnipeg, MB: Environmental Conservation Laboratory, 2014).

8. Jocelyn Edwards, "Oil Sands Pollutants in Traditional Foods," *Canadian Medical Association Journal* 186, no. 12 (Sept. 2, 2014): E444; Laura Eggertson, "High Cancer Rates among Fort Chipewyan Residents," *Canadian Medical Association Journal* 181, no. 12 (Dec. 8, 2009).

9. Nenshi is also from Alberta, which means that he is definitely and defiantly pro-pipeline and pro oil. There is almost no way for any (elected) politician in Alberta to be otherwise. And understandably: those are his people.

10. Since June 2014, when the slide started for real. See http://pubdocs.world bank.org/en/339801451407117632/PRN01Mar2015OilPrices.pdf.

11. Isaac Arnsdorf, "OPEC Is Winning the Price War," *Bloomberg*, June 2, 2015, http://www.bloomberg.com/news/articles/2015-06-02/opec-is-winning-the-oil-price-war.

12. Justin Giovannetti, "Alberta Budget to Include More Taxes, Reveals $5 Billion Deficit Over Next Year," *Globe and Mail* (Toronto), Mar. 26, 2015, http://www.theglobeandmail.com/news/alberta/alberta-budget-reveals-record-5-billion-deficit-over-next-year/article23645459/.

13. Justin Giovannetti, "Low Oil Prices, Costly Wildfire Push Alberta's Deficit to Nearly $11 Billion," *Globe and Mail* (Toronto), Aug. 23, 2016, http://www.theglobeandmail.com/news/alberta/fort-mcmurray wildfire-adds-500-million-to-albertas-projected-deficit/article31515924/.

14. Michelle Bellafontaine, "Alberta's Debt Soars to $45B, but Budget Has no Big Cuts, no New Taxes," *CBC News*, March 16, 2017, http://www.cbc.ca/news/canada/edmonton/2017-alberta-budget-speech-1.4028447.

15. Kevin P. Timoney and Peter Lee, "Does the Alberta Tar Sands Industry Pollute? The Scientific Evidence," *Open Conservation Biology Journal* 3 (2009): 65–81. The opprobrium for Alberta and the tar sands is international (Rebecca Leber, "The World's Worst Climate Change Villains? Step Forward, Prime Ministers of Australia and Canada," *New Statesman*, Oct. 21, 2014, http://www.newstatesman.com/sci-tech/2014/10/worlds-worst-climate-change-villains-step-forward-prime-ministers-australia-and), national (Yael Berger, "David Suzuki Compares Oil Sands Industry to Slavery," *Macleans Magazine*, Nov. 24, 2015, http://www.pressreader.com/canada/edmonton-journal/20151125/281 917361991097), and even local (Catherine Griwkowski, "Edmonton Marchers Want Climate Action," *Edmonton Sun*, Sept. 21, 2014, http://www.edmontonsun.com/2014/09/21/edmonton-marchers-want-climate-action).

16. "Sunny ways" was Justin Trudeau's signature electoral tag line and was prominently featured in his televised election night speech. Often described as looking like a Disney prince or Ken doll come to life, his election campaign and subsequent reign as prime minister has been marketed as a return to positive, progressive politics in Canada. See http://news.nationalpost.com/news/canada/canadian-politics/sunny-ways-my-friends-sunny-ways-lessons-of-wilfrid-laurier-not-lost-on-trudeau-115-years-later.

17. Marc Huot and Jennifer Grant, *Clearing the Air on Oilsands Emissions: The Facts about Greenhouse Gas Pollution from Oilsands Development* (Edmonton, AB: Pembina Institute, 2012), 3, https://www.pembina.org/reports/clearing-the-air-climate-oilsands.pdf.

18. Stéphane M. McLachlan, *"Water Is a Living Thing."*

19. Ed Struzik, "With Tar Sands Development, Growing Concern on Water Use," *Yale Environment 360*, Aug. 5, 2013, http://e360.yale.edu/feature/with_tar_sands_development_growing_concern_on_water_use/2672/.

20. Edward Struzik, *Future Arctic: Field Notes from a World on the Edge.* (Washington, DC: Island Press, 2015), 31–40.

21. Quoted in Damian Carrington, "Tar Sands Exploitation Would Mean Game Over for the Climate, Warns Leading Scientist," *Guardian*, May 19, 2013, http://www.theguardian.com/environment/2013/may/19/tar-sands-exploitation-climate-scientist

22. The IPCC is the Intergovernmental Panel on Climate Change. See, e.g., "The Council of Canadians, IPCC Head Says Canada Should Consider Closing Down the Tar Sands," *Council of Canadians*, Sept. 21, 2009, http://canadians.org/fr/node/5076. *Nature* is the world's most-cited scientific journal. See Christopher McGlade and Paul Ekins, "The Geographical Distribution of Fossil Fuels Unused When Limiting Global Warming to 2°," *Nature* 517 (Jan. 8, 2015): 187–190.

23. Christopher McGlade and Paul Ekins, "The Geographical Distribution of Fossil Fuels," 190: "Although such a decarbonization would be extremely challenging in reality, cumulative production of Canadian bitumen between 2010 and 2050 is still only 7.5 billion barrels. 85% of its 48 billion of barrels of bitumen reserves thus remain unburnable if the 2C limit is not to be exceeded."

24. Young's "Honor the Treaties" tour (http://www.honourtheacfn.ca/) was in support of the Athabasca Chipewyan First Nations legal defense fund, their fight against the tar sands expansionism in general, and Shell's Jackpine Mine in particular. Young stirred up a huge hornet's nest with his tour, visit to Fort Chip, and fundraising efforts. Ole Neil was attacked ferociously, especially in Alberta when he said the tar sands look like Hiroshima and when he pointed to the devastation of Indigenous communities. *Traitor* is among the gentlest accusations tossed in his direction.

25. Cape Breton University business professor Doug Lionais, speaking to the *Financial Post*: Greg McNeil, "Oil Sands Pain Spreads All the Way to Canada's Far-Flung Eastern Shores," *Financial Post*, Mar. 15, 2015, http://business .financialpost.com/news/energy/oil-sands-pain-spreads-all-the-way-to-canadas -far-flung-eastern-shores.

26. "Petrocultures is a research group at the University of Alberta (founded in 2011) whose aim is to support, produce, and distribute research related to the social, cultural and political implications of oil and energy use on individuals, communities, and societies around the world" (http://petrocultures.com/about/).

27. Petrocultures Research Group, *After Oil* (Edmonton: University of Alberta, 2016), 24, http://afteroil.ca/resources-2/after-oil-book/.

28. Government of Canada, "Leaders' Declaration G7 Summit Germany," *Global Affairs Canada*, June 7–8, 2015, http://www.international.gc.ca/g7/g7 _germany_declaration-g7_allemagne_declaration.aspx?lang=eng. The official communiqué from G7: http://www.international.gc.ca/g7/g7 germany _declaration-g7_allemagne_declaration.aspx?lang=eng.

29. Francis, *Laudato Si': On Care for Our Common Home, Encyclical Letter* (Vatican City, Italy: Libreria Editrice Vaticana, 2015), 26, http://w2.vatican.va /content/francesco/en/encyclicals/documents/papa-francesco_20150524 _enciclica-laudato-si.pdf.

30. Sortinget, "Innstilling fra energi- og miljøkomiteen om Samtykke til ratifikasjon av Paris-avtalen av 12. desember 2015 under FNs rammekonvensjon om klimaendring av 9. mai 1992," *Sortinget*, June 7, 2016, https://www .stortinget.no/no/Saker-og-publikasjoner/Publikasjoner/Innstillinger /Stortinget/2015-2016/inns-201516-407/?lvl=0KatieHerzog. Cited in "Norway Talks a Big Game, Promises to Go Carbon-Neutral by 2030," *Grist*, June 16,

2016, http://grist.org/climate-energy/norway-talks-a-big-game-promises-to-go-carbon-neutral-by-2030/.

31. Hawaii (State), House of Representatives, *A Bill for an Act Relating to Renewable Standards*, HB623, 2015, http://www.capitol.hawaii.gov/session2015/bills/HB623_CD1_.HTM.

32. Allison Lampert, "Quebec Aims to Reduce Oil Consumption by 40% by 2030," *Reuters Canada*, April 7, 2016, http://ca.reuters.com/article/business News/idCAKCN0X42HJ.

33. Lisa Friedman, "Mexico Makes Landmark Pledge to Cut Greenhouse Gas Pollution," *Scientific American*, March 30, 2015, http://www.scientificamerican.com/article/mexico-makes-landmark-pledge-to-cut-greenhouse-gas-pollution/.

34. See the report from the Federal Democratic Republic of Ethiopia, "Intended Nationally Determined Contribution (INDC) of the Federal Democratic Republic of Ethiopia" (2015), http://www4.unfccc.int/ndcregistry/Published Documents/Ethiopia%20First/INDC-Ethiopia-100615.pdf.Cited in Mail and Guardian Africa, "Showing the Way: Ethiopia to Cut Carbon Emissions by Two-Thirds by 2030, Leads Rest of the World in Setting Targets," June 11, 2015, http://mgafrica.com/article/2015-06-11-ethiopia-to-cut-carbon-emissions-by-two-thirds-by-2030-leads-rest-of-the-world-so-far-in-setting-targets.

35. The second thing we noticed was how hard it was to make connections and arrangements. Normally when any one of us plans to write about a place, we make as many contacts as we can well in advance to set up interviews, get advice, and identify people who are willing to talk. This time, though, it was difficult, complicated and complicating. We had no shortage of contacts, but one after the other, people declined to talk with us, said they didn't want to go on record, or refused to talk to any "reporters" who might be slandering the town or tar sands. We ran into such sentiments and reproaches repeatedly, and warnings came from unexpected places, including surprisingly emotional admonishments from friends. A defensive stance is hardly unusual in resource-dependent communities, including our hometowns. As one guy told us after we emailed him a friendly inquiry via an introduction from a pal: "The people of McMurray are all too used to getting poked and prodded in this way. The last thing they need when they are fearing for their jobs and their families is outsiders coming to satisfy their own curiosities. I'm afraid I won't be of much help to you."

36. *This Changes Everything* is actually not just a book, it's an elaborately choreographed media spectacular: film, website, speaking events, tours, and so on. See http://www.thischangeseverything.com.

37. At one level it is totally obvious. It is a great book: the writing is accessible and flows easily, it reveals a tremendous depth of research, and her analysis

squares to the climate crises that is on all of our minds, especially when we're boarding a plane. Still, the book always seems anomalous amid the romance novels, detective series, and lousy get-rich-quick advice manuals.

38. Klein, *This Changes Everything* (Toronto: Knopf Canada: 2014), 21.

39. Ibid., 7.

40. Ibid., 43.

41. Here we are excluding the Fox/Republican/fossil-fuel industry respondents who have attacked her with utterly predictable vitriol, mostly with very little substantive content.

42. Elizabeth Kolbert, "Can Climate Change Cure Capitalism," *New York Review of Books*, Dec. 4, 2014:

> To have a reasonable shot at limiting warming to two degrees, the general consensus among scientists is that aggregate emissions since industrialization began in the mid-eighteenth century must be held to a trillion metric tons. Almost 600 billion of those tons have already been emitted, meaning that humanity has already blown through more than half of its "carbon budget." If current trends continue, it will burn through the rest in the next twenty-five years. Thus, what is essential to preserving the possibility of 2 degrees is reversing these trends, and doing so immediately.

43. Ibid.

44. Timothy Mitchell, *Carbon Democracy* (New York: Verso, 2011). What follows is a synthesis of some of the themes of the book.

45. Alternatively, some suggest that solar power will necessarily be the basis for a form of communism in the twenty-first century. David Schwartzman, "From Climate Crisis to Solar Communism," *Jacobin*, Dec. 1, 2015, https://www .jacobinmag.com/2015/12/cop-21-paris-climate-change-global-warming-fossil -fuels/.

46. Anthropocene Working Group, "Media Note: Anthropocene Working Group (AWG)," *University of Leicester*, Aug. 29, 2016, http://www2.le.ac.uk /offices/press/press-releases/2016/august/media-note-anthropocene-working -group-awg.

47. Gaia Vince, quoted in Jonathan Amos, "Case Is Made for the Anthropocene Epoch," *BBC News*, Jan. 8, 2016, http://www.bbc.com/news/science-environment -35259194.

48. The Subcommission on Quaternary Stratigraphy (SQS) is a constituent body of the International Commission on Stratiagraphy (ICS), the largest scientific

organization within the International Union of Geological Sciences (IUGS). See http://quaternary.stratigraphy.org/workinggroups/anthropocene/.

49. P. J. Crutzen, "Geology of Mankind," *Nature* 415, no.6867 (2002): 23.

50. Simon L. Lewis and Mark A. Maslin, "Defining the Anthropocene," *Nature* 519 (March 2015): 171–180.

51. See Jan Zalasiewicz et al., "When Did the Anthropocene Begin? A Mid-Twentieth-Century Boundary Level Is Stratigraphically Optimal," *Quaternary International* 383 (Oct. 2015): 196–203.

52. The hockey stick is maybe the most famous and contested graph in recent scientific history. It was first proposed by climatologist Michael Mann and colleagues in 1998 to demonstrate the sharp upturn in planetary temperatures beginning in the late-twentieth century and since has become the focal point for a maelstrom of attacks on climate science in general and rising temperatures specifically. The original graph just showed temperatures, but since then it has been repurposed to visualize population growth, urbanization, methane emissions, ocean acidification, and a whole raft of dashboard indicators of human environmental impacts. All the graphs look basically the same: a straight horizontal temporal line that shoots up dramatically in the second half of the twentieth century.

53. Mark Lynas, *Six Degrees: Our Future on a Hotter Planet* (London: Fourth Estate, 2007).

54. Mark Lynas, *The God Species: Saving the Planet in the Age of Humans* (Washington, DC: National Geographic, 2011).

55. James Lovelock, *The Revenge of Gaia: Earth's Climate Crisis and the Fate of Humanity* (New York: Basic Books, 2007).

56. Roy Scranton, *Learning to Die in the Anthropocene* (San Francisco: City Lights Books, 2015), 16, 17, 21.

57. Ibid., 60, 68.

58. Jason Moore, *Capitalism in the Web of Life* (London: Verso Books, 2015), 170.

59. Andreas Malm is among the most articulate critics of Anthropocenic fantasies, as clearly laid in *Fossil Capital* (New York: Verso, 2016). He nicely congeals the argument in "The Anthropocene Myth," *Jacobin*, Mar. 30, 2015, https://www.jacobinmag.com/2015/03/anthropocene-capitalism-climate-change/:

> The most extreme illusions about the perfect democracy of the market are required to maintain the notion of "us all" driving the train. ... Perhaps most obvious: few resources are so unequally consumed as energy.

The 19 million inhabitants of New York State alone consume more energy than the 900 million inhabitants of sub-Saharan Africa. The difference in energy consumption between a subsistence pastoralist in the Sahel and an average Canadian may easily be larger than 1,000-fold—and that is an *average* Canadian, not the owner of five houses, three SUVs, and a private airplane.

A single average US citizen emits more than 500 citizens of Ethiopia, Chad, Afghanistan, Mali, or Burundi; how much an average US millionaire emits—and how much more than an average US or Cambodian worker—remains to be counted. But a person's imprint on the atmosphere varies tremendously depending on where she is born. Humanity, as a result, is far too slender an abstraction to carry the burden of culpability. Ours is the geological epoch not of humanity, but of capital.

60. Interview with Jason Moore, *Entitle* blog, "Jason W. Moore: Anthropocene or Capitalocene," *YouTube*, Jan. 4, 2016, https://www.youtube.com/watch?v=q1YZym_abPU.

61. Richard Heede, "Tracing Anthropogenic Carbon Dioxide and Methane Emissions to Fossil Fuel and Cement Producers, 1854–2010," *Climatic Change* (2014): 122–229:

The analysis presented here suggests a somewhat different, and perhaps useful, way to consider responsibility for climate change. ... A total of 914 billion tonnes of CO_2 equivalent ($GtCO_2e$) has been traced to 90 international entities based on analysis of historic production records dating from 1854 to 2010. ... The emissions traced to t carbon majors represent 63% of global industrial CO_2 and methane from fossil fuel combustion, flaring, venting, fugitive or vented methane, own fuel use, and cement between 1751 and 2010. ...

Cumulative emissions attributed to the twenty largest investor-owned and state-owned energy companies between 1854 and 2010 total 428 $GtCO_2e$, or 29.5% of global industrial emissions from 1751 to 2010. The ten largest investor-owned companies alone contributed 230 $GtCO_2e$, or 15.8% of global emissions through 2010. ...

The analysis presented here focuses attention on the commercial and state-owned entities responsible for producing the fossil fuels and cement that are the primary sources of anthropogenic greenhouse gases that are driving and will continue to drive climate change. The results show that nearly two-thirds of historic carbon dioxide and methane emissions can be attributed to 90 entities.

62. Erick Swyngedouw, "Anthropocenic Promises, the End of Nature, Climate Change and the Process of Post-Politicization," Lecture at Humbolt University, https://www.youtube.com/watch?v=Yz2UQrKcwJ8&feature=youtu.be.

63. Christophe Bonneuil and Jean-Baptiste Fressoz, *The Shock of the Anthropocene* (London: Verso Books, 2016).

64. Donna Haraway, "Anthropocene, Capitalocene, Plantationocene, Chthulucene: Making Kin," *Environmental Humanities* 6 (2015): 159–165.

65. Mackenzie Wark, *Molecular Red: Theory for the Anthropocene* (New York: Verso, 2015), 223.

66. Catherine Malabou, "The Brain of History or the Mentality of the Anthropocene," *South Atlantic Quarterly* 116, no. 1 (2016): 1.

67. Zoe Todd, "Indigenizing the Anthropocene," in *Art in the Anthropocene*, ed. Heather Davis and Etienne Turpin (London: Open Humanities Press, 2015), 241–254.

68. There is also an impressive body of environmental literature that focuses on justice and inter- and intranational inequality, which we admire and draw on significantly. Noteworthy examples include Peter Dauvergne, *Environmentalism of the Rich* (Cambridge, MA: MIT Press, 2016); Carl A. Zimring, *Clean and White: A History of Environmental Racism in the United States* (New York: NYU Press, 2015); Kevin Bales, *Blood and Earth: Modern Slavery, Ecocide, and the Secret to Saving the World* (Berlin: Spiegel & Grau, 2016); J. Timmons Roberts and Bradley Parks, *A Climate of Injustice: Global Inequality, North–South Politics, and Climate Policy* (Cambridge, MA: MIT Press, 2006); JoAnn Carmin and Julian Ageyman, *Environmental Inequalities beyond Borders: Local Perspectives on Global Injustices* (Cambridge, MA: MIT Press, 2011).

69. No continent will be struck as severely by the impacts of climate change as Africa—in part because of existing endemic poverty that reduces the mitigation and adaptation efforts, but also because of specific geographic and climactic features. The UN and IPCC suggest that by 2020, "between 75 and 250 million people in Africa are projected to be exposed to increased water stress due to climate change. By 2020, in some countries, yields from rain-fed agriculture could be reduced by up to 50%. Agricultural production, including access to food, in many African countries is projected to be severely compromised" (*Fact Sheet: Climate Change in Africa—What Is at Stake? Excerpts from IPCC reports, the Convention, and BAP, Compiled by AMCEN Secretariat*, http://www .docucu-archive.com/view/73db38bf034090d454ee45caf9a47c19/FACT -SHEET-Climate-Change-in-Africa-What-is-at.pdf).

70. And of course, the middle class is differentially and intersectionally exposed to the repercussions of global warming. For example, in 2010, "with 68 percent of African-Americans and 40 percent of Latinos living within 30 miles of a pollution-spewing, coal-fired power plant and over 50 percent of Asian-Americans living in counties with unhealthy air quality ... African-American

children were twice as likely to be hospitalized with an asthma attack and four times as likely to die from the disease as white children. Hispanics were 60 percent more likely than non-Hispanic whites to visit the hospital for asthma" (Laurie Mazur, "Racial Equity, Poverty and the Promise of Clean Power," *Island Press Blog*, Nov. 22, 2015, https://www.islandpress.org/blog/racial-equity -poverty-and-promise-clean-power). This is just one of a near-endless list of disproportionately felt environmental effects at local and regional levels. For some excellent explication and analysis, see Rob Nixon, *Slow Violence and the Environmentalism of the Poor* (Cambridge, MA: Harvard University Press, 2011).

71. See Stewart Brand, *Whole Earth Discipline: Why Dense Cities, Nuclear Power, Transgenic Crops, Restored Wildlands, and Geoengineering are Necessary* (New York: Penguin Books, 2010).

72. Eileen Crist, "On the Poverty of Our Nomenclature," *Environmental Humanities* 3 (2013): 140.

73. Paul Crutzen, "Albedo Enhancement by Stratospheric Sulfur Injections: A Contribution to Resolve a Policy Dilemma?" *Climatic Change* 77 (2006): 211.

74. See Fareed Zakaria's interview with Nathan Myhrvold, "Solving Global Warming with Nathan Myhrvold," *CNN News*, Dec. 20, 2009, http://www.cnn .com/TRANSCRIPTS/0912/20/fzgps.01.html.

75. See this and other proposals developed at Keith's Harvard lab: "The Keith Group": http://keith.seas.harvard.edu.

76. Honestly, we're not making this up. For a good overview see Graeme Wood, "Re-engineering the Earth," *Atlantic*, Jul.–Aug. 2009, http://www.theatlantic .com/magazine/archive/2009/07/re-engineering-the-earth/307552/.

77. Mark Lynas, "Geoengineering: Why All the Fuss?" *MarkLynas.org*, Jun. 2011, http://www.marklynas.org/2011/06/geoengineering-why-all-the-fuss/.

78. Leo Hickman, "James Lovelock. Humans Are Too Stupid to Prevent Climate Change," *Guardian*, Mar. 29, 2010, https://www.theguardian.com/science /2010/mar/29/james-lovelock-climate-change.

79. Paul Kingsnorth. See the Dark Mountain Project (http://dark-mountain .net/), among many other pieces of his writing, on giving up, withdrawing, and the like in the face of planetary collapse.

80. The framing of global warming as a war is critical for creating states of exception discourses where moral hazards are rendered irrelevant. Listen to military analyst Gwynne Dyer: "it is sheer fecklessness to fail to investigate such possibilities aggressively, because we are currently conducting an unplanned experiment in global climate alteration through massive carbon dioxide release without any kind of safety net. It would be comfortable to have at least one

reserve position to fall back on, in case all those promises of future emissions cuts don't come true. Three or four different tested and proven options for how to stop the temperature from soaring if the Kyoto process or its son or niece or second cousin doesn't deliver the goods in time would be even nicer. Moral hazard be damned. This is serious." Gwynne Dyer, *Climate Wars* (Toronto: Random House, 2008), 217.

81. We should note here that there is often considerable nuance to geoengineering discussions. We are antagonistic to most every techno-fix claim, but that doesn't mean that everyone involved in geoengineering is a retrograde quasi authoritarian. There are many reasonable and thoughtful people who have concluded that technical solutions to global warming are inevitable and that mitigation is the only realistic response. Much of the best thinking on the subject is well intentioned and highly sensitive to the social and philosophical quandaries embedded within. See, e.g., the Forum on Climate Engineering Assessment (http://ceassessment.org) for clear-headed discussion, or the foundational text by Wil C. G. Burns and Andrew L. Strauss, *Climate Change Geoengineering* (Cambridge: Cambridge University Press, 2013), or even the National Academies Reports on climate intervention: https://nap.edu/catalog/18988/climate-intervention-reflecting-sunlight-to-cool-earth or https://nap.edu/catalog/18805/climate-intervention-carbon-dioxide-removal-and-reliable-sequestration.

That being said, the starting point for all geoengineering discussions necessarily revolves around the inevitability of global warming. Inevitability discourses are deployed to subsume social and political discussions, and should always be interrogated.

82. Elizabeth Bast et al., *Empty Promises: G20 Subsidies to Oil, Gas and Coal Production* (London: Overseas Development Institute with Oil Change International, 2015), 11, http://priceofoil.org/content/uploads/2015/11/empty_promises_full_report_update.pdf.

83. Bruno Latour, "Love Your Monsters: Why We Must Care for Our Technologies as We Do Our Children," *Breakthrough* (winter 2012), http://thebreakthrough.org/index.php/journal/past-issues/issue-2/love-your-monsters.

84. We probably have more in common with Latour than we care to admit, but it is hard to tell. He often descends into veiled accelerationist claims, but then turns in other directions. Our struggle with a new definition of ecology relates to what Latour names "political ecology," but with land and decolonization woven far more explicitly in to it.

85. Joseph Schumpeter, *Essays* (Cambridge, MA: Addison-Wesley, 1951), 293.

86. Justin Trudeau, "Prime Minister Justin Trudeau's Pipeline Announcement," Nov. 30, 2016, http://pm.gc.ca/eng/news/2016/11/30/prime-minister-justin-trudeaus-pipeline-announcement.

87. Thanks Hilda Fernandez!

CHAPTER 4

1. Census Profile, 2016 Census, http://www12.statcan.gc.ca/census-recensement/2016/dp-pd/prof/details/page.cfm?Lang=E&Geo1=POPC&Code1=0292&Geo2=PR&Code2=13&Data=Count&SearchText=Fort%20McMurray&SearchType=Begins&SearchPR=01&B1=All&TABID=1.

2. See, e.g., Zoë Todd, "Ft. McMurray Wildfire—by the Numbers," *CBC News*, May 8, 2016, http://www.cbc.ca/news/canada/edmonton/fort-mcmurray-wildfire-by-the-numbers-1.3572193.

3. As local historian Peter Fortna put it, "There's three kinds of people who come to Fort McMurray. There's people who come to make a quick dollar and get out. There's other people who come with a five-year plan. ... And then there's people who come here and want to make a community of it. Those first two types of people put a lot of pressure on the third type, because it takes a lot to build a community." Quoted in Peter Scowen, "From Boom Town to Family Town: Meet the real Fort McMurray," *Globe and Mail* (Toronto), June 12, 2015, http://www.theglobeandmail.com/news/alberta/meet-the-real-fort-mcmurray/article24915022/.

4. Political theorist Chantal Mouffe argues that an agonistic politics is a necessary and productive antidote to deliberative democracy. Deliberation and consensus are based around an inadequate liberal form of politics that does not adequately address genuine political difference. Rather than be evacuated from the space of politics, difference ought to be viewed as a necessary part of the process, according to her:

> One of the principal theses that I have defended in my work is that properly political questions always involve decisions which require a choice between alternatives that are undecidable from a strictly rational point of view. This is something the liberal theory cannot admit due to the inadequate way it envisages pluralism. The liberal theory recognises that we live in a world where a multiplicity of perspectives and values coexist and, for reasons it believes to be empirical, accepts that it is impossible for each of us to adopt them all. But it imagines that these perspectives and values, brought together, constitute a harmonious and non-conflictual ensemble. This type of thought is therefore incapable of accounting for

the necessarily conflictual nature of pluralism, which stems from the impossibility of reconciling all points of view, and it is what leads it to negate the political in its antagonistic dimension. (Chantal Mouffe, "Agonistic Democracy and Radical Politics," *Pavilion*, Dec. 29, 2014, http://pavilionmagazine.org/chantal-mouffe-agonistic-democracy-and -radical-politics/)

5. David Harvey, "The Nature of Environment," *Socialist Register* 29 (1993): 3.

6. Ibid., 3–4.

7. Ibid., 4.

8. For a couple of seminal and highly germane theoretical approaches related to the interaction between humans, technology, and nature that get at this first question, see Martin Heidegger, *The Question Concerning Technology, and Other Essays* (New York: Harper & Row, 1997), and Herbert Marcuse, "Some Social Implications of Modern Technology," in *The Essential Frankfurt School Reader*, ed. Andrew Arato and Eike Gebhardt (New York: Continuum, 1982), 138–162.

9. Although we rely on Bookchin considerably throughout this section and in several other parts of this book, ours is not a carte-blanche affiliation with his analyses nor of social ecology. We admire so much of Bookchin's work, especially his pre-1990 writings, but we have taken some of his core principles here and reworked and reconfigured them in ways that he would surely abhor. We have used what we consider some of his tremendously valuable theorizing, shorn it of some regrettable intransigencies, and tried to find a more generous, more mutualistic, less dogmatic reading of his insights. We hope in this way to contribute to a revival of some of Bookchin's best ideas.

10. Murray Bookchin, *The Ecology of Freedom: the Emergence and Dissolution of Hierarchy* (Palo Alto, CA: Cheshire Books, 1982), 315.

11. Ibid.

12. Murray Bookchin, *The Philosophy of Social Ecology* (Montreal: Black Rose Books, 1995), 86. It is also worth noting here Felix Guattari's 1989 book *The Three Ecologies*, translated by Ian Pindar and Paul Sutton (New York: Continuum, 2008). Guattari presents the term "ecosophy" that argues for "an ethico-political articulation ... between the three ecological registers (the environment, social relations and human subjectivity)" (19–20). He notes not only the erosion of the relationship between the human and the other-than-human world, but equally of human subjectivity and social relationships themselves. He writes, "So wherever we turn, there is the same nagging paradox: on the one hand, the continuous development of new techno scientific means to potentially resolve the dominant ecological issues and restate socially useful activities on the surface of the planet, and, on the other hand the inability of

organised social forces and constituted subjective formations to take hold of these resources in order to make them work" (22). Guattari's work is a useful addendum and counterpart to reading Bookchin, echoing similar themes but expressed in very different languages.

13. Bookchin, *The Philosophy of Social Ecology*, 87.

14. Brian Massumi, *What Animals Teach Us about Politics* (Durham: Duke University Press, 2014), 91–93. One of our favorite and most challenging books in the last few years.

15. Bookchin, *Philosophy of Social Ecology*, 20.

16. It's actually not technically a city, or a town, or anything municipal. In 1995, Fort McMurray changed its official designation from "city" to "urban service area"—a shift so creepy we are just going to pretend it didn't happen.

17. We went there five times over two and a half years, and we were basically the only people there aside from the dozen or so eager employees who were marginally suspicious of our naive questions and repeated visits.

18. See comments from a Canadian Natural Resources Ltd. Spokesperson in "122 Birds Died after Landing on 3 Northern Alberta Tailings Ponds," *CBC News*, Nov. 5, 2015, http://www.cbc.ca/news/canada/edmonton/122-birds-died-after -landing-on-3-northern-alberta-tailings-ponds-1.2825350.

19. Brent Wittmeier, "Energy Regulator Now Says 122 Birds Confirmed Dead at Tailings Ponds in Athabasca Oilsands," *Edmonton Journal*, Nov. 6, 2014, http://www.edmontonjournal.com/energy+regulator+says+birds+confirmed+ dead+tailings+ponds+athabasca+oilsands/10356200/story.html.

20. "Syncrude Bison Left Behind as Fort McMurray Fires Force Further Oilsands Shutdown," *Edmonton Journal*, May 8, 2016, http://edmontonjournal .com/storyline/syncrude-bison-left-behind-as-fort-mcmurray-fires-force -further-oilsands-shutdown.

21. Lauren Krugel, "Syncrude Says Bison Herd Holding Up Well as Fort McMurray Wildfires Rage Nearby," *CBC News*, May 20, 2016, http://www.cbc .ca/news/canada/calgary/syncrude-bison-herd-holding-up-1.3592739.

22. Mordor is the fictional land in J. R. R. Tolkien's *The Lord of the Rings*. Leonardo DiCaprio actually calls the tar sands Mordor while flying over them in a plane in the recent National Geographic documentary *Before the Flood*. Mordor is the way a lot of enviro-types reflexively describe Fort Mac and the tar sands. There's reason for sure, but it always makes us wonder: if that's Mordor, does it make the people who live there orcs, or trolls? And is DiCaprio then Frodo, or some other Tolkeinesque hero charging in to save the day?

23. Vincent McDermott, "Recent Crime Stats Show the 'True Reality' of Ft. McMurray: Blake," *Fort McMurray Today*, Aug. 17, 2016, http://www.fort mcmurraytoday.com/2016/08/17/recent-crime-stats-show-true-reality-of-fort -mcmurray-blake.

24. Sara O'Shaughnessy, "Women's Gendered Experiences of Rapid Resource Development in the Canadian North: New Opportunities or Old Challenges?" (PhD diss., University of Alberta, 2011), 17.

25. Sara O'Shaughnessy and Goze Dogu, "The Gendered and Racialized Subjects of Alberta's Oil Boomtown," in *First World Petro-Politics: The Political Ecology and Governance of Alberta*, ed. Laurie Adkin (Toronto: University of Toronto Press, 2016), 263–296.

26. Sheena Wilson, "Gendering Oil: Tracing Western Petrosexual Relations," in *Oil Culture*, ed. Ross Barrett and Daniel Worden (Minneapolis: University of Minnesota Press, 2014), 258. Other speculative movements such as xenofeminism engage in important polemical interventions that pierce conceptual frames of gender and political scale. Here is a short excerpt from the manifesto, section 0x05, "INTERRUPT": "Whilst capitalism is understood as a complex and ever-expanding totality, many would-be emancipatory anti-capitalist projects remain profoundly fearful of transitioning to the universal, resisting big-picture speculative politics by condemning them as necessarily oppressive vectors. Such a false guarantee treats universals as absolute, generating a debilitating disjuncture between the thing we seek to depose and the strategies we advance to depose it." Laboria Cuboniks, "Xenofeminism: A Politics for Alienation," *LaboriaCuboniks.net*, http://www.laboriacuboniks.net/#interrupt/1.

27. MacDonald Island Park, "About MacDonald Island Park," http://www .macdonaldisland.ca/about-us.

28. Peter Scowen, "From Boom Town to Family Town: Meet the Real Fort McMurray," *Globe and Mail* (Toronto), June 12, 2015, http://www.theglobe andmail.com/news/alberta/meet-the-real-fort-mcmurray/article24915022/.

29. Bernard is a Vancouver-raised millennial trying to pay off student loans by working in the tar sands: "Please, not just for me, but the guys who have kids and are losing their marriages." Quoted in Elizabeth McSheffrey, "'Put Me Back to Work' Pleads Struggling Kinder Morgan Pipeline Supporter," *National Observer*, August 23, 2016, http://www.nationalobserver.com/2016/08/23 /news/put-me-back-work-pleads-struggling-kinder-morgan-pipeline-supporter.

30. Rockefeller Brothers Fund, "Divestment Statement," *Rockefeller Brothers Fund*, March 3, 2017, http://www.rbf.org/about/divestment.

31. In 2016, the tar sands, with some variance from project to project, needed oil prices to stick somewhere above US$50 a barrel to break even and prices

well above that to make profits. See Yadullah Hussain, "How High Break-Even Costs Are Challenging New Oilsands Projects," *Financial Post*, Jan. 22, 2015, http://business.financialpost.com/news/energy/how-high-break-even-costs-are -challenging-new-oilsands-projects.

32. In 2014, its direct contribution to GDP was 9.8 percent: https://www.neb -one.gc.ca/nrg/ntgrtd/mrkt/vrvw/2014/index-eng.html.

33. See the National Energy Board's statement that in 2014 energy accounted for $128.7 billion in exports: https://www.neb-one.gc.ca/nrg/ntgrtd/mrkt/vrvw /2014/index-eng.html.

34. David Parkinson, "Panic Time: As Oil Goes, So Does Canada's Economy," *Globe and Mail* (Toronto), Oct. 15, 2014, http://www.theglobeandmail.com/ report-on-business/industry-news/energy-and-resources/panic-time-as-oil -goes-so-does-canadas-economy/article21116012/.

35. Dale Jackson, "How OPEC Is Likely Ruining Your Retirement," *Globe and Mail* (Toronto), Oct. 29, http://www.theglobeandmail.com/globe-investor/how -opec-is-likely-ruining-your-retirement/article27016937/.

36. "According to market research by IBISWorld, a leading business intelligence firm, the total revenues for the oil and gas drilling sector came to [USD] $5 trillion in 2014. This sector is composed of companies that explore for, develop and operate oil and gas fields. It is also sometimes referred to as the oil and gas exploration and production industry, or simply as E&P. Since the 2014 estimates for global gross domestic product range between [USD] $77 trillion and [USD] $107 trillion, the oil and gas drilling sector makes up between 4.6% and 6.5% of the global economy." http://www.investopedia.com/ask /answers/030915/what-percentage-global-economy-comprised-oil-gas -drilling-sector.asp. Original report: https://www.ibisworld.com/industry/global /global-oil-gas-exploration-production.html.

CHAPTER 5

1. Amnesty International Canada, "The Lubicon Cree: Ongoing Human Rights Violations," *Amnesty International Canada*, http://www.amnesty.ca/our-work /issues/indigenous-peoples/the-lubicon-cree-ongoing-human-rights-violations.

2. Melina Laboucan-Massimo, "Awaiting Justice: Indigenous Resistance in the Tarsands of Alberta," *Open Democracy*, April 22, 2015, https://www.open democracy.net/5050/melina-loubicanmassimo/awaiting-justice-%E2%80%93 -indigenous-resistance-to-tar-sand-development-in-cana.

3. "A History of Struggle: A Chronology of the Lubicon Cree Land Rights Struggle," *Briarpatch Magazine*, Feb. 28, 2012, http://briarpatchmagazine.com/articles /view/a-history-of-struggle.

4. Karen Cooper, *Spirited Encounters: American Indians Protest Museum Policies and Practises* (Lanham, MD: AltaMira Press, 2007), 22.

5. "Submission to the Fourth Session of the Working Group of the Universal Periodic Review Regarding Canada's Human Rights Record, 5–16 February 2009," http://lib.ohchr.org/HRBodies/UPR/Documents/Session4/CA/LLIN_CAN _UPR_S4_2009_LubiconLakeIndianNation.pdf.

6. Amnesty International, *Canada: 20 Years of Denial of Recommendations Made by the United Nations Human Rights Committee and the Continuing Impact of the Lubicon Cree* (2010), 5, https://www.amnesty.ca/sites/amnesty/files/2010-03 -17amr200032010en20yearsdeniallubicon.pdf.

7. Melina Laboucan-Massimo, "Awaiting Justice: Indigenous Resistance in the Tar Sands of Canada," *50.50 Inclusive Democracy*, April 22, 2015, https://www .opendemocracy.net/5050/melina-loubicanmassimo/awaiting-justice-%E2 %80%93-indigenous-resistance-to-tar-sand-development-in-cana.

8. "A History of Struggle," http://briarpatchmagazine.com/articles/view/a -history-of-struggle.

9. Mario Blaser, Harvey Feit, and Glenn McCrae, eds., *In the Way of Development: Indigenous Peoples, Life Projects and Globalization* (London: Zed Books, 2004).

10. "Issues," *Cultural Survival*, https://www.culturalsurvival.org/who-are-indig enous-peoples.

11. Say post-development thinkers such as Arturo Escobar, Gustavo Esteva, Madhu Prakash, and Majid Rahnema, among others. A good place to start investigating these thinkers is with *The Post-Development Reader*, edited by Majid Rahnema and Victoria Bawtree (London: Zed Books, 1997).

12. Nick Cullather, "Development? It's History," *Diplomatic History* 24, no. 4 (2000): 644–653.

13. Douglas Lummis, *Radical Democracy* (Ithaca, NY: Cornell University Press, 1996), 46.

14. Mario Blaser, "Life Projects: Indigenous People's Agency and Development," in *In the Way of Development* (London: Zed Books, 2004).

15. See http://www.who.int/topics/millennium_development_goals/hunger/en/.

16. Harry S. Truman, "Inaugural Address," Jan. 20, 1949, http://www.bartleby .com/124/pres53.html.

17. Ibid.

18. Simon Kuznets, "National Income, 1929–1932" (1934), 73rd US Congress, 2nd session, Senate document no. 124, p. 7, http://papers.nber.org/books /kuzn34-1.

19. Perhaps the most famous excoriation of the GDP is Robert Kennedy's powerful 1968 speech at the University of Kansas:

> Our Gross National Product, now, is over $800 billion dollars a year, that ... counts air pollution and cigarette advertising, and ambulances to clear our highways of carnage. It counts special locks for our doors and the jails for the people who break them. It counts the destruction of the redwood and the loss of our natural wonder in chaotic sprawl. ... Yet the gross national product does not allow for the health of our children, the quality of their education or the joy of their play. It does not include the beauty of our poetry or the strength of our marriages, the intelligence of our public debate or the integrity of our public officials. It measures neither our wit nor our courage, neither our wisdom nor our learning, neither our compassion nor our devotion to our country, it measures everything in short, except that which makes life worthwhile. (https://www.jfklibrary.org /Research/Research-Aids/Ready-Reference/RFK-Speeches/Remarks-of -Robert-F-Kennedy-at-the-University-of-Kansas-March-18-1968.aspx)

20. Herman Daly, *Steady-State Economics* (Washington, DC: Island Press, 1977), 248.

21. Vandana Shiva, "How Economic Growth Has Become Anti-Life," *Common Dreams*, Nov. 1, 2013, http://www.commondreams.org/views/2013/11/01/how -economic-growth-has-become-anti-life/.

22. Marilyn Waring, *If Women Counted: A New Feminist Economics* (San Francisco: Harper & Row, 1988), 386.

23. Arturo Escobar, *Territories of Difference* (Durham, NC: Duke University Press, 2008), 305-6.

24. Gonzalo Oviedo, Luisa Maffi, and Peter Bille Larsen, *Indigenous and Traditional Peoples of the World and Ecoregion Conservation: An Integrated Approach to Conserving the World's Biological and Cultural Diversity* (Gland, Switzerland: WWF—World Wide Fund for Nature, 2000).

25. Quoted in Oliver Balch, "*Buen Vivir*: The Social Philosophy Inspiring Movements in South America," *Guardian*, Feb. 4, 2013, https://www.theguardian .com/sustainable-business/blog/buen-vivir-philosophy-south-america-eduardo -gudynas.

26. Eduardo Gudynas, "*Buen Vivir*: Today's Tomorrow," *Development* 54 (2011): 441.

27. "Republic of Ecuador, 2008 Constitution in English," *Political Database of the Americas*, Oct. 20, 2008, http://pdba.georgetown.edu/Constitutions /Ecuador/english08.html.

28. Séverine Deneulin, "Justice and Deliberation about the Good Life: The Contribution of Latin American *Buen Vivir* Social Movements to the Idea of Justice," Working paper, *Bath Papers in International Development and Wellbeing*, Centre for Development Studies University of Bath, June 2012.

29. Catherine Walsh, "Development as *Buen Vivir*: Institutional Arrangements and (De)colonial Entanglements," *Development* 53 (2010): 15.

30. "Human Development and *Buen vivir*: An Interview with Catherine Walsh," http://www.sidint.net/content/human-development-and-buen-vivir-interview -catherine-walsh.

31. In 2007, Correa offered to permanently suspend oil extraction activity in the Ishpingo-Tambococha-Tiputini area of the Yasuni National Park if the international community would contribute $3.6 billion (half of what the estimated revenues would be if fully exploited) into a UN-administered trust fund. The money would support a transition to a sustainable economic basis in the region, support new job creation, and protect the unique biodiversity of the region. The money failed to materialize (only $200 million was pledged) and now the Ecuadorean government is moving to develop the oil possibilities. See http://mptf .undp.org/yasuni.

32. Rickard Lalander, "The Ecuadorian Resource Dilemma: *Sumak Kawsay* or Development?" *Critical Sociology* 42, nos. 4–5 (July 2016): 623–642.

33. Derrick Hindery, *From Enron to Evo: Pipeline Politics, Global Environmentalism, and Indigenous Rights in Bolivia* (Tucson: University of Arizona Press, 2013).

34. Or as Johannes Waldmuller nicely puts it: "*Buen vivir* discourses have become a tricky minefield to engage with, also because actors and authors themselves shift between pro- and contra-governmental positions. Leading questions for any reading of *Buen vivir*/Sumak Kawsay should therefore be: who are the authors? What are their goals and political as well as academic roles? What is the purpose of their publications?" http://www.alternautas.net/blog/2014/5/14 /buen-vivir-sumak-kawsay-good-living-an-introduction-and-overview.

35. The term *Washington Consensus* was first used by British economist John Williamson and has been deployed to describe a set of neoliberal economic development policies driven by the IMF, the World Bank, and the US Treasury Department. It denotes opening up markets in domestic economies for greater competition, lowering taxes, reducing regulation for foreign direct investment, and selling off of public assets. It has also been characterized as market fundamentalism.

36. Melina Laboucan-Massimo, personal interview with the authors, March 30, 2016.

37. Ibid.

CHAPTER 6

1. Vincent Emanuele, "Christian Parenti on the State, Humanity as Part of Nature, and the Malleability of Capitalism," *Truthout*, May 17, 2015, http://www.truth-out.org/news/item/30756-christian-parenti-on-the-state-humanity-as-part-of-nature-and-the-malleability-of-capitalism. See also Christian Parenti, "Why Climate Change Will Make You Love Big Government," *Nation*, Jan. 26, 2012, https://www.thenation.com/article/why-climate-change-will-make-you-love-big-government/ and "A Radical Approach to the Climate Crisis," *Dissent* (summer 2013), https://www.dissentmagazine.org/article/a-radical-approach-to-the-climate-crisis.

2. Richard Day, *Gramsci Is Dead* (London: Pluto Press, 2005), 8.

3. Joel Wainwright and Geoff Mann, "Climate Leviathan," *Antipode*, 45 (2013): 24.

4. Alain Badiou, *The Subject of Change: Lessons from the European Graduate School*, ed. Duane Rousselle (New York: Atropos Press, 2013), 7.

5. Ibid., 6.

6. Ibid., 4.

7. Ibid., 6.

8. Alain Badiou, *Ethics*, ed. and trans. Peter Hallward (London: Verso, 2001), 113. In his lecture "From Logic to Anthropology, or Affirmative Dialectics," Badiou states, "I think the burden today is to find a way of reversing the classical dialectical logic inside itself so that the affirmation, or the positive proposition, comes before the negation instead of after it. Or in some sense, my attempt is to find a dialectical framework where something of the future comes before the negative present" (https://www.scribd.com/document/144383594/Badiou-From-Logic-to-Anthropology-or-Affirmative-Dialectics). Badiou differentiates his approach from the versions of dialectics presented by Hegel and Adorno. Badiou proposes affirmation as the first move, as opposed to negation as the beginning point of dialectics. We are interested in the dialectics of both Badiou and Bookchin in clarifying and reimagining ecological questions.

9. Alain Badiou, *Metapolitics*, trans. Jason Barker (London: Verso, 2005), 145.

10. See Leanne Simpson's lecture, "Restoring Nationhood," to SFU's Vancity Office of Engagement, Nov. 13, 2013, https://www.youtube.com/watch?v=SGUcWih74Ic.

11. Giorgio Agamben, *What Is an Apparatus*, trans. David Kishik and Stefan Pedatella (Redwood City: Stanford University Press, 2009), 14.

12. Ibid., 19.

13. Agamben has developed a theory of what he calls "bare life" by building on Aristotle's and Hannah Arendt's distinction between *zoe* (biological life) and *bios* (the political life of speech and action): the difference between mere life and the good life. For Agamben, this distinction between *zoe* and *bios* leads to new forms of domination and the transformation of democracy into more authoritarian, surveillance-infused models of the state and its practices. Because the state distinguishes between bare life and political life, it captures, limits, and enforces the possibilities of what the good life can be. See Giorgio Agamben, *Homo Sacer: Sovereign Power and Bare Life* (Stanford: Stanford University Press, 1998).

14. See Giorgio Agamben, *State of Exception* (Chicago: University of Chicago Press, 2005). The state reserves the right to exempt itself from the law. It enacts laws, but also reserves the right to suspend the law, especially in times of crises. Pure violence is included in the law through its very exclusion. Agamben argues there is no law without violence. The crisis of *law* and *the decision* become also a crisis of legality and legitimacy. For Agamben, the state of exception, the suspension of the law within the law, is the imbalance between public life and political fact at the intersection of the legal and the political. Politics suffers through its contamination with the law. The very potential of the state of exception being implemented, as the state's right to self-preservation, works against the good life of the people.

15. Timothy Morton, *Hyperobjects: Philosophy and Ecology after the End of the World* (Minneapolis: University of Minnesota Press, 2013). Morton defines hyperobjects as "things that are massively distributed in time and space relative to humans" (5).

16. Perhaps the best source we know of on glaciers is the National Snow and Ice Data Center: https://nsidc.org/.

17. Henri Bergson (1859–1941) was a highly influential French philosopher who is perhaps best known for his foundational work on duration. Bergson noted the deep inadequacies of measurement in a dynamic world, and argued for intuition and imagination in grasping a constantly disappearing/emerging reality.

18. Giorgia Agamben, *The Use of Bodies*, trans. Adam Kotsko (Redwood City: Stanford University Press, 2016), 209.

19. See Giorgio Agamben, *The Open: Man and Animal* (Stanford, CA: Stanford University Press, 2004).

20. Mack Lamoureux, "Heavy Rain Causing Localized Flooding in Fort McMurray," *CBC News*, July 31, 2016, http://www.cbc.ca/news/canada/edmonton /fort-mcmurray-flooding-1.3702663.

21. We looked at maps of the region and then tried to trace the fire's movement on the ground, but it still made little sense to us. The clearest thing we left with was the sheer heroism and skill of the firefighters. It must have been terrifying to be in the middle of that massive, capricious, burning ocean, but somehow they contained the damage. Maybe it was the spectacular media coverage fanning the flames of disaster, but for a while it had been hard to imagine how the fire was ever going to be stopped.

22. In 2016, only five countries in the world are without debt: Palau, Macao, Liechtenstein, the British Virgin Islands, and Brunei. See http://www.therichest. com/rich-list/rich-countries/the-only-5-countries-in-the-world-living-debt -free/?view=all.

23. There are many ways to talk about and measure personal debt, but across the Global North debt is an everyday, assumed, and expected feature of our lives. In Canada, for example, 2016 marked the first time cumulative household debt surpassed the GDP (http://business.financialpost.com/news/economy /canadas-household-debt-is-now-bigger-than-its-gdp-for-the-first-time). Interestingly, Alberta has the highest average consumer debt in the country (http:// www.cbc.ca/news/canada/calgary/alberta-calgary-consumer-debt-equifax -1.3484940) but also the lowest debt-GDP ratio (http://www.rbc.com/economics /economic-reports/pdf/provincial-forecasts/prov_fiscal.pdf).

24. See http://rollingjubilee.org/; https://roarmag.org/magazine/debt-collective -debtors-union/.

25. Maurizio Lazzarato, *The Making of the Indebted Man: An Essay on the Neoliberal Condition* (South Pasadena, CA: Semiotext(e), 2011), 151.

26. See Gilles Deleuze and Felix Guattari, *Anti-Oedipus: Capitalism and Schizophrenia* (New York: Penguin, 2009).

27. Lazzarato, *The Making of the Indebted Man*, 88.

28. Massive thanks to Carmen Aguirre for the back-and forth translations of our discussions with Alberto Acosta.

29. There is no shortage of ideas for a post-tar-sands Alberta. One recent, particularly promising initiative is called RAFT (Reclaiming Alberta's Future Today) that is being driven by a couple of Albertan guys—one has worked in the

patch forever and the other is a roofer. They are motivated by global warming, the ruinous volatility of the petro-economy, and the massive clean-up liabilities the oil industry is accumulating. It's the latter, massive issue that is at the heart of their proposal.

They estimate that there may well be north of $100 billion in cleanup costs facing Alberta from the oil industry: leaking, aging, and abandoned wells and pipelines, discarded equipment, bankrupt exploration sites, seeping tailings ponds, spills, garbage, etc.: "Current liabilities for the conventional sector, the plan notes, include 444,000 oil and gas wells (only 200,000 are actually pumping liquids), 430,000 kilometres of pipelines (the distance to the moon is 384,000 kilometres), 30,000 oil and gas facilities, 900 square kilometres of oil sands development, 220 square kilometres of tailing ponds and 'a 11.2 million ton sulfur pile that dwarfs the great pyramids of Egypt.' (The sulphur is another waste stream from bitumen upgrading)" (https://thetyee.ca/Opinion/2016/11/04/Clean-Up-Plan-for-Alberta-Oil-Pollution/).

RAFT's plan is to force industry to fulfill 100 percent of their legal obligations to cover the cleanup costs (currently companies routinely slither out from their responsibilities via a variety of financial and legal tactics). As they put it, the plan will not cost Albertans anything: "It's simple; the Government of Alberta has the responsibility and authority to direct the DOE—Department of Energy, and the AER—Alberta Energy Regulator, to manage the LLR liability as a 'Super priority' and take whatever steps are required to ensure tax payers do not get stuck with the cleanup bill and to make sure the environmental impact of fossil fuel production is minimized." This fund would then be directed to re-employ tens of thousands of current tar sands employees, repurposing their existing skillsets for cleanup rather than extraction. RAFT estimates that it will take "1000 rigs 50 years and every willing Canadian to clean up our mess" (https://thetyee.ca/Documents/2016/11/03/RAFT-Doc.pdf).

The RAFT proposal echoes the Yasuni-ITT in several important ways and is exactly the kind of ecological thinking we are interested in. Most importantly for us, these initiatives are a critical break in the clouds, a rupture of certainties that opens the door to so many other kinds of creativity and hopefulness.

30. Gilles Deleuze, *Nietzsche and Philosophy*, trans. H. Tomlinson (New York: Columbia University Press, 1982), 103.

31. Glen Coulthard, personal interview with the authors, March 20, 2016.

32. Ibid.

INDEX

—

Note: Page numbers in italic type refer to illustrations. Page numbers followed by "n" refer to footnotes and page numbers followed by, for example, "n14," refer to endnotes.

Acosta, Alberto, 167–171

Adorno, Theodor, 94, 203n8

Affirmative dialectics, 147, 203n8

Affirmative visions, for social and environmental transformation, 15, 21, 29, 112–114, 131, 147, 167, 172–173

Africa, effect of global warming on, 60, 192n69

Agamben, Giorgio, 28–29, 150, 152, 204n13, 204n14

Alberta. *See also* Tar sands of Alberta
characteristics of, 34–35
and extractivism in Lubicon Territory, 118–121, 137–140
finances of, 35
oil in, 5, 31–32, 35–38, 111, 118–121, 137–140, 162
politics in, 35–36

Alberta Energy Board, 6

Al Haq, Mahbub, 128

Al Jazeera (news outlet), 42

Amazon, 168

Amiskwacîwâskahikan. *See* Edmonton

Anarchism, 148

Angel, Roger, 61

Anthropocene (Age of Man)
alternative terms for, 58–59
concept of, 52
critique of, 55–63, 190n59
delineation of, 52–55
as grand narrative, 55–59
uniformity suggested by concept of, 55–63

Anxiety
authoritarianism as response to, 22
and capitalism, 17, 69–70, 172, 174–175
and debt, 165
and development, 112
of resource town residents, 49, 108

Apparatus, 150

Arendt, Hannah, 204n13

Aristotle, 204n13

Authoritarianism, as political response to global warming, 21–24, 62

Badiou, Alain, 24–25, 145–148, 150, 203n8
Bates, Lisa K., 16
Beaver Creek Wood Buffalo Ranch Viewpoint, 97–98, *98*
Beeson, Mark, 23
Before the Flood (documentary), 197n22
Benjamin, Walter, 26
Bergson, Henri, 151, 204n17
Bhutan, 128
Biodiversity, 122, 168
Birds, dangers of oil pollution for, 98–99
Bison. *See* Buffalo
"Bitumen or Bust" (Sacco), *71–80*
Bitumen "sail," *207*
Black people, 17
Blaser, Mario, 122–123
Bolivia, 132, 134–135
Bonneuil, Christophe, 58
Bookchin, Murray, 90–91, 94, 196n9
Bretton Woods, 51, 126
British Columbia, vii, 180n30
Buen vivir (good life/right living), 131–136, 167–171, 202n34. *See also* Sweetness of life
Buffalo, 95–97, 100, 140, *141*
Butler, Judith, 93

Calgary, 35
Cameron, James, 41
Canadian Natural Resources, 106
Cancer, 34
Cannons, 98–99
Cape Breton, 43
Capitalism
  Anthropocene in relation to, 58
  critique of, 19–20, 29, 46–47
  debt as component of, 164–166
  destruction as component of, 26, 64, 109, 145, 166, 172
  development spurred by, 122, 166
  exploitation as element of, 16, 27
  global hegemony of, 149
  global warming in relation to, 19–20, 26, 46–48, 58, 136
  modernity linked to, 27
  narratives of, 17
  ordering function of, 26
  politics coopted by, 150
  religious character of, 26
  resistance to, 28–29
  shame as tool of, 69–70
  the state as aligned with, 147
Carlson, Keith Thor, 18
Caygill, Howard, 165
Change
  affirmative and progressive notion of, 146
  destructive, 145–146
  in energy transition, 136
  obstacles to, 64
  reimagining, 27
  tradition in relation to, 24, 26–27
China, 128
Chlorofluorocarbons (CFCs), 19
Class
  as ecological concern, 19
  effects of global warming by, 60
  environmental movement's blind spot for, 84
Climate change, 5, 178n10
Coal, transition to oil from, 50
Cobb, John, 128
Colonialism
  concept of, 13n
  development spurred by, 122
  domination at root of, 130–131
  ecology in relation to, 12–13, 20
  land as foundation of, 15
  settler, 13n, 18, 66–69
  shame as tool of, 69–70
Communism, 145
Correa, Rafael, 134, 167–170, 202n31

Coulthard, Glen, 14, 24–25, 27–28, 173, 174
Crist, Eileen, 60
Crutzen, Paul, 52, 54, 61

Daily Show, The (television show), 42
Dakota Access Pipeline (DAPL), 6
Daly, Herman, 127, 128
Debt, 164 167
Debtor's Universe, 166
Decolonization
  Buen vivir and, 132–133
  ecology as practice of, 14–15, 25–26, 30, 114, 130, 175
  of land, 15, 25
  materialization of, 25
  as means addressing global warming, 20
Deleuze, Gilles, 166, 172
Development
  agenda of, 123–125
  of Alberta tar sands, 32
  alternatives to, 129–136, 168–169, 173–174
  Buen vivir and, 134
  capitalism and colonialism at root of, 122, 166
  critiques of, 129
  defined, 122
  as exploitation, 123
  GDP linked to, 125–127, 129
  Indigenous perspective on, 68–69, 142
  land viewed from perspective of, 17
  life projects contrasted with, 122–123
  notion of debt in relation to, 166
Dialectical naturalism, 94
Dialectics, affirmative, 147, 203n8
DiCaprio, Leonardo, 41, 197n22
Dogu, Goze, 104
Domestic workers, 102–103

Domination. *See also* Exploitation
  colonialism based on, 130–131
  ecology opposed to, 16, 19, 94
  land implicated in, 14, 30
  in Latin America, 135–136
  neoliberal, 144–145
  of other-than-human world, 14, 19, 94
Douglas Treaties, 180n30

Ecology
  affirmative vision of, 114, 172–173
  and class, 19, 29
  colonialism in relation to, 12–13, 20
  concept of, 11–12
  critique of existing politics of, 19
  debt and obligation in perspective of, 167
  decolonization and, 14–15, 25–26, 30, 114, 130, 175
  dichotomies in, 10–11
  exploitation as issue for, 27–28
  future orientation of, 172
  and human-nature relationship, 89–92
  land as basis of, 171
  land politics and, 15–16, 26, 30
  politics and, 12, 19, 92–94, 145–146, 150
  restructuring of relationships in, 172–175
  science-politics relation in, 11
  and tradition, 146
Ecuador, 132–134, 167–171
Edmonton, 31–70
  multiple users and uses of, viii
  oil-based economy and culture of, 38–39, *39*, 49, 51–52
  transformations in, 35, 39–40
Education, environmental degradation linked to lack of, 83–84
Ehrlich, Anne, 22
Ehrlich, Paul, 22

Enbridge Line 3, 6
Energy, economic structures based
    on, 50–52
Enlightenment, 145–146
Environmental accidents
    ideological responses to, 9–10
    in Lubicon Territory, 137–139
    in Vancouver, 1–2, *3*, 8–10, *9*
Environmental crises. *See also* Global
    warming
    Alberta tar sands and, 41
    Anthropocene concept and, 52–63
    human responsibility for, 52–57,
        60, 62–63
    language of, 23–24, 49, 61–62,
        66–67, 147, 193n80
    political solutions to, 21–24
    socioeconomic consequences of, 49
    technological solutions to, 8–10,
        19–20, 21, 47–48, 60–63, 194n81
Environmental initiatives
    for Alberta tar sands, 77–78
    governmental, 45
    technology-based, 8–10, 19–20, 21,
        47–48, 60–63
Environmental movement
    critical of tar sands, 41–42, 72,
        82–84, 86–89, 105–106
    socialism in relation to, 89
Escobar, Arturo, 130
Ethics
    grounded in nature, 91–93
    and other-than-human world,
        92–93
Ethiopia, 45
Exploitation, 16, 27–28, 123. *See also*
    Domination
Extractivism
    Canadian economy based on, 111
    controversies over, 34
    equipment for, *209*
    health consequences of, 34, 121, 137

hostility and violence of, 139, 142,
    162
in leftist Latin American countries,
    134–135
in Lubicon Territory, 118–121, *125*,
    137–140
process used by, in tar sands, 40, 73
socioeconomic consequences of,
    for residents, 49, 74–76, 80,
    105–106, 109–110, 164–165
ExxonMobil, 37

Fascism, 182n39
Fire, in Fort McMurray, 99–100
Fitoussi, Jean-Paul, 128
Forest-clearing, *210–211*
Fort Chipewyan, 34
Fort McMoney (video game/film/
    documentary), 41–42
Fort McMurray, 81–88, 94–114
    buffalo in, 94–98, 100–101
    cartoon history of, 74–76
    crime in, 103–105
    description of, 81
    diversity in, 104–107
    economy of, 31
    fire in, 99–100, *149*, 153–158, *154*,
        205n21
    negative views of, 32, 41–42, 46, 155
    political classification of, 197n16
    recreational opportunities in,
        106–107
    residents of, 75, 82, 84–88,
        101–103, 105–110, 156–159, 164
    women in, 103–105
Foucault, Michel, 152
Fracking, 37, 82
Francis, Pope, 45
Freedom, 29, 167
Fressoz, Jean-Baptiste, 58
Fuhr, Greg, 100–101

GDP. *See* Gross domestic product

Genuine progress indicator (GPI), 128

Geoengineering. *See* Technological solutions to environmental crises

Giants of Mining (museum), 95

Glaciers, 151

Global warming. *See also* Environmental crises
  agency in the face of, 150–153, 171–172
  Alberta tar sands linked to, 41–42
  Canada's responsibility concerning, 41
  capitalism in relation to, 19–20, 26, 46–48, 58, 136
  challenge posed by, 29, 52
  climate change in relation to, 5, 178n10
  complexity of, 150–151
  decolonization as means of addressing, 20
  defined, 5
  distribution of effects of, 59–60
  ecology concept affected by, 12
  glaciers affected by, 151
  governmental initiatives on, 45
  language of crisis applied to, 147
  notion of debt in relation to, 166
  official (state and industry) responses to, 130, 150–151
  as opportunity for social change, 47
  remoteness of effects of, 150–152
  scientific conclusions on, 10

Greenhouse gases, 5, 40

Green politics, 19, 182n39

Grimshaw Accord, 120

Gross domestic product (GDP), 125–129, 201n19

Gross national happiness (GNH) index, 128

Grounded normativity, 14

G7 summit, 45

Guardian (newspaper), 42

Guattari, Felix, 196n12

Gudynas, Eduardo, 131–132

Haeckel, Ernst, 11

Hansen, James, 41

Haraway, Donna, 58

Hardin, Garrett, 23

Harvey, David, 88–90

Hawaii, 45

Heede, Richard, 58

Hegel, G. W. F., 94, 203n8

Herman, Dennis, 160–162, *160, 161*

Herman, Diane, *160*

Herman, Melissa, 159–163, *160*

Herman, Renee, *160*

Hern, Matt, *96, 98, 102, 160*

Hitler, Adolf, 182n39

Hockey stick graph, of planetary temperatures, 54, 190n52

Holdren, John, 22

Huffington Post (online news outlet), 42

Human development index (HDI), 128

Humans
  relationship of, to nature, 89–92
  relationship of, to other-than-human world, 10, 16, 26, 92–94, 114, 133, 142, 171, 173
  responsible for environmental crises, 52–57, 60, 62–63
  uselessness of, 152–153

Hunt, Sarah, 59

Hyperobjects, 151, 204n15

IMF. *See* International Monetary Fund

Index of sustainable economic welfare (ISEW), 128

Indigenous peoples
  dispossession of, 66–68, 121–122
  ecology and, 12–13
  in Ecuador, 134, 167–171
  in global population, 122
  knowledge possessed by, 14
  and land, 12–14, 66–67
  stable social systems of, 64–65
International Covenant on Civil and
    Political Rights, 120
International Geological Congress, 52
International Monetary Fund (IMF),
    51, 136, 202n35
International Petroleum Council, 51
International Union of Geological
    Sciences, 52

Jamieson, Dale, 23
Janvier, 159–163
Janvier, Ja-Nene, *160*
Johal, Am, *98*
Jorolan, Reinalie, 101–103, 156, 158

Kazakhstan, 82
Keith, David, 61
Kennedy, Robert, 201n19
Keystone XL, 6
Kinder Morgan Trans Mountain
    Expansion pipeline, 6
Klein, Naomi, *This Changes
    Everything*, 46–48, 188n36
Kojeve, Alexandre, 28
Kolbert, Elizabeth, 48
Kothari, Miloon, 120
Kuznets, Simon, 125, 126–127

Laboucan-Massimo, Melina, 119,
    137, 140–141
Land
  as analytical/critical tool, 15–16, 25
  ceded/unceded, vii–viii, 181n31
  colonial foundations in, 15

decolonization of, 15, 25
  development perspective on, 17
  domination of, 14, 30
  ecology based on, 171
  human relationship to, 14, 16–17,
    20, 25, 30, 70, 131, 172
  Indigenous peoples and, 12–14,
    66–67
  love of, 174–175
  in Lubicon Territory, 120
  politics of, 12, 15–16, 26, 30
  rematriation of, 114, 142, 167
  as resource, 16
  taken from Indigenous peoples, 15
  treaties involving, vii–viii, 180n30,
    181n31
Latham, John, 61
Latin America, radical politics in,
    131–135, 168–171
Latour, Bruno, 63
Lazzarato, Maurizio, 166
Left, the
  condescending attitude of, 83–84
  future political strategies of,
    143–145
  as ineffective on global warming, 48
  Latin American, 131–135
  linked with capitalism, 131
  NDP and, 35–36
  and the state, 143–145, 148
  tar sands activism of, 42
Leopold, Aldo, 89
Life projects, 122–123
Linkola, Pentti, 23
Little Buffalo, 115, 135, 137
Love, 174–175
Lovelock, James, 22–23, 55, 62
Lubicon people, 118–121, 137–142
Lubicon Territory, 115–122, 135–141
  environmental consequences of ex-
    tractivism in, 137–139
  extractivism in, 118–121, *125*,
    137–140

history of, 118
Lynas, Mark, 55, 61

Malabou, Catherine, 58
Malcolm X, 147
Malm, Andreas, 190n59
Mann, Geoff, 21, 145
Mann, Michael, 190n52
Marathassa (tanker), 1–2, 6, 8
Marathon Oil, 37
Marx, Karl, 89, 94
Marxism, 27, 29
Masculinity, 103–104
Massumi, Brian, 93
McHalsie, Albert (Sonny), 18
Mendez, Ana Maria, 107
Mexico, 45
Mississauga Anishnabec people, 16
Mississauga Nishnaabeg Nation, 67
Mitchell, Timothy, 50
Modernity, 27
Montecristi Constitution, 132–134,
    167, 169–170
Moore, Jason, 57–58
Morales Bolivia, Evo, 134–135,
    181n36
Mordor, 101, 197n22
Morton, Timothy, 151, 178n10
Mouffe, Chantal, 195n4
Musqueam people, vii, 12
Myhrvold, Nathan, 61

Nation (magazine), 42
National Film Board (Canada), 41
Nature. *See also* Other-than-human
    world
  ethics grounded in, 91–93
  first vs. second, 90–92
  human relationship to, 89–92
  rights of, 132–133, 167, 170
  as social construction, 92
Nazi Party, 182n39

NDP. *See* New Democratic Party
Nenshi, Naheed, 35
Neoliberalism
  development policies of, 202n35
  in Latin America, 135–136
  misconceptions of, 144–145
  notion of debt in relation to, 166
  oil-based economy and, 50–51
  and state power, 144–145
New Democratic Party (NDP), 35–36
New York Times (newspaper), 42
Nexen, 106
Nisga'a First Nation, 180
Nistawayou. *See* Fort McMurray
Norway, 45
Notley, Rachel, 110

Obama, Barack, 6
Oil
  in Alberta, 5, 31–32, 35–38, 111,
    118–121, 137–140, 162
  cultural impact of, 38
  economic structures based on,
    50–51, 110–111
  as food ingredient, 43
  hypocrisy concerning, 43, 45
  international reserves of, 184n1
  investment in, 108
  pipelines for transporting, 5–6
  politics linked to, 51
  price of, 35, 36, 80, 108–111, 164
  transition from coal to, 50
  universal implication in economy
    of, 43, 45, 79, 84
  Vancouver and, 4–5, 8
Oil Sands Discovery Centre, 73,
    76–78, 96–97, *102, 107*
Olson, Charles E., 37
Organization of the Petroleum
    Exporting Countries (OPEC), 109
O'Shaughnessy, Sara, 104

Other-than-human world. *See also* Nature
  domination of, 14, 19, 26, 94
  Enlightenment view of, 145–146
  ethics and, 92–93
  exploitation of, 16, 26, 27–28
  as first nature, 90
  human relationships with, 10, 16, 26, 92–94, 114, 133, 142, 171, 173
Overburden removal, *210–211*

Parenti, Christian, 143–144
Petrocultures Research Group, 43
Petro-feminism, 104
Pipelines, 5–6, *7, 125, 163*
Polanyi, Karl, 170
Politics. *See also* Left, the
  agonistic, 84, 195n4
  authoritarian responses to global warming, 21–24, 62
  capital's cooptation of, 150
  of "climate change" language, 5, 178n10
  eclipse of, 150
  ecology and, 12, 19, 92–94, 145–146, 150
  of human-caused environmental crises, 54–55, 60, 62–63
  Indigenous, 65
  land as subject of, 12, 15–16, 26, 30
  law, state power and, 204n14
  oil-based economy and, 51, 110–111
  radical Latin American, 131–135, 168–171
  science/technology and, 11, 62–63
  the state in relation to, 147–150, 171–172
  without parties, 145
Poverty, 130
Power, outside of the state, 147–150, 169, 171–172

Progress
  capitalism grounded in notion of, 17
  modern concept and narrative of, 11, 13, 26–27
  tradition in relation to, 24, 26–27
Progressive Conservative Party, 36

Quebec, 45

Race, effects of global warming according to, 192n70
Rainbow Pipeline, 137
Reclaiming Alberta's Future Today (RAFT), 205n29
Redefining Progress project, 128
Refusal, 14
Relationships
  ecology as restructuring of, 172–175
  of humans and nature, 89–92
  of humans and other-than-human world, 10, 16, 26, 92–94, 114, 133, 142, 171, 173
  to land, 14, 16–17, 20, 25, 30, 70, 131, 172
  nondominating and nonexploitative, 26, 28
  security in life maintained through, 65, 175
Rematriation of land, 114, 142, 167
Resource towns, 103–104
Reversal of production and consumption ethos, 47
Robertson, Gregor, 4
Rockefeller Brothers Fund, 108
Rolling Jubilee, 166
Rotterdam, 4
Royal Dutch Shell, 37
Russia, 82

Sacco, Joe, *98, 107*
  "Bitumen or Bust," *71–80*
Salter, Stephen, 61

Sarkozy, Nicolas, 128
Saudi Arabia, 109
Scarcity, 17, 173–174
Schumpeter, Joseph, 64
Scranton, Roy, 55
səlil'wətaʔɬ . *See* Tsleil-Waututh people
Sen, Amartya, 128
Serres, Michel, 12
Settlers
  anxieties and hunger of, 17–18, 112–114
  colonialism of, 13n, 18, 66–69
  concept of, 17n
Shale oil deposits, 82
Shame, 69–70, 86
Shell, 106
Shiva, Vandana, 127
Simpson, Audra, 14, 24–25
Simpson, Leanne Betasamosake, 1, 13–17, 24–25, 64–70, 142, 147–148, 173, 175, 180n24
Singapore, 4
Sḵwx̱wú7mesh. *See* Squamish people
Slade, Leithan, 100
Slag piles, *208*
Socialism, 89, 148, 181n36
Solar power, 140–141
Squamish people, vii, 12
Standing Rock Indian Reservation, 6
State, the
  law in relation to, 204n14
  the left and, 143–145, 148
  neoliberalism and, 144–145
  political power outside of, 147–150, 169, 171–172
  response of, to change, 147, 169
Steffen, Will, 52
Stiglitz, Joseph, 128
Stoermer, Eugene, 52
Stó:lō people, vii, 18
Strike Debt, 166

Subcommission on Quaternary Stratigraphy, 54, 189n48
Sulfur, *212–213*
Sumak kawsay (good life/right living), 131–135, 169–170, 202n34. See also *Buen vivir*; Sweetness of life
Suncor, 95–96, 99, 106, 136
Sundberg, Juanita, 59
Sweetness of life (*la dolce vita/ douceur de vivre*), 28, 30, 171–175, 183n56. See also *Buen vivir*; *Sumak kawsay*
Swyngedouw, Erick, 58
Syncrude, 95–97, 99–100, 106, 136
Syncrude plant, *83, 88*

Tailings ponds, 40, 95, 97–99, 101
Tar sands, global reserves of, 82
Tar sands of Alberta, 82
  environmental criticism aimed at, 41–42, 72, 82–84, 86–89, 105–106, 187n24
  environmental impact of, 40–42, 73–74, 77–79, 96–97, 110
  extraction process in, 40, 73
  global warming linked to, 41–42
  health consequences of, 34
  investments in, 37
  map of mineable, *214*
  museum exhibition about, 73, 76–78, 96–97
  oil reserves in, 5, 31–32, 40
  pipeline structure for, 7
  terminology related to, 72
  visual description of, 101
  workers and residents connected to, 42–43, 49, 74–76, 80–82, 84–89, 101–103, 105–110
Technological solutions to environmental crises, 8–10, 19–20, 21, 47–48, 60–63, 194n81
Theory, 84
Todd, Zoe, 59

Total Fitness, 106
Toxic: Alberta (documentary), 42
Tradition
  change in relation to, 24, 26–27
  defined, 24n
  ecology and, 146
  progress in relation to, 24, 26–27
  reimagining, 21, 24, 24n, 27, 29
Treaties, vii–viii, 68, 180, 181n31
Trudeau, Justin, 6, 64, 110, 186n16
Truman, Harry, 123–124
Trump, Donald, 6, 36
Tsawwassen First Nation, 180
Tsilhqot'in First Nation, 180n30
Tsleil-Waututh people, vii, 12
Tuck, Eve, 25
Tutu, Desmond, 41

United Nations, 120, 128
United Nations Human Rights
  Committee, 119
United States, 82
Uselessness, 152–153

Vancouver
  environmental accidents in, 1–2, *3*,
    8–10, *9*
  as gateway city, *3*
  neoliberal urbanism in, 4
  and oil, 4–5, 8
  politics of, 4
  port of, 4
Venezuela, 82
Vice (website), 42
Vince, Gaia, 53
Volatility, 37, 40, 104, 108–109,
  111, 153

Wainwright, Joel, 21, 145
Waldmuller, Johannes, 202n34
Walsh, Catherine, 134
Waring, Marilyn, 127–128
Wark, Mackenzie, 58

Washington Consensus, 136, 202n35
Water
  in glaciers, 151
  as human right, 170
  related to tar sands oil extraction,
    40–41, 73
Whiteness, and theories of environ-
  mental crisis, 59
Williamson, John, 202n35
Wilson, Sheena, 104
Winter Olympics (Calgary, 1988),
  119
Women, in resource towns, 103–105
Wood bison. *See* Buffalo
Workers, in tar sands of Alberta, 42–
  43, 49, 74–76, 80–82
World Bank, 51, 202n35
World Council of Churches, 119
World Wildlife Fund, 122

Xenofeminism, 198n26
Xwelitem (non-Indigenous arrivals),
  18
xʷməθkʷəy̓əm. *See* Musqueam people

Yang, Wayne, 25
YASunidos Collective, 169
Yasuni-ITT Initiative, 134, 167–169,
  202n31
Young, Neil, 41, 187n24

Zapatistas, 59